CENTRAL LABOR COUNCILS
AND THE REVIVAL OF
AMERICAN UNIONISM

CENTRAL LABOR COUNCILS AND THE REVIVAL OF AMERICAN UNIONISM

ORGANIZING FOR JUSTICE IN OUR COMMUNITIES

Immanuel Ness • Stuart Eimer

editors

M.E. Sharpe
Armonk, New York
London, England

Copyright © 2001 by M. E. Sharpe, Inc.

Library of Congress Cataloging-in-Publication Data

Central labor councils and the revival of American unionism : organizing for justice in
our communities / Immanuel Ness and Stuart Eimer, editors.
    p. cm.—
  Includes bibliographical references and index.
  ISBN 0-7656-0599-6 (cloth : alk. paper)
    1. Central labor councils—United States—case studies. I. Ness, Immanuel. II. Eimer,
Stuart, 1967–

HD6508.C35 2001
331.88′0973—dc21
                                     00-053161

Printed in the United States of America

BM (c)   10   9   8   7   6   5   4   3   2   1

To Frances Fox Piven
and the memory of
Saul Mills, CIO
Greater New York Industrial
Union Council.

Contents

List of Tables and Figures

Tables

Figure

Acknowledgments

We thank all those who helped us put this volume together, particularly the authors. Thanks are also due to the members of the AFL-CIO Field Mobilization Department in Washington, D.C.—Marilyn Sneiderman, Bruce Colburn, Charles Stott, and Scott Reynolds—for patiently explaining to us the details of the union movement's new efforts to revitalize councils. We also thank leaders and members of labor councils—James Cavanaugh, Ron Judd, Doug Kratsch, John Goldstein, Charley Richardson, and Ian Robertson—for explaining to us the constraints they face in activating their councils. We would also like to thank the Professional Staff Congress of the City University of New York for helping to fund this project. For advice and assistance, we thank Frances Fox Piven, JoAnn Wypiejewski, Jody Knauss, Brian McLaughlin, Ed Ott, Nick Unger, Sean Sweeney, Sarah Zimmerman, and Enid Eckstein. We also thank countless labor leaders and activists across the country who helped us understand the importance of reaching out to workers on a community and regional basis across industrial lines and craft. We also thank Sean Culhane and Elizabeth Granda, our editors, who recognized the importance of this project and provided important advice on the editing process, and Christine Florie, our project editor. Finally, personal thanks go out to our colleagues, friends, and families, whose lived experience instilled in us an appreciation of the labor movement's importance and potential, and to Alyson Wiecek for her patience and support.

CENTRAL LABOR COUNCILS

AND THE **REVIVAL** OF

AMERICAN UNIONISM

Introduction

Immanuel Ness and Stuart Eimer

> Had the city bodies been given autonomy in organizing new shops, helping strikes, guiding local unions, and in political affairs in their areas, there might have been greater involvement of the rank and file in union affairs. As it was, the national unions became all-powerful and to a considerable extent inflexible.
>
> —*Sidney Lens, 1959*

As local federations organized on a regional basis, central labor councils (CLCs) are responsible for unifying local unions, long separated by craft and industrial jurisdictions, around common legislative, political, and economic goals. Over the course of the last century, the ability of CLCs to carry out their mission effectively has ebbed and flowed as times and conditions have changed. In the late nineteenth century and the first half of the twentieth century, despite constraints imposed by national federations, CLCs were often formidable institutions that wielded significant power at the local level. They helped advance the economic interests of affiliate unions by mobilizing rank-and-file workers in support of one another's collective bargaining struggles. Many CLCs also had well-developed grass-roots political operations that were used to elect candidates and lobby for a broad range of social legislation.

By the 1950s, however, the power of CLCs had waned, and many had become relatively moribund institutions. Though the causes of their decline have not been adequately researched, it seems likely that the "post-war labor accord," which demobilized labor in general, also functioned to weaken CLCs. Changes in labor law, the increasingly national scope of collective bargaining, and the corresponding centralization of union activities, as well as shifts in labor's political ideology and tactics, diminished the importance of local-level activity. As a unionist reflecting on the situation told Sidney Lens in 1959, "[L]ocal unions starve to death simply for lack of things to do" (Lens 1959). Not surprisingly, as federations comprised local unions with little to do, CLCs became less vibrant organizations. By the mid-1980s it was generally agreed in the AFL-CIO that CLCs were "problem spots" that in some cases had ceased to function altogether (Wallihan 1985).

Despite the lack of local union and CLC activity, the postwar labor accord advanced the economic interests of most American workers for the quarter century following World War II. Unfortunately, it also left organized labor ill prepared for the challenges it faced when the American economy began to sputter in the early 1970s. Automation, deregulation, and global competition, combined with an increasingly antiunion climate, created a crisis for a labor movement that had been more or less demobilized since the 1950s. Union density began to plummet, real wages declined, and the once powerful body of organized labor became but a shadow of its former self.

In the early 1990s, frustrated by the failure of the union movement to fight back, several labor leaders independently launched efforts to reinvigorate the power of their local labor councils. The most prominent of these initiatives occurred in Atlanta, Milwaukee, Seattle, and San Jose. In 1994 these CLC leaders organized a meeting to discuss strategies for revitalizing councils, and with the ascent of the Sweeney administration in 1995, these effort were given moral and material support by the national AFL-CIO. In July 1996 a national conference for AFL-CIO central labor councils was held in Denver, under the slogan "Organizing for Justice in Our Community." The following winter, the AFL-CIO launched its Union Cities program, with the goal of reestablishing the councils as support centers for local organizing and focal points for expanding labor's economic and political power. To date, 160 CLCs have committed to the Union Cities project.

However, many of the participating and nonparticipating councils do not have the resources to adopt the principles of the Union Cities program. In response, the AFL-CIO launched the New Alliance in 1999, perhaps the most significant transformation of organized labor's institutional structure since the merger of the AFL and CIO in 1955. The plan aims to transform the institutional basis of labor councils by encouraging international affiliates and local unions to participate more fully in the revitalization of councils and state federations. The New Alliance plan grew out of the need to develop activist programs for local and state labor movements with defined roles and responsibilities. It called for the reorganization of the labor movement at the local level with a focus on creating sixty to seventy-five area labor federations around the country capable of carrying out that program.

At present, the form, content, and extent of CLC initiatives vary widely across the country. Some councils devote resources to mobilizing rank-and-file members for solidarity activities aimed at organizing new workers or winning better contracts. Other councils have created alliances with nonlabor organizations to support economic-development projects and to increase their collective political capacity. Sadly, a majority of councils have hardly changed at all and limit their activities to monthly meetings, Labor Day parades, and the provision of basic informational services to member unions.

Given the current efforts to revitalize CLCs, it seems an appropriate time to inquire into the changing role and function of these bodies. The essays in this book examine the opportunities and constraints that challenge the labor movement as it attempts to reinvigorate central labor councils. Mindful of unfulfilled past efforts, the bulk of the chapters focus on successful efforts to organize and build political and economic power for working people throughout the nation. The essays demonstrate that an active, committed labor movement can successfully transform labor councils into effective and consequential organizations dedicated to improving the lives of working people. Part I contains three chapters that place the current revitalization efforts in a larger context. They provide a sense of the contemporary landscape, the theoretical possibilities, as well as the institutional constraints. In chapter 1, Immanuel Ness explores the tensions within the labor movement that precipitated the decline of CLCs. He then recounts the events leading up to the current efforts to rejuvenate labor councils and describes the Union Cities projects. Ness notes that the successes of councils that have adopted Union Cities have motivated the AFL-CIO to call for the restructuring of the councils through the New Alliance program, which among other important goals consolidates long-dormant councils and creates area labor federations to mobilize for political and economic goals in larger metropolitan regions. Through the program, the AFL-CIO seeks to increase participation and resources for local councils and state federations that have been unable to change through the Union Cities program alone. Ness concludes by arguing that while there is great potential for CLCs to become centers of union activity once again, there are serious obstacles to be overcome.

Chapter 2 presents a more general analytic framework for thinking about CLCs. Wade Rathke and Joel Rogers argue that metropolitan regions are the natural building blocks of labor's national strength. In this chapter, they offer a broad-based strategy for how labor in general, and CLCs in particular, can leverage union strength in metropolitan areas in pursuit of organizing, legislative, and political goals. Rogers and Rathke suggest that this will require more patient budgeting of organizing campaigns, active membership in minority settings, strengthened coordinating capacity (particularly at the local level) among unions, in-place local organizers, and a "use it or lose it" approach to jurisdiction.

In chapter 3, Stuart Eimer provides a historical overview of CLCs, concentrating on the evolution of the relationship between national federations and local councils. He highlights the tensions that exist between occupational unionism and territorial unionism, and considers some of the rules that were enacted to mediate the conflicts that arose. He pays particular attention to decisions that skewed power within the AFL toward the national unions and to the subsequent decision to make affiliation with CLCs voluntary. After a look at AFL, CIO, and AFL-CIO history, he concludes that the policy of voluntary affiliation has severely hampered the capacity of CLCs. In recounting this history, he reminds readers that the New Alliance is by no means the first effort to reinvigorate local councils and that past efforts have achieved very little. He concludes by suggesting that mandatory affiliation might be the only way to solve the problems that CLCs have struggled with over the past century.

In part II, we present four chapters written by academics who have researched contemporary CLC activity. Each of the pieces touches on a different component of CLC activity and provides an opportunity both to learn about the projects and to evaluate their success. In chapter 4, Fernando Gapasin examines how the Los Angles County Federation of Labor has transformed the local labor movement through working with independent labor organizations and labor educators and energizing local unions with living-wage campaigns and other common projects to improve the conditions of workers. Gapasin demonstrates that by encouraging the participation of Latinos and other previously excluded groups, central labor councils can appeal to the concerns of the broader population, helping to build the power of the local and regional labor movements. The Los Angeles labor federation presents a model for building the political and economic power of labor through linking the interests of established labor forces with new communities now no longer excluded from the labor movement.

In chapter 5 Eimer examines efforts of the Milwaukee County Labor Council (MCLC) to design a proactive economic development plan for the Milwaukee metropolitan area. Combining participant observation with interviews, he details the emergence of the Campaign for a Sustainable Milwaukee (CSM), a broad-based labor–community coalition instrumental in crafting and pursuing policies that advance the interests of a broad cross-section of working people in the region. He pays particular attention to projects that aim to improve the standard of living of minority residents in the central city. Eimer concludes by arguing that the key to MCLC's success has been its willingness to put time and resources into campaigns that benefit the broader community.

In chapter 6, drawing on ethnographic data and results of empirical research, Roland Zullo investigates the role of another Wisconsin labor council in establishing and sustaining a regional, multiunion political coalition. Zullo argues that labor councils are uniquely positioned to facilitate effective member-to-member political outreach by resolving many of the collective-action problems that plague political coalitions. A critical factor is whether local leaders can establish mechanisms for affiliates to achieve their unique political goals without undermining the common pursuit of a unified political agenda.

In chapter 7, Stephanie Luce explores the role of CLCs in the living-wage movement now sweeping the country. Her work draws on dozens of interviews with CLC leaders and living-wage activists to determine the extent of CLC involvement in these campaigns. She finds that councils have played a leading role in almost half the successful campaigns that have been waged to date. When asked why they participate, CLC leaders provide a range of motivations that include improving the standard of living of low-wage workers, building political power and coalitions, and spawning new organizing. Luce suggests that the degree to which these goals have been realized has varied from city to city, as has the actual enforcement of living-wage ordinances. Reflecting on the strengths and weaknesses of the strategies CLCs have employed, she concludes, "labor council leaders can use living-wage campaigns to build coalitions, political power, an atmosphere that supports unionization, and tools that can be used as leverage in new organizing."

In part III, we present three chapters written by people who are intimately involved in efforts to create more active CLCs. These articles provide a unique opportunity to hear from leaders as they reflect critically on their councils' efforts to actualize the goals stated by Union Cities. In chapter 8, Jonathan Rosenblum reviews an innovative multiunion organizing project, Seattle Union Now (SUN), developed by the King County Labor Council (KCLC). As a participant in the creation of SUN, Rosenblum is uniquely positioned to reflect on the key events and developments that led up to the project. In recounting this history, he reveals a slow but steady process of ratcheting up the militancy and capacity of the KCLC. By 1997, after several years of increasing activity, a critical mass of unions made the commitment to increase the level of organizing in the Seattle area. In 1998, with the help of the national AFL-CIO, this commitment was institutionalized in the form of SUN. Since its creation, the project has provided technical assistance to affiliates and mobilized interunion solidarity in support of a variety of organizing campaigns. In some cases, it has moved beyond the provision of support to initiate and coordinate organizing drives. Rosenblum concludes by noting that though SUN has benefited from greater national and local support than many CLCs enjoy, the key ingredients of CLC leadership, commitment to organizing and involvement of rank-and-file members, can be developed in communities anywhere in the country.

In chapter 9, Amy Dean examines a far-reaching effort by the South Bay Labor Council in Silcon Valley to build labor's capacity to be a player in regional economic development. Recognizing that labor can no longer leave questions of investment, training, and economic development to management, the South Bay council has become actively involved in economic planning at the local level. In 1995 it developed Working Partnerships USA, a labor–community partnership that seeks to "bring a wider range of voices to the table in discussions around regional economic development, and state and national employment policy." Dean reflects on the larger societal changes that precipitated this project and then describes the evolution of Working Partnerships USA, which today is engaged in research, education, policy generation, and grass-roots activism.

Finally, in chapter 10, Stewart Acuff reflects on the various strategies and tactics that the Atlanta Labor Council has utilized to build political and economic power in the community. He considers the key components of labor-council success and emphasizes the need for CLCs to ensure that their leadership reflects the face of the community they hope to mobilize, organize, and influence politically. Acuff describes how the Atlanta council vigorously addressed the issue of diversity, eschewing cronyism, to obtain diversity in its own ranks. He notes that white males no longer command a majority of the executive board and suggests that this lends the local labor movement the credibility necessary to reach out to people of all races and ask them to join a diversified alliance. Acuff describes how a more diverse organization has built political power for working people through organizing new members into unions and by advocating economic development and job creation.

Bibliography

Lens, Sidney. 1959. *The Crisis of American Labor.* New York: Sagamore.
Willihan, James. 1985. "The CIO: Industrial Union Council (IUC) Miscellaneous Notes," in *The CIO: 1935–1955.* Chapel Hill: University of North Carolina Press. Or *Union Government and Organization in the United States.* Washington, DC: Bureau of National Affairs.

I

The Task at Hand

1

From Dormancy to Activism

New Voice and the Revival of Labor Councils

Immanuel Ness

Labor councils, the only existing body capable of organizing the common interests of workers—whether they belong to unions or not—reach beyond the individual differences of unions and form the basis for a more unified labor movement. Individual unions, frequently viewed by the media as special interests, do not have the equivalent capacity of labor councils to reach beyond narrower labor market, cultural, and jurisdictional boundaries. But, even as the AFL-CIO has sought to restore councils, it remains unclear how these local labor bodies, steeped for decades in a traditional service model of representation, can transform themselves into organizations capable of mobilizing to fight corporate efforts to depress wages and worsen working conditions.

The longstanding failure of the labor movement to unify around a common program of building local and regional power by increasing member participation and energizing central labor councils has allowed employers to dominate the economic and political agenda with little resistance from organized labor. But one significant question remains unanswered in addressing this problem. If labor councils are doing little to mobilize from among their own ranks, how can they build political and economic power for the majority of workers not organized into unions? One of the most significant initiatives of the new AFL-CIO leadership that assumed power in 1995 is the effort to expand union power locally by urging the central labor councils to transform themselves from declining service organizations to organizing centers for the labor movement.

Vertical to Horizontal Production

A major factor that influences the labor movement's interest in energizing labor councils is the growing importance of the spatial dispersion of work and concomitant declining capability of industrial unions to organize workers in these new workplaces. Industrial restructuring and the growth of subcontracting to small businesses that have never been organized by industrial unions have sustained the rapid expansion in the number of low-wage jobs in the United States over the last two decades. Trade union members who are experienced in industrial organizing techniques increasingly require new organizing strategies that can reach workers in these new sectors. The union organizing campaigns that have depended on preexisting institutional arrangements covering large segments of industry are much less likely to succeed in this new environment. Ironically, the growth in the global economy and capital mobility increases the relevance of metropolitan and community-organizing strategies that target smaller, spatially dispersed firms employing a smaller number of workers across a larger number of industries.

In the late nineteenth century, labor councils formed to unify craft unions around demands for the eight-hour day and improved working conditions. In chapter 3, Stuart Eimer notes that, since the origins of organized labor in the late nineteenth century, proponents of industrial, or vertical, unionism and proponents of geographic, or horizontal, unionism have been in conflict. In each historical era, industrial unionism won out over geographic unionism. The rise of industrial unionism in the first three decades of the twentieth century reduced the significance of central labor councils by shifting resources from local councils to the international affiliates, reducing the relevance of labor councils and promoting sector-based industrial unionism.

The growth of national unions in the late nineteenth and early twentieth centuries altered the institutional ties between international unions and local communities. By the 1950s, industrial-organizing strategies supplanted community and metropolitan organizing, and the relative resources and mobilizing capacity of local labor councils shriveled and disappeared. Since the 1950s, the AFL-CIO contributed to the weakening of councils' ability to mobilize locally by shifting institutional bonds away from local unions to international union leaders. While the labor councils have remained in name, many severely lack resources. Many small labor councils across the nation operate without any staff and without ties to unions, other labor councils, or state federations. Moreover, if the state labor federations are to have an effective political and legislative role, they will require active councils that are capable of mobilizing and organizing members and nonmembers to support labor's program.

Unions fought their own sectarian battles in discrete labor markets, often at the expense of reducing local trade-union solidarity (interview with Bruce Colburn, AFL-CIO field mobilization department, August 1998). As Colin Gordon notes, the viability of metropolitan unions was reduced by the shift in industrial production from local to national markets—calling for a commensurate response by labor to organize and bargain on a national basis (Gordon 1999, 564). By the early 1990s, even large unions with significant rank-and-file support could not overcome management opposition, due in no small way to the unions' failure to build local and regional alliances.

Although there is evidence that industrial unions supported the notion of metropolitan unionism, the shift in institutional focus away from locally based organizations toward larger national structures effectively foreclosed the practicality and political necessity of building community alliances. By the mid-1990s, the more than six hundred CLCs in the United States were dinosaurs of that bygone era when labor united to defend the common interests of workers across diverse categories of skill and craft. Few among the six hundred or so labor councils were performing collective support activities for organizing. Most CLCs limited their activities to public proclamations in support of union organizing or criticizing employer antilabor actions. Only a handful of councils actually directed resources and organizational support to union organizing. The most that councils did was pass on organizing leads to local union affiliates (McLewin 1999, 4). Indeed, AFL-CIO and international union leaders did not view CLCs as integral partners in the future of the American labor movement. Labor councils were not seen as support centers for union organizing or union collective political action but as organizations established to provide information and services to union affiliates (Ulman 1966).

Resistance to change was not only limited to the national labor hierarchy, but was evident on the regional and local level too. CLC leadership, far from being representative of the composition of the local work force, has historically lacked gender, racial, and ethnic diversity and has often been dominated by "old-boy" networks. Councils have often been led by older union leaders, who view their positions as preretirement sinecures and do not see the CLCs as centers for mobilization. Election to CLC leadership was not based on democratic voting by rank-and-file members. Consequently, in many cities, a conservative leadership elected by the numerous but far smaller craft and building-trades unions, which dominated CLCs. These factors contribute to a view of labor councils as irrelevant to serious organizing efforts, and this image hinders the recruitment of promising leaders more representative of labor's diversity and increasing affiliation with and participation by international and local unions.

In theory, international and local trade unions affiliated with the AFL-CIO consider CLC leaders the political voice of the local labor movement, responsible for local policy and political action. However, many central labor councils have had a reputation for taking conservative positions on political and economic issues. In recent decades, the councils have seldom used their position for anything beyond providing perfunctory services and organizing obligatory Labor Day parades.[1]

In other instances, labor councils have been known to use union contributions intended to run the organizations to pay for school scholarships for union members' children. By the mid-1950s, central labor councils and spatial forms of labor organizing were largely overshadowed by the growth of sectoral forms of industrial organizing, and as a consequence, the organizing role of CLCs diminished greatly. For more than sixty years, the typical CLC passed along organizing leads to international and local labor unions (Gapasin and Wial 1998).

Rise of New Voice

The sentiment among international union leaders who deposed Lane Kirkland as AFL-CIO president in 1995 seemed obvious to most observers of organized labor in the United States. For the two decades of Kirkland in leadership, he failed to advance organized labor's legislative agenda of reforming labor law, protecting welfare-state programs, and advancing neo-Keynesian policies deemed vital to labor's success in the post–New Deal era. For many, Kirkland's legacy was his promotion abroad of the U.S. model of trade unionism—a model in which organized labor is conceived as just one interest group among many, rather than as the basis for defending and increasing the economic and political power of workers. By the early 1990s, a growing number of international union leaders recognized this interest group strategy as having contributed in large measure to the paralysis of organized labor as a political force in American society.

The spiraling decline in organized labor's density in the work force from about 35 percent in the mid-1950s to about 13 percent in the mid-1990s was indicative of labor's lost political clout under Kirkland's leadership. At century's end, union density in the private sector hovered below 10 percent—threatening to call into question the future status of unionized workers in the public sector, where density hovered around 60 percent. This decline has been linked to labor's decreasing capacity to organize the majority of workers who are not in unions—and therefore to its growing irrelevance in national political debates. While many unions had abandoned organizing new workers to focus on collective bargaining, by the mid-1990s, it was clear that antiquated labor laws and the renewed willingness of employers to use union-busting tactics to break organizing drives made it nearly impossible to organize workers into unions.

By the mid-1990s, labor leaders were grudgingly recognizing that they could not hold Democrats accountable for not supporting legislation important to unions. Democratic candidates were taking labor's money and resources to get elected, only to take union support for granted once in office. Under Kirkland's stewardship, labor had been acclimating itself to Democratic ambivalence. But President Bill Clinton's active support of the North American Free Trade Agreement (NAFTA) over strident union objections deepened an already profound sense of powerlessness among labor leaders. In the wake of the NAFTA debacle, key international union leaders concluded that simply electing a Democratic majority to Congress would not be enough. What seemed to mark the Kirkland era was the continued transformation of labor from a social movement to just another interest group. Although labor activists had long before called for the transformation of the AFL-CIO and its affiliates into effective organizing and political forces, by the mid-1990s the international union leadership was now also holding this view. To reverse its fortunes, the AFL-CIO needed to make the Democratic Party more accountable to organized labor.

"New Voice" emerged in response to this posture of inertia and lack of a coherent vision for rebuilding labor's power. The New Voice slate, led by John Sweeney, Secretary-Treasurer Richard Trumka of the United Mine Workers, and Executive Vice President Linda Chavez-Thompson of AFSCME (American Federation of State, County, and Municipal Employees) had recognized the need to revitalize the AFL-CIO as a political and organizing force in American society. They won the leadership of the AFL-CIO in October 1995 on a platform that called for devoting greater national federation resources to labor mobilization and new organizing through building interunion alliances. The new leadership maintained that central labor councils must coordinate new organizing as a means of mobilizing all the available resources and support of the labor movement (Rosier 1996). The New Voice leaders considered energizing state federations and central labor councils critical to revitalizing the labor movement on a national scale.

The Road to Union Cities

The critical question then became whether the planned revitalization of the AFL-CIO's national leadership under Sweeney's New Voice would lead to increased political and economic power for U.S. workers. Clearly, its slogans and rhetoric sound more determined, but to what extent has the new leadership met the challenge of achieving concrete gains? After taking office, the New Voice group crafted the Changing to Organize, Organizing to Change campaign to concretely expand labor-union membership by shifting resources to new organizing.

In the late 1980s, while CLCs largely abandoned membership mobilization and new organizing, Jobs With Justice, ACORN, and other locally based, activist labor organizations saw the potential of community-based organizing through labor councils as a means to rebuild labor's political and economic power. In Los Angeles and other major cities, the Justice for Janitors campaign demonstrated the effectiveness of coordinated labor action in winning organizing drives (Bronfenbrenner et al. 1998). Energetic community and labor activists with a history of organizing were elected to council leadership positions in several metropolitan areas—Bruce Colburn in Milwaukee, Stewart Acuff in Atlanta, Amy Dean in South Bay (San Jose, California), and Ron Judd in Seattle. What these leaders share is their determination to change the culture of their local councils to promote new organizing and expand labor's political influence. In 1994, even before John Sweeney and the New Voice slate were elected AFL-CIO officers, the new, activist labor-council leaders, frustrated by a lack of support from the national leadership, met in Las Vegas to discuss an activist strategy for councils. According to Dean, executive officer of the South Bay Labor Council:

> The only thing we had in common was that we understood the power of labor councils to invigorate the labor community. We saw them positioned at the crossroads that could bring together a diversity of unions. The potential for building a progressive majority was enormous even after we showed the movement how to build a constituency and the value of local councils. (Interview with Amy Dean, July 1998)

A central component of the effort was the discussions held with CLCs and international unions seeking to expand membership mobilization and new organizing across the nation. To convince local unions of their importance, the councils needed to prove they could deliver organizing resources to the labor movement.

The new AFL-CIO leadership provided much of the new energy needed to do this, although its capacity remained constrained by limited resources. In January 1996, a labor council advisory committee was formed, chaired by Dean, with the goal of persuading an ambivalent labor movement of the potential for expanding union power through the councils. The following July, the AFL-CIO convened a national meeting of CLCs in Denver, the first such meeting ever held. Council leaders were asked to confront the question of how they could help reverse the decline in union membership (Interview December 1999). Two questions dominated the discussion: how union culture could be changed from one of stagnation and decline to one dedicated to organizing and mobilizing, and how labor councils, given their limited energy and resources, could jump-start local union organizing on a mass scale.

At the Denver conference, smaller councils concerned about decidedly different issues were separated from larger big-city councils to discuss strategies for change. Leaders of councils of all sizes agreed unanimously that the labor movement needed to build political and economic power on the local level to revitalize the labor movement. In Denver in July 1996, the AFL-CIO Field Mobilization Department and interested labor councils convened a meeting of key council leaders to plan a strategy to support the program of change and organizing. At the Denver meeting, a Central Labor Council Advisory Committee was organized on the Future of Labor Councils—a twenty-two-member committee of more active labor councils to develop a national strategy that could be implemented on a local basis (AFL-CIO Central Labor Council Conference, Denver, Colorado, July 1996).

The Union Cities program that emerged from the Denver meeting was motivated by recognition of the need to target organizing to the distinct needs of unions in local communities (interview with Marilyn Sneiderman, June 1998). The program was designed by the new leadership to shift significant federation and international union resources and energy to the effort to unionize more workers. Its goal was to revitalize labor councils as support centers for expanding labor's economic and political power. The new leadership of the AFL-CIO believed that workers needed to trust their unions as viable alternatives to corporate control of the economic and political agenda, a situation caused in part by the declining ability of local unions to organize and mobilize their membership on a geographic basis, a decline that led to a downward spiral in union organizing and membership density. Many local unions simply lacked the resources, organizing culture, and experience to organize new members and to promote issues vital to the interests of working families. Moreover, local unions were more wedded to the culture of their international union and tended to have few ties to their communities.

The eight-point strategy—developed by the local councils with the assistance of the AFL-CIO Field Mobilization Department includes the following objectives: (a) make organizing a priority; (b) mobilize against antiunion employers; (c) build political power through community councils; (d) promote economic growth and protect communities; (e) provide economics education; (f) support the right to organize; (g) promote diversity; and (h) increase union membership.

Make Organizing a Priority

The primary goal of the union and the local councils is to develop union power in local communities by shifting to an organizing perspective. Research showed that, on average, about 3 percent of unions' budgets were devoted to organizing. To increase union power through building membership, union and council resources are to be redeployed to organizing. The AFL-CIO, which had already devoted 30 percent of its budget to organizing, set a target of moving 30 percent of each CLC and local union budget to organizing within three years.

Mobilize Against Antiunion Employers

The aim is to recruit and activate local union members who will serve as solidarity and rapid-response teams available for rallies, demonstrations, and other forms of support for worker struggles against antiunion employers. The AFL-CIO has set a goal for each council to activate at least one percent of members in a given area.

Build Political Power Through Community Councils

The AFL-CIO is seeking to organize grass-roots lobbying and political action committees to work on local, state, and national issues by building community alliances, supporting political candidates committed to working families, and holding those officials accountable after they are elected. All too often, Democratic Party candidates have taken trade unions and CLCs for granted, articulating pro-worker positions during campaigns only to forget about them after they are elected.

The labor–community approach has grown out of successful campaigns conducted in the early 1990s, including the Justice for Janitors campaign by the Service Employees International Union (SEIU), which built solidarity among custodial workers employed in the Los Angeles central business district. In some cities unions have established relations with a political party, in some instances with both major parties. It is hoped that as the labor agenda sharpens, greater pressure for change will come from the rank and file. The general perception of unions as special-interest groups is in fact grounded in the stark reality that unions at present lack the political clout to promote an agenda embracing all workers, and that CLCs frequently endorse candidates who agree to promote the narrower interests of some unions while ignoring broader, class-based issues.

Promote Economic Growth and Protect Communities

The councils are encouraged to work with community supporters in devising economic-development programs, including private and public investment, to maintain and improve public health, environmental, employment, and labor-management standards. For example, publicly funded development projects could prohibit employers from opposing union organizing efforts. During the 1990s, councils throughout the country promoted successful living-wage campaigns, paving the way for broader economic-development strategies directed at increasing union power.

Provide Economics Education

To counter prevailing hype regarding the triumph of the free market, education in economics will show how and why economic conditions are actually declining for most working families. The goal is to give workers the knowledge to make informed decisions during organizing drives and political campaigns.

Support the Right to Organize

CLCs should initiate efforts in city councils and other local bodies to pass resolutions supporting the right of workers to organize and to fight illegal opposition from employers. The councils should hold political candidates accountable as a condition of continued support. The objective is to generate political and community support for worker empowerment and labor law reform.

Promote Diversity

Too often the leadership of CLCs does not reflect the diversity of union members and unorganized workers in local communities. The Union Cities campaign set a goal of promoting gender, racial, and ethnic diversity in CLC leadership positions to reflect the diverse membership of affiliated locals. Already several councils have checked and appointed women, African Americans, Latinos, Asian Americans, and members of other minorities to key leadership positions.

Increase Union Membership

The strategy is to reverse the last four decades of declining union membership. The program set a goal of increasing membership in CLC jurisdictions by 3 percent by the end of the year 2000. The councils are instrumental in this process, generating support for organizing across diverse affiliate unions, as well as building the strength and solidarity necessary for successful strikes, organizing campaigns, and political and legislative initiatives.

Evaluation of Union Cities

Critics argue that revitalized local councils would have achieved many of these goals in absence of the Union Cities program because some councils were already organizing around the principles codified in the national program. For example, the efforts in Atlanta; Milwaukee; Seattle; Lynn, Massachusetts; and San Jose—all of which spearheaded the national effort—were administered on a local basis with little national support. But not all CLCs had the resources to attain these goals, and some achieved dramatic organizing and political victories that can be directly attributed to the Union Cities effort. In its first three and a half years, 160 CLCs nationwide, home to 8.2 million union members (more than 50 percent of all unionized workers in the United States), signed on to the goals of Union Cities.

A survey conducted by the AFL-CIO Field Mobilization Department in July 1998 revealed substantial changes in CLCs representing a majority of workers in the labor movement. Of the 100 CLCs responding in 1998, 69 percent participated in Street Heat actions (mass labor demonstrations) in support of organizing drives; 55 percent participated in the June 24, 1998, Right to Organize Day; 56 percent are participating in economics education; and 51 percent have held a regional organizing conference (see Table 1.1). Moreover, 62 percent are devoting greater resources to new organizing; and 66 percent have elected, developed, or recruited more officers, delegates, and activists of color (AFL-CIO Field Mobilization Department 1998).

Another study, by Philip McLewin of 190 councils (96 Union Cities councils and 94 councils not enrolled in the program), found that labor councils that had adopted the Union Cities program were more likely to engage in activities supporting the mission of the AFL-CIO of mobilizing members, building voice (education, communications with affiliates, and diversity), devoting resources to organizing, and expanding organized labor's political power (McLewin 1999). When size is taken into consideration, the study found, small labor councils that adopted the program had significantly outpaced nonenrollees in the four key categories.[2] Although McLewin found that many councils that went on to enroll in Union Cities were already engaging in activities promoted by the AFL-CIO, labor councils that had embraced and were implementing the program had made substantial gains, compared with those councils that had not yet enrolled. The survey's key finding is that 90 percent of

Table 1.1

Council Participation in Organizing Activities

Activity	Participation (%)
Member/student recruitment for organizing institute	39
National right to organize day of action	55
Commonsense economics training	56
Introduction of right to organize resolutions	34
Street heat actions to support organizing campaigns	69
Regional organizing conference	51

Source: AFL-CIO Field Mobilization Department. "Statistical Report on Central Labor Councils." Washington, DC: AFL-CIO, 1998.

Union City councils were engaged in mobilization efforts, compared to 55 percent of those councils that were not enrolled. Councils not yet enrolled in the Union Cities program were engaged in training rank-and-file volunteers and mobilizing to support organizing at slightly higher rates than cities enrolled in the program.[3] The study's most significant finding is that resources available to all councils, including those unions embracing the program, are in short supply.

Significantly, the survey shows that while Union Cities had engendered more active councils, the program had not altered their relationship with state labor federations. McLewin found that "The Union Cities process had had no measurable effect (better or worse) on CLC-State FED relationships" (McLewin 1999, 7). The absence of significant support for local activities from state federations limited the Union Cities success, because as centers of political activity, state federations are considered vital in implementing labor's program. Thus, while Union Cities has fostered an environment conducive to organizing and has begun to achieve structural changes in localities across the country, because of a lack of financial resources and political backing from state federations, the program cannot build new organizing structures or resolve interunion conflicts and differences in the labor movement.

Limitations

The preliminary experience indicates that labor councils that embrace the Union Cities program have achieved major political and organizing victories through adopting some or all actions in the eight-point program and demonstrates that, if put into practice more systematically, the program could substantially alter the balance of power between capital and labor. However, significant structural changes are needed in CLCs if they are to realize their potential as centers of mobilization and organizing.

While the Union City model has transformed council behaviors in fifteen to twenty larger cities, AFL-CIO and international union leaders maintain that the program needs to expand dramatically if its prescriptions are to have a tangible influence on rebuilding the national power of the labor movement. Thus, if the program is to succeed, large and small labor councils will need to be strengthened by increasing international and local union affiliation and participation. To have a significant influence, the AFL-CIO believes it must increase the number of energized and well-funded councils from the current fifteen to twenty to seventy-five (Sneiderman and Colburn 2000).

Funding limitations are perhaps the most serious impediment to the revitalization of labor councils. In McLewin's survey the average annual per capita revenue of nonenrolled councils was $16,500, while average per capita revenue for councils enrolled in the Union Cities program was $59,600 (McLewin 1999, 7). Not funded by the AFL-CIO, local councils and state federations must rely on contributions from affiliated internationals and local unions. But there has been no requirement that local unions affiliate with councils. Some council leaders and activists resent the fact that the AFL-CIO leadership has recommended change without providing the necessary financing for its implementation. In turn, union leaders maintain that councils must first demonstrate to local unions that they matter. If councils are to transform into activist organizations, they will have to convince under-affiliated unions and prospective affiliates that they provide tangible benefits and can build power for labor in the local community. According to Colburn:

> You can't have a labor movement unless you build local centers of power that transcend differentiated unions. Central labor councils may develop as centers of organizing economic and political power, but the structure of councils' funding and organizing needs to change first to have significant results. (Interview with Bruce Colburn, August 1998)

To improve the stature of labor councils, the AFL-CIO believes it will need to convince international unions that they have a stake in enhancing the local and state labor movements. International unions must, in turn, convince local and state unions to increase affiliation with councils.

Committee 2000 and New Alliance

Although the Union City model succeeded in energizing local labor councils to support political action, mobilize members, and organize drives in nearly one hundred cities across the nation, the AFL-CIO is faced with the dilemma of how to invigorate the hundreds of labor councils that have not embraced the program. Anticipating this problem, John Sweeney formed Committee 2000 in 1998 as an exploratory body empowered to improve the synergy of the AFL-CIO, international affiliates, and local labor unions and to explore a new strategy to activate CICs. The primary charge of Committee 2000 was to recommend programs to coordinate the AFL-CIO effort with affiliated state federations and labor councils through proposing initiatives to assist international unions reach their political and organizational objectives by utilizing state federations and labor councils. Committee 2000 functioned as an international central labor council advisory committee to Sweeney.

Through much of 1999, members of the Executive Council visited communities throughout the United States with the objective of listening to the concerns of workers, trade unionists, and labor leaders. Committee 2000 members found overwhelming support among unions across the country for making better use of labor councils as a tool for mobilizing diverse unions around specific organizing and political objectives. Still, operating on a geographic, rather than an industry level, Committee 2000 found that labor councils remain remote from the concerns of international unions, whose major priority has always been building their own industrially oriented organizations (Sneiderman and Colburn 2000). Consequently, international unions have resisted forcing their local unions to affiliate with labor councils, particularly since state federations and labor councils did not have a uniform program for change that would lead to new organizing. Despite these limitations, the committee members also found that political and economic decentralization have increased international reliance on local and statewide community support for achieving labor's political and organizational objectives.

Task-force members documented the success of the Union Cities in labor councils where the program was adopted. Committee members also documented the urgent need to rebuild state and local organizations across the country. As expected, a significant observation was the criti-

cal role played by state and local bodies and the need to link state federations of labor with local council programs. In most localities, state
federations and labor councils did not adequately coordinate their political and organizing activities. In cases where such activities were coordinated, both state and local bodies lacked the resources to implement
coherent programs, discouraging international affiliates from tangibly
supporting the program (AFL-CIO, August 3, 1999).

New Alliance is the result of three-and-a-half years of experience,
research, and deliberations. It is an ambitious plan that aims to transform the institutional basis of labor councils by pushing international
affiliates and local unions to participate more fully in the revitalization
of councils and state federations. The AFL-CIO maintains that the creation of New Alliance signals the most significant transformation of
organized labor's institutional structure since the merger of the AFL and
CIO in 1955. According to the executive committee:

> In order to balance the need to have both strong, well-resourced local
> organizations—as well as organizations that are rooted in as many com-
> munities as possible—we propose to recreate the central labor council
> structure for the 21st century by working to construct both strong areawide
> labor councils in larger cities and regions, while at the same time insuring
> the continuation of central labor councils in smaller union communities.
> (AFL-CIO, August 3, 1999, pp. 6–7)

New Alliance's primary objective is to integrate the union movement
on a community, regional, and state level, and create more effective bodies
through increasing union participation with the goal of "forging a stronger, more effective and more militant labor movement" (AFL-CIO August 3, 1999, 2). New Alliance's objective is to streamline and restructure
the union movement in communities through integrating and coordinating organization on the state and local level. The program seeks to balance the different needs and perspectives of local unions of differing
size, in different states, regions, and localities, and in different industries and occupations.

Restructuring and Remapping Labor Councils

While the state federations generally serve state political and legislative issues and the labor councils address local issues, Committee 2000
found that neither state nor local bodies were capable of coordinating

labor actions on a metropolitan level. Thus, political action and new worker organizing on the regional level was frequently neglected.

To address the need to coordinate regional action, the New Alliance plans to create areawide federations that will combine the functions of smaller councils that have been inactive or marginalized. The AFL-CIO considers the six hundred chartered central labor councils in the United States to be critically important to the national labor movement. Area labor federations, as they will come to be known, are to be created in metropolitan regions that have reached what the AFL-CIO characterizes as "a sufficient critical mass" of unionized workers that can maintain a minimum of three full-time staff members capable of establishing at least the minimum features of the Union Cities program. To achieve this "critical mass," drafting committees composed of local union leaders may redraw the jurisdictional boundaries of labor councils and merging existing central labor councils where the committee believes resources can be reorganized to bolster and expand council activities to meet the needs of these areas that have been unable to expand their capacities.

The creation of areawide federations is not intended to replace central labor councils in small communities where union membership and resources are not adequate to support the Union City program. Many smaller labor councils do not have full-time staff members or funds to operate viable programs approaching the goals of the Union Cities model. For these councils with limited resources, New Alliance hopes to facilitate partnerships with state federations or areawide federations to achieve the desired level of activities to meet the needs of organized labor in their areas. According to Dean:

> More and more decisions—political and economic—are made at the local and state level. We must have strong, coordinated organizations that can contest for power at the local level, and we have to have these organizations across the country. The New Alliance gives us the opportunity, for the first time in the history of the labor movement, for all three levels of the union movement—national, state, and local—to come together to rebuild our organizations into front-line fighting machines. (Amy Dean, quoted in AFL-CIO, August 3, 1999)

Thus, the intent is not to eliminate local councils, but to improve the ability of smaller councils with less union density to function through linkages with areawide federations. The program is also expected to help build union presence in suburban areas where organized labor has had less of a presence.

State Federations and Labor Councils

The New Alliance program recognizes the problem of fragmentation and decentralization for the national organization and the dispersion of power to the internationals, which are less able to coordinate political affairs on a state and regional basis. Thus, New Alliance aims to central-ize and strengthen the authority of the national AFL-CIO over its re-gional and local bodies through coordinating the programs of state federations and labor councils. State federations will have primary re-sponsibility for advancing the political agenda of labor through repre-senting the interests of workers in the legislative and executive branches of state and national government and coordinating grass-roots mobili-zations. State federations will be responsible for unifying the diverse union interests and developing a common agenda for labor appropriate to the particular state. On a metropolitan level, area federations and la-bor councils are to direct efforts at mobilizing and educating through organizing, contract campaigns, grassroots lobbying, progressive eco-nomic development, and a common political action (AFL-CIO August 3, 1999, 2–3).

Implementation of the New Alliance in the States

The AFL-CIO established broad guidelines encouraging the highest level of international union and statewide participation in approving New Alli-ance state plans and in the approval of work plans and budgets facilitated through regional and state directors. To generate local and state support, the program seeks direct participation of the largest local unions in each state and the approval of the final draft by all local unions. By including international and local union participation in its planning, New Alliance hopes to encourage affiliation with councils and federations.

The process of drafting the New Alliance plan in each state is to be initiated by national AFL-CIO, with the goal of gaining representation from the current leadership in state federations, central labor councils, and other major unions, and the participation of the major national unions in the state. The New Alliance will organize state drafting committees that will propose plans to reorganize and remap the state labor move-ments through reorganized state federations and the formation of new areawide labor councils with sufficient resources to carry out the goals of the plan. Smaller labor councils will affiliate with the new state federation or new areawide councils. One of the objectives is to maximize the effectiveness of the labor movement in states by eliminating duplication of responsibilities and assuring complete coordination among the reorganized affiliated organizations.

Smaller, community-based councils will be maintained or created in cases where membership is sufficient to require the presence of labor councils, but where there are too few members to sustain areawide councils. The state labor federations will take into account the interests of smaller councils and their unions in planning strategies and actions.

Full Participation and Diverse Leadership

The major limitation of current labor councils is the lack of full participation among major unions in states and communities. Insufficient participation reduces the resources available to labor councils to implement Union Cities programs. Since only 55 percent of unions nationwide are affiliated with state federations and about 50 percent are members of labor councils, the financial resources available for mobilization, organizing, and political action are severely limited. The goal is to have all national unions participate actively and fully with each affiliate in state federations and labor councils throughout the country. As remnants of the 1930s, councils tend to be led by a small number of craft unions that frequently do not represent the unions in states and communities. Thus, to justify greater participation and affiliation among unaffiliated and underaffiliated unions, the AFL-CIO seeks to meet its broader concerns and interests by increasing the diversity of membership in the state and local bodies on the basis of gender, race, ethnicity, industry and craft, geography, and size to represent the broad composition of the labor movement more accurately. By establishing criteria and guidelines for participation and leadership, the goal is to make organized labor look like the workers it represents.

Affiliation, Work Plans, and Budgets

New Alliance also aims to develop a coherent central-labor-council strategy that appeals to a broader labor base that will spur unions to affiliate fully. Full affiliation will lead to increased budgets and more effective state federation and labor council programs. Because organized labor does not require mandatory affiliation in state and local bodies, AFL-

CIO organizers believe that the New Alliance must persuade national unions to encourage local unions to affiliate through developing effective programs that help build the power of organized labor through building cross-union mobilization for organizing and contract support.

The plan calls for underaffiliated unions to phase in increased affiliation over time with the assistance of national unions, with the goal of encouraging unions to participate fully once New Alliance plans are adopted in their state federations and councils. Where there are gaps in funding, the AFL-CIO is expected to sustain state federations and labor councils with subsidies and other support.[4] The national unions will encourage local unions to remain affiliated with federations and labor councils at agreed-upon levels.

Conclusion

The institutional and bureaucratic resistance to change labor councils to activist organizing bodies has endured within the AFL-CIO and within the American labor movement since its origins in the late nineteenth century. However, despite this opposition, the transformational potential of labor councils as a geographic organizing force has always remained formidable. Central labor councils occupy a unique position in assisting local unions, long separated by competing industrial traditions, to unify around common issues.

The struggle for leadership in the AFL-CIO in 1995 demonstrably reflected organized labor's obvious recognition of its inability to mobilize and organize American workers for political and social change. As labor union density declined and political capacity evaporated, this apparatus of the labor movement that was built in the 1930s did not seem responsive to the real needs of organized and unorganized American workers of the 1990s. The new leaders of the AFL-CIO saw the stagnation of labor councils as a primary failure of organized labor. Because the American labor movement is wedded exclusively to an industrial-union mentality, they have been unable to respond to corporate restructuring and geographic decentralization of production.

The basic premise of the AFL-CIO effort to revitalize labor councils is that the decentralized nature of the American federal system of government compels organized labor to operate effectively on the national, state, regional, and local level. Industrial restructuring and decentralization of production has imposed greater demands on organized labor to be able to challenge corporate power effectively through building local power in America's cities and communities. Union Cities demonstrates that labor councils can become decisive in transforming unions into forces to challenge capital for economic and political power for workers. But if the program is to be more than a chimera, the AFL-CIO will have to compel unions to affiliate with councils and state federations. The New Alliance initiative recognizes that the AFL-CIO will not achieve full affiliation through coaxing and persuading union leaders, but will have to institute a concrete program to mandate the affiliation that is so necessary to enhance labor's power.

New Alliance recognizes labor's belief that the AFL-CIO and its constituent unions must operate effectively on a state, regional, and local level to achieve the goals that were articulated under Union Cities and that are necessary to rebuild organized labor's organizational and political strength. The New Alliance drastically transforms the relationship among the AFL-CIO, state federations, and labor councils because it potentially redefines the relationship through supporting geographic organizing. Since the program potentially treads on entrenched union interests that are comfortable with old ways of doing things, it is essential that it gain the support of leading international unions. Critical to its success is increasing funding through increasing affiliation with international and local unions. Without greater funding New Alliance will remain a good idea without a good result.

Notes

1. In 1994, even this tradition was challenged, when the New York Central Labor Council decided to hold its parade down Fifth Avenue only once every two years. Ted Jacobsen, CLC secretary, rationalized this change as a reflection of the culmination of the labor movement's success: "We're a victim of our own success. We've created this big middle class, and it likes an extra day's rest at the end of the summer like everyone else" (Kaufman 1994). This version of a victorious labor movement belies the reality of a divided union leadership struggling to stay afloat. Rarely, if ever, did CLC's actively mobilize support for new organizing.

2. McLewin found that, in forty activities important to the AFL-CIO mission, Union City councils contribute 41 percent more than councils not yet enrolled. Union cities had a 68 percent value added in mobilizing, 53 percent in community voice, 30 percent in organizing, and 28 percent in building political power. The study also found that among small councils with an average annual budget below $40,000, union cities maintained a 40 percent value-added advantage over small councils that were not enrolled in the program. McLewin's survey compared councils on levels of participation, differences in participation, rankings of importance of CLC activities, and differences in levels of ranking.

3. McLewin found that councils not enrolled in the program typically held one mobilization effort per year—while councils enrolled in the program were engaged in monthly mobilizations (McLewin 1999, 5).

4. After adoption of New Alliance by national and local unions, state federations, and labor councils, newly reorganized state federations and new area labor federations, they are expected to develop two-year work plans and budgets designed to meet the goals and objectives of the New Alliance (AFL-CIO, August 3, 1999). Each state federation and council is required to submit work plans and budgets that are to be reviewed and approved by governing state bodies and national AFL-CIO for review and approval.

Bibliography

AFL-CIO. 23rd Biennial Convention. Home Convention 99 Resolution Book One, No. 12. Los Angeles, CA, October 1999.

AFL-CIO. Building A New Labor Movement in Our Communities: The New Alliance. Chicago, IL: AFL-CIO Executive Council Statement, August 3, 1999.

AFL-CIO. Committee 2000 Site Visit to the Atlanta Labor Council, AFL-CIO and the Albany/Southwest Georgia Labor Council. Washington, DC: AFL-CIO Field Mobilization Department, April 22, 1999.

AFL-CIO. Field Mobilization Department. Statistical Report on Central Labor Councils. Washington, DC: AFL-CIO, 1998.

AFL-CIO. State Federation Visits: Executive Summary. Washington, DC: AFL-CIO, 1999.

Bronfenbrenner, Kate, Sheldon Friedman, Richard W. Hurd, Randolph A. Oswald, and Ronald L. Seeber, eds. *Organizing to Win: New Research on Union Strategies*. Ithaca, NY: Cornell University Press, 1998.

Gapasin, Fernando, and Howard Wial. "The Role of Central Labor Councils in Union Organizing in the 1990s." In *Organizing to Win: New Research on Union Strategies*, ed. Kate Bronfenbrenner, Sheldon Friedman, Richard Hurd, Ronald Seeber, and Rudolph Oswald. Ithaca, NY: Cornell University Press, 1998.

Gordon, Colin. "The Lost City of Solidarity: Metropolitan Unionism in Historical Perspective." *Politics and Society* 27, no. 4 (December 1999): 561–85.

Greenhouse, Steven. "Growth in Unions' Membership in 1999 Was the Best in Two Decades." *New York Times*, January 20, 2000, A15.

Kaufman, Michael T. "Labor Day Approaches for Harvard." *New York Times*, September 3, 1994, B1.

Kriesky, Jill. *Working Together to Revitalize Labor in Our Communities: Case Studies of Labor Education-Central Labor Body Collaboration*. Orono, ME: University and College Labor Education Association, University of Maine, 1998.

Lazarovici, Laureen. "Launching a New Alliance." *America @ Work*, June 1999.

Luria, Daniel, and Joel Rogers. "A New Urban Agenda." Boston Review 22, no. 1 (February/March 1997).

McLewin, Philip. *Has Union Cities Made a Difference? An Analysis of the 1999 AFL-CIO Central Labor Council Survey.* Washington, DC: AFL-CIO Field Mobilization Department, 1999.

Ness, Immanuel. "The Road to Union Cities." *Working USA* 2, no. 4, (November/December 1998).

Rosier, Sharolyn A. "Energized Central Labor Councils Explore New Roles." *AFL-CIO News*, August 5, 1996, 5.

Segrue, Thomas. *Origins of the Urban Crisis: Race and Inequality in Postwar Detroit*. Princeton, NJ: Princeton University Press, 1996.

Shefter, Martin. "Trade Unions and Political Machines: The Organization and Disorganization of the American Working Class in the Late Nineteenth Century." In *Working Class Formation: Nineteenth-Century Patterns in Western Europe and the United States*, ed. Aristide Zolberg and Ira Katznelson. Princeton, NJ: Princeton University Press, 1986.

Sneiderman, Marilyn, and Bruce Colburn. New Strength: Union Cities and the New Alliance. Draft paper, February 3, 2000.

Ulman, Lloyd. *The Rise of the National Trade Union*. Cambridge, MA: Harvard University Press, 1966.

Wial, Howard. "The Emerging Organizational Structure of Unionism in Low-Wage Services." *Rutgers Law Review* 45 (1993): 680–92.

Interviews

Interview with Amy Dean, South Bay Labor Council, January 8, 2000.

Ibid., December 1999.

Interview with Bruce Colburn and Marilyn Sneiderman, AFL-CIO, October 29, 1999.

2

"Everything That Moves"

Union Leverage and Critical Mass in Metropolitan Space

Wade Rathke and Joel Rogers

Of the more than 3 million new members American unions gained in 1937, more than 99.9 percent did not join through the NLRB (National Labor Relations Board) certification process. If the mid-1950s level of union win rates and growth through NLRB elections had continued through the mid-1990s, private-sector union density would be roughly identical to what it is now.

Is there a lesson in these facts? For a self-rejuvenating labor movement intent on reclaiming its place in this economy—a movement with declared ambitions to organize tens of millions of new members in the next decade—many think that there must be a lesson and that it is well past time that labor learned it. But just what the lesson is, how to learn it under contemporary conditions, and what learning it might imply for labor's present structure and organizational life all remains obscure.

It is clear enough that exclusive reliance on NLRB certifications is a loser for a labor movement that wants to increase its share of the total workforce.[1] And it is clear that many of the most interesting examples of new organizing, even some startling successes, occur largely or completely outside the tried and untrue routine of NLRB elections. Among the examples in recent years:

- The Hotel and Restaurant Employees union (HERE), using a combination of aggressive organizing, aggressive bargaining for card check at new facilities, direct action, select strike activity, and a large amount of local political muscle, has picked up 15,000 workers in Las Vegas over the last decade and driven membership in its Health and Welfare Fund to one in seven Las Vegas residents.
- The Service Employees International Union's (SEIU) Justice for Janitors (JFJ) campaign has preserved or enhanced market share in Los Angeles, San Jose, Philadelphia, and other cities through aggressive public campaigns and leverage off the existing organized employer base. Recently it achieved card check union recognition without an election in a small nursing-home chain by building off organized parts of the industry. And SEIU Local 880, making use of "members only/pay as soon as you join" tactics largely unknown in the private sector since the 1930s, has continued to grow—and grow, and grow.[2]
- The United Food and Commercial Workers union (UFCW), using pressure campaigns built on heavy advertising and telepicketing (calling union households to encourage them to boycott nonunion grocery stores), has successfully defended or increased market share in a number of regions. Elsewhere, it has used "stop the purchase" contract language to influence the bidding on the unionized but going-out-of-business Woodies grocery chain in Washington, D.C., and it has won union card check and neutrality at the historically antiunion Hecht's grocery chain that wanted a share of the old Woodies market.
- The United Brotherhood of Carpenters and Joiners (UBCJ), which captured and extended the insurgent success of the heavily Latino California Drywallers (dominating a market segment and driving up wages throughout it), has organized carpenters' associations in Calgary, Canada; Gainesville; and Boise. These associations have made wage demands and have organized and signed up enough members to move to significant or even numerically dominant membership shares of relevant labor markets—again, largely outside the NLRB.
- The Union for Needletrades Industrial and Textile Employees (UNITE) had leveraged agreements with lead plants of large employers (Levi Strauss, Tultec) to gain either card check or less resistance in other operations (evidenced in the 600-member Levi

Strauss facility organized in Albuquerque). Whether in its Montreal campaign against Peerless, an apparel company—where UNITE used its immigrant rights to challenge a company union that discriminated against them—or in its Dominican Republic campaign against Bibong—where UNITE gained the assistance of other employers in curbing the clothing maker's union abuse by threatening a Generalized System of Preferences–based lawsuit undermining Caribbean Basin Initiative export rights—it has freely used legal tactics outside labor law proper to improve its bargaining position. UNITE's Justice Centers in Los Angeles and New York, meanwhile, provided another example of worker service associations, as defined on a broad industry basis.

- The International Brotherhood of Electrical Workers (IBEW) has supplemented the longstanding building-trades practice of controlling work through (non-NLRB) prehire agreements—negotiated top-down with employers—with more aggressive bottom-up salting practices aimed at holding or extending market share through placing union members on nonunion jobs. In the Pacific Northwest, the trades are now considering a unified strategy, employing both tactics to pursue the area's home-building labor market.
- The International Longshoremen's and Warehousemen's Union (ILWU), building off its historic base among agricultural workers in Hawai'i, has bargained with landholders to extend its power in hotel and other commercial developments in Hawai'i. Back on the mainland, the growth in membership of the International Brotherhood of Teamsters (IBT) Sacramento United Parcel Service division remains a classic of systematic non-NLRB accretion to existing, growing strength.[3]

As impressive as much of this activity is, however, the numbers tell us it is clearly not enough. There are as many reasons for this as variations in the tactics described. With rare exceptions, the organizing is not at regional or industry wage scales. Some cases, including some of the most dynamic and truly membership-mobilizing ones, appear to depend on extraordinary leaders or conditions. They are heroic, not clearly replicable, with practice outrunning theory. Other cases show almost too much theory and too little real mobilization. They feature a literal application of the injunction to "organize employers, not employees"—resulting in employer organization without new members and resulting in mediocre contracts—or a weak "associational unionism" that provides new services for old bases, or old services for new ones, but builds little self-sustaining organization among either.[4] Most important, even the best examples face the limits (isolation, previous alliance, the broader combustion breaking out of both could bring) of being exceptions—limits imposed by a labor movement that has generally not recognized or secured the institutional conditions to grow and expand its membership.

This will not do. Along with heroism and variety, labor needs organizational routines and replicable models subject to wide application, without prohibitive expense, by unexceptional individuals and organizations (or at least no more exceptional than those who have already chosen the benefits of union representation), in a movement structured to reward only those who actually expand it. Labor needs a plausible and disciplined organizing *strategy*—one that will inevitably rely in part on NLRB procedures, but draw on its overriding strength from actions outside that process—and clarity about what its execution requires institutionally. At present it has neither.

Of course, the beginning of wisdom in finding that strategy is to recognize that the search is never-ending. Nobody has all the answers now, and nobody ever will. Still, we believe labor could be much clearer on what some of the elements of a winning strategy are, and how they depart not just from discredited practices of old, but from some of the "cutting edge" practices of the present.

In the text that follows, we will provide a broad-brush outline of how labor's strategy in the future needs to depart from its strategy of the past. Second, and showing their natural linkages to that new strategy, we identify some of the mechanisms that explain recent organizing success outside the NLRB. Third, we identify the changes in labor's own targeting and organizational routines necessary to bring these examples to scale.

Broad Strokes

Post–World War II labor's organizational practice was defined by four basic elements.[5]

Just Service

Provide members with good wages and benefits, and the unorganized will join up. Effectively, this was the theory of union growth trade union leadership offered in the postwar period. With the exception of a 1960s explosion in the public sector, organizing expenditures as a percentage of total revenues stagnated or declined throughout the period—even as increased workforce heterogeneity, spatial isolation, and changing firm size and structure were raising the effective costs of organizing. The union wage-and-benefit premium rose; but the new members did not come into unions as fast as the old members were disemployed or new labor-market entrants were integrated into a "unionfree" environment. Where new units were targeted for organizing, the basic pitch was "first contract and, thereafter, peace." The basic goal was to gain majority status among the workers—seen as necessary to the economics of servicing, of contract enforcement, and of the protections offered only to *exclusive bargaining representatives* that had demonstrated such status. Dues were seen to be collectible only following achievement of majority status, and after contract negotiation, union members were asked for little else. When organizing failed to achieve majority support within a limited time frame, it was generally abandoned.

Production Control

Encouraged by law and their own organizational sense, with rare exceptions (in particular, the building trades) unions steered clear of making demands on issues lying at the *core of entrepreneurial control.* They reacted to firm decisions on training, technology, investment, relocation, product strategy, and work organization; they negotiated job descriptions and defended their boundaries in administration of the internal labor market; they engaged in productivity bargaining tying compensation to success in raising the rate of output. But they did not typically seek to take responsibility for steering the firm's product strategy or organizing the inputs necessary to implement preferred strategies. In a weaker position than the employer, unions saw such assumption of responsibility as promising only responsibility without power and blurring the distinctions between "us" and "them" critical to maintaining solidarity in the unit. Needless to say, the prospect of changing the strategies of the entire industry was considered even more daunting and unattractive as a task.

Specific Sites

Despite lead agreements, pattern bargaining, and the labor market sectoral jurisdictions of the Congress of Industrial Organizations (CIO), collective bargaining agreements were generally negotiated on a firm-by-firm, and often plant-by-plant, basis. Contract administration was highly decentralized, with wide variation in agreements across sites. Within regional labor markets, there was little effort (again, the prevailing wages of the trades loom as an exception) to generalize wage or benefit norms beyond organized employers. Efforts at multiunion bargaining, much less organizing, were infrequent. Murderous jurisdictional disputes were not. And if relations among unions were not close in regional labor markets, relations between the labor movement and community organizations were generally confined to charitable giving, with no coordination of organizing strategies.

Liberal Democrats

With very rare exceptions, unions were loyal supporters of the Democratic Party and deeply hostile to independent politics or even sharp programmatic definition. In contrast to the weight of union activity and need, political work—understood throughout as support for candidates—was also heavily skewed toward national, as against state or local, government.[6]

Without attending to its origins, or the suppression of alternatives that was required for its consolidation, or the flaws that many pointed out at the time, we say only this about this "traditional model" of unionism. It worked passably well—though as the steadily declining union-density figures attest, chiefly for those already in unions—in a relatively closed economy dominated by large, spatially concentrated firms generally featuring "Taylorist" time-management forms of work organization; occupied by semi- or unskilled labor, composed overwhelmingly of men; and faced with a "nationalizing" state in which even Richard Nixon declared his loyalty to Keynes. But it works much less well in today's world, with lower average firm size; more widely dispersed production, a working class not "ready made" but repeatedly "unmade" through increased educational opportunity, work heterogeneity, and spatial dispersion; composed increasingly of minorities and women in firms subject to increased competition (owing both to international pressures and, more important in our view, technology, deregulation, and the failure to foreclose "low-road" restructuring options at home that seek to increase worker exploitation) and policy makers hostile to union presence or utterly confused about the vital contribution organized workers can make to a productive economy.[7]

More precisely, the service model proves hopelessly expensive, while not producing active and engaged memberships; the two conditions together inhibit organizing, which requires a vast increase of expenditures on paid organizers and recruitment and mobilization of the existing base. Particularly in large units, the preoccupation with majority status imposes too demanding a condition of success and slows the needed coordination across sites, sectors, regions, and even different branches of large, national, but decentralized employers. It also carries enormous opportunity costs for membership growth, since in virtually all workplaces some significant percentages of workers wish now to belong to unions.[8] Meanwhile, economic restructuring has made investment, relocation, technology, and training decisive for member well-being, the defense and advance of which requires that unions be as deeply involved in "baking" the pie as carving it up. Where unions can best do this, however—and gain the ability to do it in part through their contribution to the infrastructure of advanced production—is less in the high politics of federal policy than the low politics of regional labor markets, where in any case their continued existence is unthinkable without substantial local political power. For both reasons, unions have found the need for closer strategic alliance with a range of community groups and populations (in particular, populations of color) traditionally operating at some distance from the labor movement. But this often sets them on a collision course with internationals much more interested in the next congressional election and with a Democratic Party that, at its best, provides real support only in up-ballot federal races, and at its more frequent worst is hostile to the idea of actually building union power.

As a general matter, then, we would argue that this traditional model should be turned on its head, as illustrated in the following four points.

"Everything That Moves"

Locally based organizing staffs and member organizers are a cheaper and more effective way to organize than parachuting international representatives in for hot shop campaigns where workers are already eager to join unions. Imagine a union movement that took the development of in situ organizing capacity—among rank-and-file members, stewards, local unions—building on the one signal strength labor still has: the loyalty of its own people. With such built-in capacity more or less permanently in place, the logic of majority-only organizing and short time-cycles for achieving it—mistaken in any case, given the need for expansive reach—additionally fails. It becomes possible to contemplate truly long-term and large-scale campaigns and, within them, clearer focus on the real goal of organizing—which is not to get to contract per se but to build the union presence in the workplace. Employees in units still lacking majority status would be given the full rights and responsibilities of other union members and accreted to the organizing machine of which they are one extension. Reciprocally, the "organizer" would become less a "parachutist" and more a "member of the community"—an on-the-scene, full-time union activist. He or she would help direct the training and administration of the local organizing machine, do ongoing targeting for new outreach (itself improved by the organizer's longer presence in the community), strategize political supports for campaign efforts, and so on.

Terms of Production

In the supply-side kingdom, the bourgeoisie is king, but only if the serfs permit. Operating across firms as well as within them, a union movement seriously interested in affecting the design and utilization of human capital systems, technology, and work organization could in fact do so. Power in these areas, moreover, could be bargained-for power in decisions further back in the production chain—investment, new technology, and product strategy. And especially in the United States, where weak employer associations operate as little more than trade associations, coordination across firms to supply the needed inputs for advanced production—regional training systems, one-stop-shopping for labor-market services, intermediaries for economically targeted investment, modernization assistance of all kinds, early-warning networks, production networks, search assistance for needed employees, among others—is something that unions are uniquely positioned to provide. Imagine then, a labor movement that did provide them—that offered itself as another force of production, but only to employers prepared to share power in decision making and comply with specified wage and production norms. Imagine this was sought not just in lead firms but in their primary and secondary suppliers, that support of lead firms was in part conditioned on their assistance in generalizing such norms to suppliers.

Coordination

To shift strategies and wage-and-benefit conditions in large industries, workers in those industries need to be organized, and growing variation across firms increasingly recommends that union organization really be "wall-to-wall," encompassing all workers, regardless of skill. Frequently, a single union simply cannot do this. Imagine, then, a labor movement that recognized this fact and devised joint organizing strategies for sectors; instead of policing existing jurisdictional boundaries, central bodies would monitor their deliberate mutual transgression. Recruited members could be divided up by unions on any number of imaginable justified bases or thrown into a new pool jointly administered by those contributing to it. The same holds, *a fortiori*, for the organization of regional labor markets. With critical mass provided by pooled resources, organizing campaigns are the natural complement and support to regional skills standards and other aspects of effective supply—especially in metropolitan labor markets—not least because they can foreclose the low-wage restructuring strategy that suppresses the demand it aims to meet. As regional labor bodies come to take a more active role in securing the infrastructure of advanced, high-wage production, it would thus be natural for them also to assume supervision of such organizing, making terms explicit in their double-barreled strategy of imposing norms on the economy (and thus punishing "bad" firms) while assisting firms in meeting them (rewarding "good" firms).

Independent Politics

Finally, we favor a labor movement that is genuinely independent in its political operations—governed in its political endorsements and supports not by party label but by the values and program of those seeking its help (discounted of course by the plausibility of their implementing the values and program). Imagine too that labor invested heavily in developing its own capacity to shape the terms of political debate and action—spending less on "hand it over" PAC contributions to individual candidates and more on membership training, candidate recruitment (and more training) from among its own ranks, development of its own program, the institution of precinct-based labor–neighbor political machines, and ongoing work with progressive elected public officials sympathetic to this program. Imagine that this effort was made first where it was most feasible and traditionally neglected—in local and state politics. There, the costs of elections are infinitely cheaper, the offices at stake are of immediate relevance to improving labor's organizing terms,[9] and the vast majority of public offices (certainly 80 percent) are nonpartisan—so support for more a more labor-friendly formation than the Demo-

cratic Party need not even raise concerns about traditional national loy-
alties. For relatively modest expenditures, in most American cities it
would again be possible for labor to help set and move the public agenda.

Nuts and Bolts

Sifting through the experience of some of the best non–NLRB-centered
organizing, we glimpse elements of this new strategy—albeit generally
not self-conscious or at needed scale. Without drawing everything from
that experience, or trying to fit all suggestions into it, we note in particular
the use of *leverage*, pay-as-you-go *organization* with broadly defined interests, the *spatial* or *sectoral* nature of the organizing frame, the explicit
use of public opinion and *politics* in advancing campaigns and increasing
union strength, and, as a master correlative of all this, increased attention
to cities or *metropolitan* regions as sites of organizing.

Leverage and Critical Mass

With a long-enough fulcrum, you can move the world; in any campaign
you know you are winning when the opportunists climb on board. These
two verities speak to what really should be an iron law of organizing:
always and everywhere devise strategies that exploit existing strengths
that seek leverage strategies that exploit those strengths while aiming
for "critical mass" effects–sufficient density and momentum that the
costs of offering support drop and the costs of not joining rise. That
many unions recognize this is apparent from the examples cited above—
IBT's accretion strategy in Sacramento, HERE's success in Las Vegas,
or the otherwise quite different UFCW and JFJ/SEIU based on existing
employer bases.

Often, of course, such critical mass is to be sought in particular industries or sectors, defined by some number of competing firms—and
here the antecedents are so familiar as to hardly bear renewed notice. A
very traditional goal of unions has been to "take wages out of competition," to make the costs of unionization felt by all competing firms. Dis-
regarding tastes for despotism, competing firms should be indifferent
between unionfree and fully unionized environments; it is only the in-
termediate case—where unionization is a cost felt by some but not all
competitive rivals—that drives them to union avoidance or rollback.
Even here, however, there are different incentives for employers depend-

ing on the extent of unionization. Imagine employer happiness as a U-curve, with the top left tail being the unionfree environment, the top right one being the fully unionized environment, and the line on which the U sits describing increasing union density. Unions need to scramble hard to get to the bottom of the curve, and they can expect to do so over general employer opposition, but once a certain density is reached they can expect something quite different: tacit or overt support from already-unionized employers for extending the benefits of unionization to their rivals. That is the point of critical mass.[10]

But this familiar effect, especially in today's world, has two additional implications or instances.

Pay-as-You-Go Organizing

While somewhat trickier given the paucity of examples, SEIU Local 880's success with "members-only" representation suggests that, especially in dense population areas, some measure of in-some-measure self-sufficing leverage is to be found everywhere. Of course, to find it again requires a break with the "contracts are us" model of unionism, a shift in the goal of organizing from union serviced contracts per se to independent worker organizations that are durable and grow *before* as well as after they reach contract. And that requires that those who would claim the benefits of such membership take the costs of union membership seriously from the start. Given the plethora of unenforced labor regulations, bad management practices, possibilities for interesting and useful alliances with allies elsewhere in the improvement of workplace conditions, it is not so very hard to convince workers in minority settings that they have something to gain from being in a union, even if a majority of their colleagues are not yet persuaded of that fact. A labor movement that turns away the energy and resources of such workers is wasting an obvious asset. Notice too that harnessing that asset would immediately vastly extend the range of labor's reach. It would be, if not dominant everywhere, then at least present almost everywhere.

Spatial and Sectoral Organizing

While leverage and critical mass, not to mention minority memberships, can be sought on a sector or employer basis, the most obvious place to seek them is within regional labor markets. It is there that the

effects of density in one firm can be most easily leveraged to its neighbor, there that the effects of density in one sector can be most easily
leveraged to another, there that the range of solidarity and service activity of a sort that would satisfy members without contracts are most
easily and efficiently realized. And it is there that the distinctive modern contribution of unions to creating a well-ordered economy would
in fact first have to be realized: regional labor-market boards and integrated human-capital systems, modernization programs, a variety of
public goods essential to the success of advanced firms and not capable of being produced by any one of them.

Politics

Public power is also organized spatially, and public power is needed to
reduce organizing costs. It is hard to imagine HERE's Las Vegas campaigns (or the Atlanta Central Labor Council campaign on Olympic work)
without local political muscle, or a JFJ campaign with a completely
hostile police presence. But while everywhere to be seen, national unions
have been slow to take the point of this explicitly—by deliberately seeking the political power, beneath the federal or even state level, that would
most directly aid them in their organizing. (However, almost behind
their backs, the Central Labor Councils (CLCs) are beginning to do it.
Look at the political operations in Milwaukee, Santa Clara, or San Francisco, led by the CLC.) Nor, it bears emphasis, does the importance of
politics consist only in the spark that some power in the state may provide to organizing. In today's world, no less than the old one, thinking
of building a union movement as an essentially "economic" project distinct from a political one is like thinking about ice without water, or
skiing without snow. Politics is necessary to lubricate the economic advance and to define the terms of what that advance is about. Most ab-
stractly, but necessary for labor to grasp, the economic project can only
command popular support if the project shows the contribution of an
organized people, and for this contribution to be seen, the demand on
the "economy" must be more stringent than rewards for shareholders.
Some broader notion of the social good and social productivity is necessary to make visible the productive contribution of people. The signa-
ture of new labor is to raise standards and then help in their achievement;
the contribution made in the second activity is invisible without the first;
the first is impossible without some measure of state power.

Cities

Put the pieces together—the need to leverage off existing strength, the gains to be had by aiming at critical mass, enough density of activity and people to support members-only organizing, the need to show union contribution in providing the productive public goods that also require those densities, a labor movement that aims at taking the political power it needed to protect itself—and what do you have as the natural targets for investment in organizing? Most important, we should think, are metropolitan regions. The degree to which the labor movement was always a distinctly metropolitan phenomenon is not something widely enough appreciated even in the labor movement. But density in metropolitan areas has always been, and continues to be, several times national density levels, and it is the failure to protect that density at critical mass levels that most explains the collapse of traditional unionism.[11] These are the most promising ruins from which to arise.

What It Takes

A union movement that wants to take these lessons seriously will do several things. With a concentration on metro areas, it will build local capacity for coordination and organizing and politics, accrete members in minority settings to those local bodies and institutions that have been refashioned as powerful organizing machines, gain additional national visibility by campaigns against partially organized lead employers. Standing in the way of such obvious moves, however, are three longstanding traditions in the labor movement: studied indifference to the strength of local coordinating bodies, the "campaign" mode of organizing that looks for quick results (as conventionally measured, again, by contracts), and norms on jurisdiction that do not require any results at all.

Local Capacity

To agitate, organize, service minority members, run candidates, or perform other useful activities, local labor bodies need staff and technical assistance. But under current rules, with antecedents in the silos-of-solidarity industrial unionism sellout of CLCs going back to the first merger of the AFL and CIO, they are effectively denied this support by a culture that sees local coordinating bodies as distinctly secondary institutions—

unworthy of mandatory comprehensive per capita contributions by the members of the larger federation. A movement that is interested in serious local capacity will take one of its central tasks to be the revival of CLCs, beginning with the necessary flow of funds. Not inconsistently, where the CLC structure is itself too fatally weak or uninteresting to hold much promise of organizing return, there should be no hesitation in supporting a particularly aggressive local, or confederation of locals, in performing the necessary coordinating and organizing function. Beyond the check, needed technical assistance to these local coordinating bodies—and this is a role that coordinated internationals, as well as the federation itself, could in fact usefully perform—would include advice on modernizing their political operations (list management, voter-file integration with membership files, candidate recruitment and training, program, message), building economic development and industrial policy capacity [sectoral training consortia, modernization services, pension- and 401(k)-based independent financial vehicles], coordinating with national solidarity, organizing, and initiative campaigns (e.g., Overnite, Detroit newspapers, Beverly Nursing Homes), living-wage initiatives, and managing and modernizing their own operations (strategic planning, use of committees, media operations, secondary leadership development, internal and external communications, links with universities, development). The problems are not dissimilar in different sites. For relatively little money, enormous gains could be made by sole-source production of standardized supports of this kind.

Patient Capital

If contracts are accepted as simply one point (not necessarily the most important one) on the continuum of building a worker organization, if what is most needed at the moment are large-scale and long-term organizing projects aimed at achieving real density and critical mass, if one of the techniques of paying for pay-as-you-go members in minority settings, if support for them as well as the more general organizing work requires the knitting together of competent coordinating capacity in local arenas, results will not be seen tomorrow. Like a rocket that will eventually go much further with a greater payload than a popgun, the organizing strategy recommended here will show slower takeoff and flatter trajectory than "three yards and a cloud of dust." That requires patience in organizing budgets. The prominent inclusion of pay-as-you-go members in the union's work provides a ready measure on accountability, and other more interesting ones abound (success in local ordinances favorable to unions, rates of job retention and measurable job improvement, rates of membership involvement in union activity, changes in membership satisfaction and pride in the union, willingness of local unions to increase organizing budgets, etc.). But still, it must be recognized that, as the saying goes, it took a while to get into this mess, and it will take a while to get out.

Jurisdiction

Organizing requires resources and measured risk taking in their application, but the labor movement is structured not to reward such risk takers, however high the collective return. Nowhere is this more apparent than in the current union practice regarding jurisdiction. In the passage from the antiraiding provision of Article XX of the AFL-CIO constitution—a good, minimal solidarity principle in building a bigger movement—to the anticompetitive rules on organizing in what has become known as Article XXI, labor has never fully confronted the ways in which traditional understandings of jurisdiction get in the way of organizing; nor have area co-ops in which members of the co-op can freely cast negative checkoffs on new targets (denying any flow or resources to their organization) or positively claim targets and stall interminably in their organization, or (as in the Disney, Superdome, and other cases) limit cooperation to a single employer, with employees simply directly shunted into one or another participating union. The fact is that most national unions have extremely uneven national coverage of employees within their historic jurisdiction. And where they have little coverage, their presumptive jurisdiction should not be permitted to get in the way of organizing "their" workers. If the International Association of Machinists (IAM) wants to organize hotel workers someplace where HERE has no power, they should be encouraged to do so. If HERE wants to organize truckers in an area where IBT has no power, it should likewise be encouraged. And if long-term cooperative campaigns are truly worthwhile, they should be truly cooperative. More resources should go to the coordinating mechanism itself, which should be more than a feeder for cooperating unions. Membership in it should be allowed to mean something for individual workers; participating unions should take respective "shares" in the dues paid the common body as a return on their initial investment, but not immediately siphon off all bodies, much less be permitted to stifle organizing by their institution. Unless labor accepts some such more relaxed approach to jurisdiction and aggressively insists on actual organizing to countenance its defense, the possibility of true coordination—of the sort that is now needed nationally for employers operating nationally and regionally in all the ways already suggested—will be forever lost. Here as elsewhere, in contrast to past practice, the structure of labor organization and the organizational culture of the movement should be disciplined by its core interest in expansion of organizing as close to possible "everything that moves."

Notes

"Everything That Moves" was written for a 1996 conference—"New Approaches to Organizing"—sponsored by the AFL-CIO and the Cornell University School of Industrial and Labor Relations. Never before published, it has had enormous impact on subsequent union strategy, as reflected in the Union Cities and New Alliance programs, the Center for Working Capital, and the current programming of the Working for America Institute.

1. Here and throughout, we do not demonize the NLRB process (there is no need, as it condemns itself), much less use of it. We only note that without very substantial changes in its terms and the correlate provisions of the Labor Management Relations Act (LMRA) regarding bargaining (which are not likely to happen anytime soon), it cannot be anywhere near the whole show.

2. This is hardly news to public-sector unions, of course, many of which were first built on less-than-majority "meet and confer" or "professional association" memberships.

3. Also, in an example of what a difference a better legal regime would make, UFCW has brought 5,000 members under contract in the last year, using the provisions of the California Labor Relations Board (CLRB)—most notably its authorization of quick (twenty-four hour) elections in times of strike. By getting enough worker support to trigger a one-day strike, UFCW can trigger an election immediately thereafter, eliminating the long grind of employer resistance. While noting it here, we do not include the example in the text because of the uniqueness of the CLRB rules. For the foreseeable future, most private-sector unions in the United States will have to operate under the LMRA framework.

4. For example, despite the Parc 55 contract win in San Francisco (after a five-year campaign), the win of majority status against MGM Grant (after two years), and enticing talk at Local 100 in New York about gearing up for area restaurants, HERE's most impressive victories are limited to Las Vegas. Indeed, even within Nevada gaming, Las Vegas is isolated. Very little is heard from HERE in Laughlin and Reno, for example, where the casino industry's staggering profits offset its Vegas concessions. UFCW's general avoidance of strategies geared to increasing direct member or worker involvement—some of their most visible campaigns (e.g., those against Food Lion and Publix supermarket chains) in fact involve few actual

workers—helps guarantee inability to win decent contracts at campaign's end, as reflected in three- or four-tiered wage scales in recent agreements. UBCJ's associations, while undeniably bottom-up, have not in fact been able to win contracts. SEIU has not cracked the problem—evident in Washington, D.C., and Atlanta, among other cities—of how to move a real base of workers (and not just make tactical assaults), especially where those workers are part-time. IBT has been plagued with problems getting to contract even after election successes (they have been trying for more than six years now at Pony Express, and Overnite trucking firms show similar problems) and has no clear industry strategy. The UBCJ and UNITE worker associations/centers, while decidedly bottom-up and useful, have not yet brought measurable results in contractual working conditions and wages.

5. We sometimes refer to this as the "traditional" model, but the accuracy of that reference of course depends on what counts as tradition. What we are talking about here is the postwar "silos of solidarity" industrial unionism of the merged AFL-CIO. What we urge in its stead has clear antecedents in the more city-based, politically active, occupationally structured unionism of previous periods.

6. While labor in the United States remains strongly local, with relative weak national coordination, and while 99.5 percent of the 100,000 odd elective offices in the United States are not national, political monies are disproportionately spent on national races. From January 1991 to June 1994 (i.e., even before the fall elections), for example, of the 151 million spent by union PACs, 43 percent was spent on federal races.

7. Here again, we have background views. We believe that worker organizations advance when their activity offers something attractive to members or potential members and where it solves broader social problems—most controversially, perhaps, problems for capitalists, on whose welfare the rest of the society depends; such contribution is needed if worker organizations are to get the policy supports needed for their own maintenance and growth. In the Keynesian world, the contribution of worker organizations was to effective demand—the stabilization and growth of markets for goods and services which led to increased investment, enhanced productivity, and the lowered real cost of consumption goods of general benefit. While a little demand stabilization could surely be used now, the contribution of modern unions, we suspect, must at least as much be seen on the supply side—in the provision of the inputs and regulatory capacities needed to secure advanced (high-wage, low-waste, high-involvement, etc.) production. Just as in the old world, where the union contribution to effective demand was beyond the power or interest of any individual firm to make, so in the new world this provision of "effective supply" lies beyond the capacity or interest of individual firms, even as it lies squarely in the social interest and the interest of a critical sector of capital.

8. In repeated polls, about one-third of private, nonmanagerial, nonunion workers—a population larger than twice the current membership of all private-sector unions—report that they would vote for a union tomorrow if given the chance. Surely some significant portion of them would be willing to pay for a union attempting to organize their workplace.

9. There should be no confusion about this. To get social services to members, assure reasonable police behavior during conflicts, build effective regional training systems and other elements in egalitarian effective supply, impose local wage norms, and end subsidy abuse to large firms in local economic development, the most important element to have is local.

10. Of course, unions often do not reach beyond that point, do not complete their domination of existing markets (or even individual employers), because the economic effects on existing members' wages are sometimes trivial. With organizing expenditures coming at the expense of services and with existing members (rather than the union itself, or unorganized workers) the deciders of how money should be spent, organizing languishes. What is typically ignored here, we would argue, is how dramatically the per capita costs of additional organizing have dropped by the time this point is reached. Consider the countless units in which only 80 percent of workers are on union dues check-off; or the countless (in particular regional) labor markets in which organizing of sectors is stagnant at 40 percent. Would anyone argue that the costs of getting beyond that point are considerably less than the costs of getting there in the first place?

11. On the relative rates of density: In 1960, at a time when the union coverage of private nonagricultural workers was just over 30 percent, density in metropolitan areas was 73 percent (77 percent in the Northeast, 80 percent in North Central, 80 percent in the West, even 48 percent in the South). As late as 1984, when overall union density had dropped to 20 percent, the metropolitan average was still above 51 percent. On the metro-based destruction of traditional unions, consider manufacturing. From 1978 to 1988, sixteen cities accounted for 70 percent of the jobs lost in manufacturing, and virtually all the unionized jobs. It was the failure to defend metro manufacturing that accounted for the nearly halving (40 percent decline) of unionized manufacturing employment between 1980 and 1990, a period when overall manufacturing employment declined just 6 percent.

3

The History of Labor Councils in the Labor Movement

From the AFL to New Voice

Stuart Eimer

The trades' union, or central body, although it is the second form of organisation of labour, is the first to arouse the public, and it repeats itself in all industrial countries. . . . It represents the uprising of a class against other classes, submerging the lines that distinguish occupations.

—John Commons, labor historian, 1918

It is unmitigated hypocrisy for the labor movement to say out one side of its mouth that all those who benefit from unionism should pay their just portion in making these benefits possible while we say in the next breath that over a thousand city central bodies and fifty state organizations can be maintained on an open shop basis as they are now.

—Sam Ezelle, Kentucky AFL-CIO, 1959

The above quotes aptly capture both the opportunities and constraints that AFL-CIO central labor councils (CLC) face. At their best, CLCs can "submerge the lines that distinguish occupations" in order to craft and advance interests that promise to benefit all workers in a given area, regardless of whether or not they are union members. Time and time again, whether fighting for unemployment insurance in the 1930s or for living-wage campaigns in the 1990s, CLCs have shown that they are capable of uniting their affiliates in order to win real gains for workers (Fink 1978; Foner 1990; Luce 2001). On the other hand, there can be no denying that AFL-CIO rules have functioned to make it unnecessarily difficult for CLCs to accomplish such feats. From the earliest days of the AFL, rules were enacted that skewed power within the federation in favor of the national unions. These unions then enacted bylaws that reduced the authority of CLCs, and that also made their very existence precarious (Burke 1899; Barnett 1913; Ulman 1955; Lens 1959; Montgomery 1983; Wallihan 1985). Of particular importance in this regard was the decision to make union affiliation with central labor bodies voluntary, thereby leading to "open-shop" conditions, which until this day allow local unions to opt out of their local CLCs. Given this option, many unions have decided that while "Solidarity Forever" is a nice song to sing at the occasional meeting, in practice solidarity costs time and resources. Thus, instead of joining their CLCs, far too many local unions have simply taken a free ride on the backs of other unions in their communities. This has hampered the ability of organized labor to build and maintain working-class movements at the local level.

In this chapter, I put current efforts to reinvigorate CLCs into a historical context by reviewing the development and consequences of some the more important bylaws that govern local bodies. I first describe how national unions in the AFL adopted rules that diminished the power of CLCs within the organization. I then consider how and why the national unions used their dominance within the AFL to limit CLC activity, and then argue that the decision not to mandate affiliation with central bodies was a grave error that created severe resource problems that persist to this day. Next, I show how both the CIO and the AFL-CIO mimicked the AFL bylaws, thereby creating affiliation problems for their respective local bodies. I conclude by reflecting on the need for the AFL-CIO to alter fundamentally the relationship between local unions and CLCs.

An Overview

CLCs have been a continuous presence in hundreds of communities across the nation for well over a century (see Figure 3.1).[1]

References to these councils can be found throughout the labor history literature, appearing in general histories (Lorwin 1933; Foner 1955:

Figure 3.1 **AFL-CIO CLCs, 1896–1994**

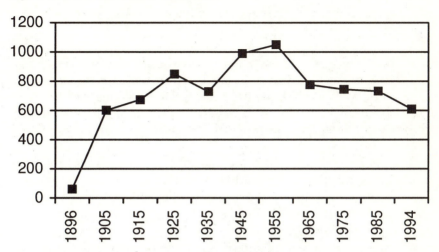

Commons et al. 1961; Zieger 1995) as well as works on other topics such as general strikes, politics, or regional labor history (Brune 1982; Kagel 1984 ; Greene 1991; Kazin 1986; Davin and Lynd 1980; Borsos 1996; Gavett 1965; Freeman 2000). To the extent that CLCs have been the focus of research, it has been through case studies, often unpublished theses, that examine one council over a period of time (Bigham 1925; Dixon 1926; King 1939; Forsythe 1956; Bizjack 1969; Javersak 1980; Skakkeback 1981).

For the few who have bothered to reflect on the general role and function of central labor councils, there is unanimity in the view that the national unions in the AFL consciously sought to limit the power of local federations. As early as 1913, George Barnett argued that the city federations had "been definitely subordinated to the national union (Barnett 1913, 474). Forty years later, Lloyd Ulman reached the same conclusion, suggesting that the national unions had implemented rules designed "to destroy the city central's ability to compete with the nationals for control over the local unions and to confine them largely to the sphere of political activity" (Ulman 1955, 381). Writing at roughly the same time, Sidney Lens went so far as to charge that AFL President Samuel Gompers himself had set a "deliberate course to whittle the power of the city bodies," and "as result one city central body after another was incorporated into the AFL and its wings clipped" turning them into a "negligible force." (Lens 1959, 61–62). In Lens's opinion, the "emasculation" of CLCs and their "reduction to minor legislative roles, lowered the curtain on a proud period in labor's history." He sadly concluded that the:

> Union protagonists can be permitted a moment of nostalgia for this "little" labor movement which no longer exists, nor can ever exist again, but which, while it lasted, was free of the specific problems that bedevil the labor movement today when by force of circumstance it has been separated a few notches farther from the rank and file. (Lens 1959, 33)

Though he aptly described the general trend, Lens probably overstated his argument. While clearly weakened and severely constrained, the case studies mentioned above suggest that some CLCs managed to overcome the obstacles they faced in order to actively pursue social legislation and political goals.

That said, regular reports at the national conventions suggest that successful CLCs were the exception that proved the rule. Most central bodies have historically suffered from affiliation problems, and without an affiliate base to pay per capita dues to the council, severe resource constraints have been generated. Without adequate resources most local bodies have lacked full-time staff and have thereby had difficulty developing much capacity.

The Rise of the AFL

The constitution adopted at the first meeting of the American Federation of Labor (AFL) in 1886 called for the organization of workers on both an occupational and territorial basis. As its first goal, the AFL declared that:

> The objects of this Federation shall be the encouragement and formation of local Trades and Labor Unions and the closer Federation of such societies through the organization of Central Trades and Labor Unions in every city, and the further combination of such bodies into state, territorial, or provincial organizations to secure legislation in the interests of the working masses. (FOTLU 1886, 1)

In laying out a dual strategy, the founders of the AFL built on past experience, which indicated that workers' grievances were best addressed simultaneously through collective action organized at the point of production as well as in society at large.

Occupational organization aimed to unite similarly situated workers in labor market institutions that could address issues pertaining to a particular workplace or industry. The AFL expected these local unions to join together to form autonomous national organizations that could address the newly emerging national economy, which had forced workers from different regions into competition with one another. It was hoped that vertically integrated national unions would be able to bargain with large business organizations and employer associations in order to take wages, hours, and working conditions out of competition (Commons et al. 1961 [vol. 2], 5, 43).

Concurrently with its efforts to organize workers along occupational lines, the AFL sought to build territorially defined labor federations, which could unite the occupationally defined labor unions in a given city or state. The reason for forming such local bodies was aptly captured in the following motion calling for the establishment of an early central labor council:

> Whereas, It has been fully demonstrated by experience that unity of action and organization among working people are imperative and essential in order to combat the ever growing encroachments of organized and consolidated capital, and as *there are many questions affecting the interest of the working classes which cannot be dealt with in special and separate Trade and Labor Unions*, as that end can be best attained by a central labor organization through which all branches of labor may prove allies to any particular one that may be oppressed, and all may form a Brotherhood for the defense and protection of the laboring masses; therefore, be it Resolved, That we the delegates of the various Trade and Labor Unions here represented, do hereby form the Central Labor Union of . . . for the purpose of organizing and concentrating the efforts of the working classes for their own mutual protection, education and social advancement. (Burke 1899; 43; emphasis added)

As this quote makes clear, local labor bodies were formed because workers recognized that individual unions could not confront business alone. There was a need for an institution that could mobilize local unions in support of one another's struggles within the labor market, as well as for an institution that could advance the interest of the more broadly defined "laboring masses" via the state.

Given the potential power of both occupational and territorial organization, it made perfect sense that the AFL would declare a need for both. It was also clear that the two logics of association conflicted, as the success both of national unions and of local federations depended to a large extent on their ability to exercise authority over local unions. If national unions were going to standardize conditions within an occupation, they required a certain level of organizational discipline from their various locals. Similarly, if CLCs were to be an effective voice for workers at the local level, local unions would have to agree to participate in the projects that the CLC initiated.

A hint of which of the two logics would come to dominate was provided at the first meeting of the Federation of Organized Trades and Labor Unions (FOTLU), the organization that would become the AFL. At this gathering, rules were adopted that granted national unions convention representation based on size, while local federations were given one vote regardless of how large they were (Ulman 1955, 379; Commons 1961 [vol. 2], 323; Barnett 1913, 461). Representatives of CLCs opposed this rule and sought to substitute language that permitted proportional representation to all labor bodies, but this move was defeated.

In 1887, fearing that weighted representation might not be enough to ensure that national union representatives would outnumber CLC delegates on the convention floor, the national unions passed a resolution that weighted the voting procedure in their favor.[2] This provision dictated that when a roll call was demanded, each national union delegate could cast a vote for every one hundred members that he or she represented, while city and state representatives could cast only their one vote. With this move, the national unions made their dominance of the AFL nearly iron clad, as they were now practically guaranteed control over convention proceedings. To illustrate the magnitude of this power shift, consider the 1911 AFL convention, which was attended by 347 delegates: 228 from national unions, 25 from state federations, 67 from local federations, 21 from federal unions, and 6 from fraternal organizations. National union delegates made up 65 percent of the floor, but held 99 percent of the roll-call votes (Barnett 1913, 462).

With power resting firmly in their hands, the national unions proceeded to institute a variety of rules that secured their authority over local federations. For example, in the late 1890s the AFL instituted constraints on locally coordinated sympathy strikes (Ulman 1955, 383; AFL 1898, 144). During such strikes, members of unions other than the one involved in a collective bargaining dispute would walk out in sympathy.

While such activities functioned to strengthen the power and identity of organized labor in a particular region by connecting local workers to one another's struggles, they also challenged the authority of national unions, which saw sympathetic strikes as a breach of contract that hurt labor's legitimacy with employers. As Ulman noted, "National unions were opposed to this practice, holding in effect that the good union doctrine of 'sanctity of contracts' should take working precedence over the good union doctrine of 'an injury to one is the concern of all'" (Ulman 1955, 383).[3]

Above and beyond limiting the power and authority of local federations, the national unions foisted rules upon CLCs that made it difficult for them to secure the membership of local unions. In 1893, a provision was put into the AFL constitution that stated that national unions had a "duty" only to instruct their locals to join labor councils. Barnett suggested that the affiliation was not mandated for a simple reason:

> If a city federation becomes unsatisfactory to a local union, it may withdraw at will, or in case a city federation pursues distasteful policies, a national union may even encourage or order its local union to withdraw. . . . Since the city federation has no power to retain local unions its conduct must commend itself to the local unions or they will leave. . . . No more effectual check on the exercise by city federations of any real power over the constituent unions could well have been devised. (Barnett 1913, 468)

As implied by Barnett, voluntary affiliation privileged exit over voice within the local bodies (Hirschman 1970). Instead of adopting rules that required unions to join CLCs and to voice their positions via a deliberative democratic process, the AFL's commitment to union autonomy led them to create a system in which locals were simply encouraged to quit councils that they did not like. In effect, this gave large affiliates a check on CLC activities since their exit might spell financial ruin for the body. The rhetoric of respecting union autonomy really functioned to protect the interests of certain affiliates (Rogin 1971).

In addition to privileging exit over voice, voluntary affiliation saddled local federations with perpetual free rider problems (Olson 1971). Since participation was not mandated, local unions had to be willing to incur the monetary and organizational costs of belonging to a CLC, despite the fact that they would benefit from many of the body's activities even if they did not join.[4] For example, consider the case of locally coordinated political action. Every union in a community has a general interest in having labor-friendly candidates elected to local office. Friendly city government might mean more tolerant police at picket lines or easier access to relief benefits during a strike. Likewise, however, failure to participate in the CLC-sponsored political activity needed to elect such candidates will not preclude a union from taking advantage of whatever benefits accrue. Unfortunately, if the leaders of all local unions reason this way, then few will join the local body, and CLCs will have difficulty providing support for labor-friendly candidates. The pursuit of narrowly selfish interests by the locals will generate suboptimal results in the aggregate and will create CLCs that lack resources and the ability to depend on the participation of member unions. The last century of CLC history stands as testament to the magnitude of this problem, as low affiliation rates have caused continual resource problems for central bodies.[5]

As the national unions used their power within the AFL to constrain local federations, central body leaders did not stand idly by. In 1900, two convention resolutions were offered that would have increased the power of CLCs. The first proposed that each delegate from a national union be allowed only one vote on a roll call. This was defeated without discussion. The second suggested that local federations be permitted to "cast the votes of local unions directly affiliated with the Federation and connected with the city federation." This proposal also was defeated (Barnett 1913, 463–464; Lens 1959, 61).

The following year, efforts were made to address the issue of affiliation. The Fort Worth Trades Assembly introduced a resolution arguing that since the goal of the AFL was to "consolidate the wage earners of America into one compact body," local unions that refused to affiliate with their CLC should have their charters revoked. Alongside this motion was one by a delegate of the Barbers Union, which called for the AFL constitution to be amended to read that "all National and International Unions shall make it compulsory on the party of their locals to affiliate with Local Central Bodies." Locals that refused to do so would be disciplined by their national unions by having their charters revoked. Moreover, national unions that refused to enforce this rule would be denied affiliation with the AFL (AFL 1901, 198).

The Committee on Laws recommended against adoption of such motions. They reminded delegates that the AFL was based on the autonomy of the national unions, noting that the federation did not have "mandatory power to legislate for National and International Unions" (AFL 1901, 198). Moreover, they suggested that officers with the AFL and affiliated unions were working "diligently" to increase affiliation, and thus there was no need to alter the constitutional language, which deemed affiliation a duty. When the motion was called, the resolutions failed, as would similar motions introduced at conventions in 1910, 1914, 1923, and 1937, to name but a few of the conventions at which the subject was brought up.

It was no doubt frustration with their subordinate position within the AFL that led the Federated Trades Council of Milwaukee to issue an invitation in 1902 to all AFL central bodies to form a federation of local federations (Barnett 1913, 463–464; Lens 1959, 61). The call urged the formation of a National Municipal Labor League, and suggested that:

> Before we can hope to do much on a national scale, we must obtain the control of city and state governments. The proper course for the toilers is to use their trade union strength . . . as the guiding spirit and rallying point for municipal campaigns. This being true, it is also important that these city and town movements work along uniform lines in full knowledge of what each other is doing. (Gavett 1965, 101)

Samuel Gompers, president of the AFL, and his organization did not take kindly to this attempt, arguing that the project would "not only destroy the unity of the labor movement of the country, but divide and endanger its very existence." As Gomper's put it in an appeal to all central bodies:

> [I]t is only necessary to give the matter a moment's thought to arrive at the inevitable conclusion that if this so called "new federation" of central bodies were launched, the conclusions it would reach would, beyond a doubt, differ from those reached by the American Federation of Labor; and then what? Rivalry and conflict, from which the workers alone would suffer and the whole past effort for unity and federation would have to be begun all over again from the very start. (Gompers 1902, 507)

Gompers' appeal, combined with pressure from national unions on their locals not to cooperate with the movement emanating from Milwaukee, succeeded in checking the formation of the new federation (Lens 1959, 62; Barnett 1913, 464; Ulman 1955, 387).

New House, Same Structure

While AFL leaders were able to prevent the development of a new national federation based on local federations, they were unable to stop the rise of a federation based on the principles of industrial unionism. By 1935, frustration with the AFL's failure to organize industrial workers had spread to the organization's highest ranks. A minority of the Executive Council had become convinced that it was necessary to set aside craft jurisdictions in order to allow for the industrial organization of mass-production workers. Plans proposed by this faction were defeated during the 1935 convention; and immediately following that meeting, unions committed to industrial unionism met to launch organizing drives on their own (Stolberg 1971; Levinson 1995; Zieger 1995).

When the Congress of Industrial Organizations (CIO) unions broke with AFL policy, they did more than create a schism between leaders at the national level. All over the country, cleavages emerged in the state federations and central labor councils where locals loyal to the AFL and the CIO were now jointly housed. This division soon created what AFL President William Green described as a "great deal of confusion" as contests for power emerged between AFL and CIO unions in local federations throughout the nation.[6]

Unwilling to allow its CLCs to become bases of power for the insurgent CIO unions, the AFL Executive Council went on the offensive. What began in early 1936 as stern warnings to central labor bodies that they were forbidden to aid the rival CIO, had by 1937 led to the expulsion of local unions loyal to the CIO from local labor councils. In April 1937, Green reported to the Executive Council that he had "found it necessary" to "take definite action in a number of cities where serious internal turmoil and differences had arisen in Central Bodies between the CIO Unions and the regular bona fide AF of L organizations." He noted that in some local federations the CIO was strong enough to create "strife" at every meeting as each side battled for control, and thus he had decided to end the problem through purges that he admitted were sometimes "done in a rather arbitrary way." As a result he "had cleaned up the situation" in Philadelphia, Worcester, Cleveland, St. Louis, Toledo, and Birmingham. Pleased with the results, the AFL Executive Council adopted a resolution that gave Green the power to continue "purging Central Bodies and Sate Federations of Labor of dual representatives."[7]

With the AFL forcing its locals out of central labor bodies, the CIO had to decide what to do. In March 1937, CIO Director John Brophy reported that there was an "increasing need for coordination of organizing efforts of CIO affiliates" and that this need had already resulted in "various forms of cooperation." The desire to launch joint organizing drives had given form to regional CIO bodies in New England, Wisconsin, and New Jersey. At the local level, CIO unions had created central bodies in Philadelphia and Toledo, and requests about the national CIO's attitude toward such federations had come in from locals in Buffalo and Los Angeles. Given the situation, Brophy argued that it was necessary to adopt a policy to guide local unions in this matter and suggested that the CIO should "authorize and encourage the formation of local CIO central bodies in cases where the situation warrants this step."[8] The CIO Executive Board heeded Brophy's counsel, and the decision to grant certificates of affiliation to city centrals when such action seemed advisable was made.[9]

To facilitate this development of industrial union councils (IUCs), the national CIO created a process by which local affiliates could form local Industrial Union Councils and apply for charter. In addition, the CIO's national staff drafted rules to define both the powers that IUCs would have and their relation to the national organization.[10] For guidance on how to best address these questions, the CIO turned to the obvious place, the AFL constitution. In 1937, CIO office manager Katherine Pollack Ellickson examined AFL bylaws, creating draft language for the CIO by literally going through text and crossing out words like "Central Labor Union" and replacing them with the term "Council."[11] Consequently, the role and function of the CIO's IUCs mirrored that of the AFL's CLCs. Substantively, their purview was broad, as it was expected that IUCs would:

> serve as center[s] of unionism in their localities, and that they will endeavor in every practical way to promote the welfare of the working people and the community in accordance with their charters through spreading bona fide organization, through securing necessary legislation, through mobilizing labor's purchasing power, and through increasing public understanding of the great aims and principles of the Committee of Industrial Organizations.[12]

In pursuing these goals, however, IUCs were not allowed to "assume . . . powers over such unions that properly belong to the unions or to the CIO or its national and international affiliates . . . ," such as calling strikes or originating boycotts.[13]

By the time of the first CIO convention in November 1938, IUCs had sprouted up around the nation, and 124 local bodies were represented at the meeting. In his opening remarks, CIO President John L. Lewis commented positively on the formation of the IUCs, noting that "CIO unions have combined in their various states and cities to set up Industrial Union Councils as the democratic expression of the whole movement in the respective states and localities" (CIO 1938, 31, 289).

The new CIO constitution formally made provision for IUCs. Like the initial rules that governed the Councils, the constitutional language was modeled after the AFL. IUCs were granted just one voting delegate at national conventions regardless of size, while national unions were granted representation proportionate to the number members they represented. Moreover, the CIO made affiliation with local bodies voluntary, using language that was virtually the same as that in the AFL constitution. The section read: "It shall be the duty of national and international unions and organizing committees to direct their locals to affiliate with the proper industrial union councils" (CIO 1938, 127).[14]

While there was no dissent on the floor regarding the rules governing convention representation, a debate did emerge over the issue of voluntary affiliation. A delegate from the Lake County Indiana Industrial Union Council took issue with the notion that it should be only a "duty" to join an IUC. He relayed his experience in Indiana, claiming his IUC did "not get the fullest cooperation from the CIO organizations." Given the importance of IUCs at the state and local level in coordinating programs and policies so that they could more effectively be pursued as "a bloc of CIO rather than as individual unions," he argued that individual unions should be compelled to join IUCs (CIO 1938, 136).

Despite declaring the Committee on Constitution's agreement in principle on this point, the chair of the committee argued that "you just cannot make this compulsory in this constitution," and suggested that the committee had tried to craft language that would have the "moral effect of requiring affiliation." As for the reasons that affiliation could not be made compulsory, the chair bluntly stated that "there are many local unions who are in a position where it is not to their advantage, possibly, to affiliate." With that point, he proclaimed that the committee had carefully considered the issue and had also heard testimony on it, and that they had gone as far as they could "without using the word 'compulsion' in this constitution" (CIO 1938, 137).

This sentiment was echoed by a representative from the Packing House Workers Organizing Committee who was "opposed to compelling local unions to affiliate with industrial union councils" because the "whole concept of the Committee for Industrial Organization is that we shall have democracy . . . so if we are to going to have democracy we certainly can't come here and try to compel anyone." Instead of compulsion, he argued that if IUCs were "organized and functioning properly they . . . [would] be able to attract all local unions to affiliate with them and pay their per capita tax." Apparently this sentiment was widely shared, as it passed by a "very large majority" (CIO 1938, 137).

As a consequence, like the AFL, the CIO adopted rules that privileged exit over voice. As the Packinghouse Worker's statement nicely illustrates, democracy was conceived as the right to reject participation. The autonomy of national and local affiliates trumped the desire for rules that would ensure well-financed local councils. Consequently, like their sister CLCs, IUCs would be faced with severe free rider problems and would continuously suffer from low affiliation.[15]

By 1941, resolutions were being passed that drew attention to affiliation problems and that called on "international unions to direct their local unions to affiliate with CIO councils (CIO 1941, 218). The following year, President Philip Murray reported that affiliation was still not what it should be (CIO 1942, 57), and in 1943 he noted that the "problem is rendered more serious by the fact that where locals of two or three Internationals fail to maintain affiliation, locals of other unions are also apt to drop out." (CIO 1943, 51). This dynamic resulted in a vicious cycle, which sometimes required that whole councils be reorganized.

Brief mention of the affiliation problems became a regular event at CIO conventions. Finally, in 1947, while in the midst of a bitter fight between left and right for control of many big city IUCs, Murray went beyond casually mentioning the problem and chastised unions for not joining their local bodies. He argued that the problems the CIO was currently having with its IUCs (a reference to the fact that many were controlled by Communist unions) stemmed "almost entirely from a lack of full affiliation. " He asserted that there "is still too much of a tendency at times for locals which disagree with the way Councils are run to withdraw from the Council or suspend or reduce per capita tax payments." He went on to pronounce that "such policies are inexcusable" and to remind the convention that the vital work that needed to be done in each state and community could not be done without "well financed and well staffed" IUCs. He concluded by pointing out that IUCs where "wholly democratic" organizations, and pledged that if "abuses creep in at any point" the national CIO has the "power to correct them on request." Consequently, it was "essential that all CIO locals affiliate" with their IUCs and pay their per caps at all times (CIO 1947, 79).

While Murray's words suggested a vision of IUCs as deliberative democratic bodies based on unions exercising voice instead of exit, nothing concrete was done to change the rules governing affiliation. Consequently, when Walter Reuther succeeded Murray as president of the CIO, his first annual report would contained a statement about the "constant problem of finding the money to carry on the all important work of our Councils" (CIO 1952, 90). The following year would be no different, as he drew attention to the financial problems that plagued IUCs, suggesting that per capitas needed to be increased, and then noting that "it is a matter of common knowledge that the financial problem of some of our Councils would be eased considerably were all the locals in their territorial jurisdiction to affiliate" (CIO 1953, 148).

Newest House, Same Rules

Just as the split between the AFL and the CIO led to the creation of hundreds of new CLCs, the merger between the two federations necessitated that hundreds of local bodies across the nation combine into one. AFL-CIO rules dictated that the newly merged councils, like those preceding them, were to be subordinate to the national federation. In late 1955, after several years of negotiations, the AFL and CIO agreed to combine forces. The reunification of the two federations necessitated that the hundreds of dual AFL and CIO local bodies that existed throughout the nation be merged together. Not surprisingly, AFL-CIO rules dictated that the newly merged councils, like those preceding them, were to be subordinate to the national federation. CLCs were again allowed only a single vote at national conventions, and affiliation would again be voluntary, with national unions having only a "duty" to instruct their locals to affiliate. As in the past, CLCs were prevented from ordering local unions to strike and could not originate boycotts (AFL-CIO 1991, 7).

Given that AFL-CIO rules governing CLCs were similar to those of the AFL and CIO, it should not come as a surprise that the convention debates surrounding these bodies resembled reruns of previous AFL and CIO gatherings. By 1959, the issue of affiliation with central bodies had reemerged as a point of contention, and a resolution was introduced that sought to change the constitution in order to mandate affiliation. A delegate from the Michigan AFL-CIO indicated that he was tired of listening to national union presidents "give the most profound lip service to political action" while telling their local unions they could freeload on the backs of the local bodies that were responsible for carrying out political functions. He then noted how ironic it was that the AFL worked against "Right to Work Laws" while failing to "provide a union shop agreement for our own subordinate organizations." He concluded by declaring:

> I am tired of freeloaders, not only the freeloader who comes into our shop and scabs and doesn't pay his dues to the local union; I am kind of tired of the freeloaders who are riding on our backs, taking all the benefits our subordinate organizations can give us and paying nothing. (AFL-CIO 1959 [vol. 1], 355)

As in the past, this plea was countered by statements that recognized the importance of increasing affiliation, but claimed that mandating affiliation was simply not possible. As AFL-CIO President, George Meany, put it:

> No one is going to argue about the desirability of cooperation at the local level. But you change the entire structure if we say to a national union, "You must compel your locals to belong," because then we are saying to that local union "You can't belong to the national union unless you belong to the central body." So if we would adopt this policy we would have to adopt the policy of absolute central control from the headquarters of Washington of every state organization and every state local body. There would be no other way. (AFL-CIO 1959 [vol. 1], 361)

Meany's position was basically a rehash of the argument that had been used since the 1890s. Mandatory affiliation violated the cherished autonomy of the national unions and thus could not be considered. Not surprisingly, the move to change the rules regarding affiliation was defeated.

While the convention was reluctant to alter the core rules governing the AFL-CIO, it did recognize that problems existed in its central bodies, and the Committee on State and Local Central Bodies recommended that the president appoint a committee to work with the national unions to increase affiliation. The committee suggested that full affiliation would "immeasurably strengthen state and local central bodies so that they will play their full role in furthering the political, legislative and economic goals of the labor movement" (AFL-CIO 1959 [vol. 1], 684). The motion was adopted without discussion, and as a result, a series of national conferences of state and central body leaders was held in 1960.

At the first conference, a resolution was adopted that outlined ways that the AFL-CIO could improve the operation of its local bodies. Suggestions included the creation of a coordinator of state and local central bodies to supervise and assist local bodies as well as the formation of an advisory committee to consider issues pertaining to these bodies (AFL-CIO 1961 [vol. 2], 52). In line with these proposals, President Meany appointed Stanton E. Smith, president of the Tennessee State Federation of Labor, to be the new coordinator of state and local central bodies.

With a mandate to secure maximum affiliation to local bodies, Smith's office first undertook a survey of the situation. Matching lists of local unions provided by national unions against state federation records, it was determined that only 48.5 percent of locals were affiliated with their respective state bodies (AFL-CIO 1961 [vol. 2], 52). While no numbers were given for CLCs, it is likely that they were about the same or lower. Writing in the *American Federationist*, Smith could only describe this as a "poor record," which represented a "waste of strength and resources which the labor movement . . . can ill afford" (Smith 1961, 8).

Unfortunately, efforts to improve the situation did not accomplish much. At the 1963 convention, "because the problem continued without substantial improvement," the convention passed resolutions urging national unions to "re-examine both their policies and practices with respect to the problem of affiliation of local unions to local bodies" (AFL-CIO 1967 [vol. 1], 635). In 1965, seeing little progress, the convention again called on national unions to "immediately develop programs to implement the policy of complete and full affiliation" (AFL-CIO 1967 [vol. 1], 635). Moreover, to provide positive reinforcement with unions that were taking action, the 1965 convention gave special recognition to national unions with 80 percent or more of their locals affiliated with state central bodies. Only 13 of the more than 100 unions in the federation qualified for recognition (AFL-CIO 1965 [vol. 1], 549). By 1967, the Committee on State and Local Central bodies could describe the response to efforts to strengthen local bodies only as "disappointing, if not disheartening" (AFL-CIO 1967 [vol. 1], 635). The Committee concluded by noting:

> The vast changes which have taken place in the social, economic and political areas of our national life, and the fact that these changes are continuing, emphasizes the need to fashion stronger and more effective

instruments to achieve the objectives of the labor movement. In an effort to meet this need, with respect to the state and local central bodies, the committee suggests that a major review be undertaken by the executive council of the AFL-CIO, of the role and functions of the state and local central bodies as the operating arms of the AFL-CIO, in the field. (AFL-CIO 1967 [vol. 1], 637)

While the committee's report was unanimously adopted, the 1960 convention proceedings indicate that the executive council never carried out the "major review" and report that "progress in improving affiliations has generally been slow and tedious" (AFL-CIO 1969 [vol. 1], 495, 491).

Through the 1970s and 1980s, little changed. Convention reports repeatedly stressed the importance of local bodies for legislative and political action, and then lamented the difficulties that these bodies had in carrying out their responsibilities. The report to the 1981convention pointed out that the most notable problem for central bodies was "the continuing low level of affiliation." Reports suggested that as of December 1980, 56 percent of union members were affiliated with state bodies, and random samples of CLCs suggested that local affiliation was "only slightly higher [affiliation with] than state bodies" (AFL-CIO 1981, 63). By 1985, the percentage of members affiliated with state bodies had dropped to 52 percent, and no numbers were given for CLCs (AFL-CIO 1985, 315).

With low affiliation and the resource problems that followed, many CLCs simply found it hard to function effectively. Wallihan noted that, where resource constraints were severe, CLCs were "barely able to perform their core functions—political representation at the state and local level and voter mobilization, coordinated through COPE, for elections at all levels" (Wallihan 1985, 163). In summarizing the general situation, he bluntly concluded that the "central body structure remains a problem spot in the AFL-CIO" (p. 164).

Same House, New Rules

As the other chapters in this book detail, the AFL-CIO is once again trying to transform its CLCs from problem spots into vital centers of union activity. In 1997 the Union Cities project was launched, and as of 1999, 157 of the AFL-CIO's 590 councils had signed on to the project (AFL-CIO Web A). While research by McLewin suggests that Union

City councils are more active than others (AFL-CIO Web B), the fact that only 27 percent of CLCs have joined the program suggests that problems still remain at the bulk of the federation's local labor bodies.

It was no doubt recognition of lingering problems that led the AFL-CIO to adopt the New Alliance Program at its 1999 convention. Described as the "first major structural change in the AFL-CIO in nearly 50 years" (AFL-CIO Web C), the program was launched with the recognition that local federations "face numerous problems—including a lack of clarity as to their core responsibilities, competing demands on them, and a lack of sufficient resources for them to do their jobs" (AFL-CIO 1999, 1). Though documents related to the project provide little discussion of why this state of affairs exists, it is noted that national unions "expressed concern about the lack of integration of their national priorities at both the state and local level as well as a lack of coordinated planning and accountability" (AFL-CIO 1999, 1).

To address this situation, the New Alliance hopes to "create and sustain consensus on the proper roles and responsibilities and the core programs of these affiliated organizations" and to "better integrate national union priorities with state and local priorities." The program will "articulate clear goals and objectives, as well as standards for these organizations, and will provide sufficient resources to meet these goals—by bringing about full participation of the entire labor movement" (AFL-CIO 1999, 2).

To accomplish this, the plan calls for the creation of "drafting committees" which will, among other things, examine the status of each state's labor councils. These committees will review the participation of each local union and will "propose a plan to reorganize and re-map the state through the creation of a reorganized state federation and as well as the creation of new area-wide councils with sufficient resources to carry out the goals established by the Executive Council." (AFL-CIO 1999, 4). To ensure adequate resources, the plan will "provide for eventual full participation and fair affiliation by the major unions in the state and each community" (AFL-CIO 1999, 5). Such affiliation will be phased in over a "reasonable period of time for those unions who need such a phase in." How this will be done remains vague. The plan states that:

> National Unions will make their best effort to work with affiliated local unions to achieve the phase in and assure full participation. Once a local union has committed to participate . . . national unions will have a special

responsibility to insure that their local unions remain affiliated at the expected level. (AFL-CIO 1999, 6)

As this quote makes clear, while the New Alliance ambitiously seeks to refashion and reinvigorate local bodies, its approach to solving affiliation problems breaks little new ground. As in the past, it prods national unions to get their local unions to join their respective local bodies. At least one delegate to the convention, Texas AFL-CIO President Joe Gunn, felt this was a problem and spoke against the proposal because it "did not go far enough to ensure full affiliation of locals in state federations" (AFL-CIO Web C). Whether he knew it or not, in taking this position, Gunn joined a century-long chorus of voices of those who were dissatisfied with the way the national federations have dealt with the issue of affiliation.

Conclusion

While it is true that from day one the AFL constitution recognized that a variety of organizational forms was needed to protect and advance the interests of workers, power within the federation was quickly skewed in favor of national unions. These unions used their control of the federation to pass a variety of rules that curbed CLC power and made affiliation to CLCs voluntary. When the CIO formed, it mimicked the AFL's position on affiliation, and when the two federations merged, the new entity did the same.

The effect of voluntary affiliation on local bodies is clear. First, it encourages local unions to exit councils when disagreements emerge, thereby giving an unfair power advantage to larger affiliates whose departure might spell financial ruin for a CLC. Second, it saddles councils with severe free-rider problems, as many locals simply choose to enjoy the benefits of CLC activity without contributing financial or human resources to the council. These two dynamics lead to low affiliation rates, which in turn lead to resource constraints. Without adequate resources, many CLCs are forced to operate without a staff, an office, or in some cases even a telephone. Obviously, a local federation without such things has little capacity to be of much use to anyone, and we should not be surprised if local unions choose not to affiliate with such a council. The result is a vicious cycle of CLC degradation.

While the New Alliance program's effort to break this cycle by restructuring local bodies should be applauded, a century of history suggests that affiliation and resources problems will not be solved by merely appealing to national unions to do the right thing. While such efforts will probably lead to increased affiliation in scattered locales where leaders are able create a sense of solidarity that trumps the incentive to free-ride, in most cases CLCs will probably continue to be plagued by affiliation and resource problems.

Given organized labor's historic support for union and agency shops that require all workers to help pay for the benefits they receive from a union, the refusal to mandate affiliation with CLCs seems odd. To repeat the quote from Sam Ezeell of the Kentucky AFL-CIO, which was offered at the outset of this chapter:

> It is unmitigated hypocrisy for the labor movement to say out one side of its mouth that all those who benefit from unionism should pay their just portion in making these benefits possible while we say in the next breath that over a thousand city central bodies and fifty state organizations can be maintained on an open shop basis as they are now. (AFL-CIO 1959, 351)

Advocates of this position have yet to succeed in convincing national unions that the AFL-CIO should once and for all mandate affiliation. While such a rule would require national unions to surrender a bit of their autonomy, it seems a small price to pay to ensure that local councils have the resources needed to develop some real capacity in their communities

Notes

1. Data compiled from *List of Organizations Affiliated with the American Federation of Labor*, 1904–05, 1912, 1920, 1928, 1936, 1946, 1955 which are now in Georgy Meany Memorial Archives, Collection RG34–00, and from the *List of Organizations Affiliated with the American Federation of Labor and Congress of Industrial Organizations*, AFL-CIO: Washington D.C., 1956–1994.

2. This fear was not unwarranted. At the 1882 meeting of the FOTLU, there were eight delegates from national unions and ten from CLCs. In 1883, there were eight from national unions and five from CLCs. See Commons 1961 (vol. 2), 328.

3. In 1901, the AFL further insulated local unions from the authority of local federations when it prohibited them from originating boycotts. Once again, national union leaders felt that such local actions threatened their relationship with employers by asking their local unions to punish firms with which they themselves had no problem. (Ulman 1955, 383; AFL 1901, 196).

4. As the report of the Committee on Local and Federated Bodies put it in its 1949 report to the convention, "[L]ocal unions that are not in affiliation share in the

benefits put forth by the local Central Body at the expense of those local unions who are affiliated and attend the meetings of their Central Bodies and work for the interest of organized labor" (AFL 1949, 415).

5. Though exact numbers were not calculated regularly, the AFL occasionally attempted to discern affiliation rates. At the 1946 convention, survey results reported that 38 percent of all eligible locals were affiliated to city centrals (AFL 1946, 42). Forsythe reports that the same year found 25 percent of AFL membership affiliated with the Detroit and Wayne County Federation of Labor (in Michigan) and 64 percent of area membership in St. Louis (Forsythe 1956).

6. AFL Executive Council (AFLEX), January 15–29, 1936, p. 50.

7. AFLEX, April 19–23, 1937, pp. 7–8, 45.

8. Report of Director of CIO Meeting, March 9, 1937, Catholic University of America (CUA), John Brophy Papers (JB), Box 1937, Folder 1937 CIO Reports.

9. *New York Times*, March 19, 1937, p. 1; Policy, prepared by Charles Howard, March 24, 1937, Archives of Labor and Urban Affairs, Wayne State University (WSU), Katherine Pollack-Ellickson Collection (PE), Box 17, Folder 17.

10. Comments on Model Industrial Union Council Constitution, Katherine Pollack, July 14, 1937, p. 1, WSU, PE, Box 19, Folder 3.

11. See "Applying for a Charter for an Industrial Union Council of the CIO- Form 24, WSU, PE, Box 9, Folder IUC (Industrial Union Council) 1937; for reliance on AFL constitution, see "Comments on Model Industrial Union Council Constitution," prepared by Katherine Pollak, July 14, 1937, WSU, PE, Box 19, Folder 2.

12. Brophy to City and County Industrial Union Councils, September 15, 1937, WSU, PE, Box 19, Folder 1.

13. Ibid.

14. The AFL language was as follows: "It shall be the duty of all National and International Unions affiliated with the American Federation of Labor to instruct their Local Unions to join chartered Central Labor Bodies" (AFL, 1936, p. xxvii).

15. While I have not come across any national-level statistics, the following IUC affiliation rates give a sense of the rate of affiliation. In 1941, the Erie County IUC reported that 53 percent of locals were affiliated. In 1952, that had increased to 58 percent. In 1946, 51 percent of eligible locals were affiliated with the Greater New York Industrial Union Council. For Buffalo numbers, see "Erie County IUC Report to Brophy," January 23, 1941, Catholic University, CIO Collection, Box 14, Folder 61; Greater Buffalo Industrial Union Council Semi-Annual Report, August 4, 1952. New York City numbers calculated from Membership Standing, October 1, 1946, Robert Wagner Labor Archives, Saul Mills Collection, Box 3, Folder 4; 1947 New York Trade Union Directory.

Sources

Depository Designations

Catholic University of America (CUA)
Archives of Labor and Urban Affairs, Wayne State University (WSU)
Robert Wagner Labor Archives (RWLA)

Collection Designations

AFL Executive Council (AFLEX)
John Brophy Papers (JB)
Pollack Ellickson Collection (PEC)
Saul Mills Collection (SM)

Bibliography

AFL. 1898. Report of Proceedings of the Eighteenth Annual Convention of the American Federation of Labor. Kansas City, MO. December 12–20.

AFL. 1901. Report of Proceedings of the Twenty-First Annual Convention of the American Federation of Labor. Scranton, PA. December 5–14.

AFL. 1936. Report of the Proceedings of the Fifty-Sixth Annual Convention of the American Federation of Labor. Tampa, FL. November 16–27.

AFL. 1946. Report of the Proceedings of the Sixty-Fifth Annual Convention of the American Federation of Labor. Chicago, IL. October 7–17.

AFL. 1949. Report of the Proceedings of the Sixty-Eighth Annual Convention of the American Federation of Labor. St. Paul, MN. October 3–10.

AFL-CIO. 1959. Proceedings of the Third Constitutional Convention of the AFL-CIO, vol. 1, Daily Proceedings. San Francisco, CA. September 17–23.

AFL-CIO. 1961. Proceedings of the Fourth Constitutional Convention of the AFL-CIO, vol. 2, Report of the Executive Council. Miami Beach, FL. December 7–13.

AFL-CIO. 1965. Proceedings of the Sixth Constitutional Convention of the AFL-CIO, vol. 1, Daily Proceedings. San Francisco, CA. December 9–15.

AFL-CIO. 1967. Proceedings of the Seventh Constitutional Convention of the AFL-CIO, vol. 1, Daily Proceedings. Bal Harbour, FL. December 7–12.

AFL-CIO. 1969. Proceedings of the Eight Constitutional Convention of the AFL-CIO, vol. 1, Daily Proceedings. Atlantic City, NJ. October 2–7.

AFL-CIO. 1981. Proceedings of the Fourteenth Constitutional Convention of the AFL-CIO, Daily Proceedings. New York, NY. November 16–19.

AFL-CIO. 1985. Proceedings of the Sixteenth Constitutional Convention of the AFL-CIO, Daily Proceedings. Anaheim, CA. October 28–31.

AFL-CIO. 1991. Rules Governing AFL-CIO Local Central Bodies, Washington, DC: AFL-CIO.

AFL-CIO. 1999. Executive Council Statement. "Building a New Labor Movement in Our Communities: The New Alliance." Chicago, IL. August 3.

AFL-CIO. Web A. http://www.aflcio.org/frong/faqs.htm

AFL-CIO. Web B. http://www.aflcio.org/convention99/sr02_mapping.htm

AFL-CIO. Web C. http://www.aflcio.org/convention99/conv_updates_res12.htm

Barnett, George E. 1913. "The Dominance of the National Union in American Labor Organization." *Quarterly Journal of Economics* 27: 455–81.

Bigham, Truman. 1925. The Chicago Federation of Labor. Doctoral diss., University of Chicago.

Bizjack, Jack. 1969. The Trade and Labor Assembly of Chicago, Illinois. Master's thesis, Department of History, University of Chicago.

Borsos, John. 1996. "We Make You This Appeal in the Name of Every Union Man and Woman in Barberton: Solidarity Unionism in Barberton, Ohio, 1933–41." In *We Are All Leaders*, ed. Staughton Lynd. Chicago: University of Illinois Press.

Brune, Lester. 1982. "'Union Holiday–Closed Till Further Notice': The 1936 General Strike at Pekin, Illinois." *Journal of the Illinois State Historical Society* 75: 29–38.

Burke, William Maxwell. 1899. *History and Functions of Central Labor Unions*, vol. 12. New York: Macmillan.

CIO. 1938. Daily Proceedings of the First Constitutional Convention. Pittsburgh, PA. November 14–18.

CIO. 1942. Daily Proceedings of Fourth Constitutional Convention of the Congress of Industrial Organizations. Detroit, MI. November 17–22, 1941.

CIO. 1942. Daily Proceedings of the Fifth Constitutional Convention. Boston, MA. November 9–13.

CIO. 1943. Final Proceedings of the Sixth Constitutional Convention. Philadelphia, PA. November 1–5.

CIO. 1947. Final Proceedings of the Ninth Constitutional Convention. Boston, MA. October 13–17.

CIO. 1952. Proceedings of the Fourteenth Constitutional Convention. Atlantic City, NJ. December 1–4.

CIO. 1953. Proceedings of the Fifteenth Constitutional Convention. Cleveland, OH. November 16–20.

Commons, John R., David J. Sapposs, Helen L. Sumner, E.B. Mittelman, H.E. Hoagland, John B. Andrews, and Selig Perlman. 1961. *History of Labour in the United States*, vols. 1, 2. New York: Macmillan.

Davin, Eric, and Staughton Lynd. 1979–1980. "Picket Line and Ballot Box: The Forgotten Legacy of the Local Labor Party Movement, 1932–1936." *Radical Labor History Review*, Winter.

Dixon, Marion. 1929. The History of Los Angeles Central Labor Council. Master's thesis, University of California–Berkeley.

Emspak, Frank. 1972. The Break-Up of the Congress of Industrial Organizations (CIO), 1945–1950. Doctoral diss., Department of History, University of Wisconsin–Madison.

Fink, Gary. 1978. "The Rejection of Voluntarism," in *Labor and American Politics: A Book of Reasonings*, ed. Charles M. Rehmus et al. Ann Arbor: University of Michigan Press.

Foner, Henry. 1990. "Saul Mills and the Greater New York Industrial Union Council, CIO." *Labor History* 31, no. 3: 347–60.

Foner, Phillip. 1955. *From the Founding of the A.F. of L. to the Emergence of American Imperialism*. New York: International Publishers.

Forsythe, Edwin James. 1956. The St. Louis Central Trades and Labor Union, 1887–1945. Doctoral diss., Columbia: University of Missouri–Columbia.

FOTLU (Federation of Organized Trades and Labor Unions of the United States and Canada). 1886. Report of the Sixth Annual Session of the Federation of Organized Trades and Labor Unions of the United States and Canada; also the Proceedings of the First Annual Convention of the American Federation of Labor, Columbus, Ohio.

Freeman, Joshua. 2000. *Working Class New York: Life and Labor Since World War II*. New York: New Press.

Gavett, Thomas. 1965. *Development of the Labor Movement in Milwaukee*. Madison, WI: University of Wisconsin Press.

Gompers, Samuel. 1902. "Attention Central Labor Councils." *The American Federationist*, September, p. 507.

Greene, Julia. 1991. " 'The Strike at the Ballot Box': The American Federation of Labor's Entrance into Election Politics, 1906–1909." *Labor History* 32, no. 2: 165–92.

Hirschman, Albert. 1970. *Exit, Voice and Loyalty*. Cambridge, MA: Harvard University Press.

Javersak, David. 1980. "Response of the O.V.T. and L.A. to Industrialism." *Journal of the West Virginia Historical Association* 4: 35–45.

Kagel, John. 1984. "The Day the City Stopped," *California History* 63: 212–33.

Kazin, Michael. 1986. "The Great Exception Revisited: Organized Labor and Politics in San Francisco and Los Angeles, 1870–1940." *Pacific Historical Review* 55, no. 3: 371–402.

King, Joseph. 1939. "The Durham Central Labor Union." *Southern Economic Journal* 5, no. 1: 55–70.

Lens, Sidney. 1959. *The Crisis of American Labor*. New York: Sagamore.

Levinson, Edward. 1995. *Labor on the March*. Ithaca, NY: ILR Press.

Lorwin, Lewis. 1933. *The American Federation of Labor: History, Policies, and Prospects*. Washington, DC: The Brookings Institution.

Luce, Stephanie. 2001. "Building Political Power and Community Coalitions: The Role of Central Labor Councils in the Living-Wage Movement." In *Central Labor Councils and the Revival of American Unionism: Organizing for Justice in Our Communities*, ed. Immanuel Ness and Stuart Eimer. Armonk, NY: M.E. Sharpe.

Montgomery, David. 1983. "New Tendencies in Union Struggles and Strategies in Europe and the United States, 1916–1922." In *Work, Community, and Power: The Experience of Labor in Europe and America, 1900–1925*, ed. James Cronin and Carmen Sirianni Cronin. Philadelphia: Temple University Press, 88–116.

Olson, Mancur. 1971. *The Logic of Collective Action: Public Goods and the Theory of Groups*. Cambridge, MA: Harvard University Press.

Rogin, Michael. 1971. "Voluntarism: The Political Functions of an Anti-Political Doctrine." In *The American Labor Movement*, ed. David Brody. New York: Harper and Row: 100–18.

Skakkebaek, Mette. 1981. "Concerns of Organized Labor, 1902–1918: The Belleville Trades and Labor Assembly, Illinois." *American Studies in Scandinavia* 14: 81–92.

Smith, Stanton. 1961. "The Challenge Facing Central Labor Bodies." *American Federationist*. May 7, 68: 5.

Stolberg, Benjamin. 1971. *The Story of the CIO*. New York: Arno.

Ulman, Lloyd. 1955. *The Rise of the National Trade Union*. Cambridge, MA: Harvard University Press.

Wallihan, James. 1985. "Union Government and Organization." In *Union Government and Organization*. Washington, DC: Bureau of National Affairs.

Zieger, Robert H. 1995. "The CIO: Industrial Union Council (IUC) Miscellaneous Notes." In *The CIO: 1935–1955*. Chapel Hill: University of North Carolina Press.

II

Case Studies

4

The Los Angeles County Federation of Labor

A Model of Transformation or Traditional Unionism?

Fernando E. Gapasin

Los Angeles is the second largest city in the United States, a Mecca of diversity, crossroads of world trade, and the manufacturing center of North America. There is no better place for a labor-movement revival. "Los Angeles Area Now a Model for Labor Revival" says the *Los Angeles Times* (September 6, 1999). In 1999, Los Angeles labor unions have added more than 85,000 new members, thus raising their union density from 18 percent to 20 percent. They have also built a network of political and community allies that is paying off in new laws and public support. Perhaps more than anywhere else in the nation, unions here have embraced the more aggressive, more sophisticated approach to organizing promoted by the leadership of the AFL-CIO (American Federation of Labor–Congress of Industrial Organizations). With its heavily immigrant, low-wage work force—which many see as ripe for organizing—the region once known for its hostility to unions is being viewed as its next great hope.

Led by a reenergized Los Angeles County Federation of Labor (LACFL) and a few committed locals and backed by money and resources from the national AFL-CIO, Los Angeles–area unions have spent millions of dollars in recent years on organizing drives and political campaigns. The political clout of the LACFL is evident in the resounding defeat of the antiworker, in the "paycheck protection act" (Proposition 226), and in recent elections in which the LACFL won fourteen of fifteen state assembly seats and two of three city council seats. The LACFL mobilized some 10,000 workers and their families for the opening convocation at the National AFL-CIO convention held in Los Angeles in October 1999. It has also strategically used resources in targeting whole industries (Cleeland 1999).

Grounded in the realities of a declining union movement, the National AFL-CIO moved its rhetoric from "business unionism" (traditional unionism) to an organizing, mobilization model. This chapter presents an examination of the transition of the LACFL from "traditional" to "transformative" (Gapasin and Wial 1998, 58–64).

The article will examine the role of local unions, the role of independent labor organizations and labor education, and the role that labor–community projects like the "Living Wage Campaign" can have in the transformation of a local labor movement. In addition, this analysis speaks to the implications that these different forces have for the ideology, culture, and structure of a central labor council (CLC).

Central Labor Councils

The challenge for the AFL-CIO leadership is to convince the leadership of the national and international unions to increase resources directed toward organizing the unorganized. There is a real relationship among rapid globalization of business, workplace restructuring, union density, political power, labor laws, and organizing, but the truth is that unions are not allocating enough resources to organizing unorganized workers.

Clearly there is a dynamic, reciprocal relationship among political power, union density, and organizing; thus, organizing increases political power and political power can facilitate organizing, for example, resulting in improved labor-law legislation and enforcement. The foundation for the AFL-CIO's culture shift from servicing to organizing will be local, county, and regional central labor councils. As Executive Vice President Linda Chavez-Thompson said, "We're aiming to create a culture of organizing throughout the union movement . . . and Central Labor Councils can and will be the center of that culture" (Rosier 1996, 3).

Until the election of the AFL-CIO's New Voice slate in 1995, central labor councils participated in organizing efforts because they had leadership that emphasized the importance of organizing, had local affiliated unions that provided resources for organizing, and had community support for organizing (Gapasin and Wial 1998, 64–65). Many of these "organizing" CLCs, which championed the 1995 election of the New Voice slate, were led by activists who had prior experience as both union and community organizers. Their efforts prior to the election of the New Voice created alliances between organized labor and communities (particularly communities of color) that have facilitated union growth and organization. These "organizing" CLCs usually have eight behaviors[1] that distinguish them from CLCs that merely refer information to international unions (see chapter 1). These behaviors include organizing new members, immobilizing against employee opposition, building political power, promoting economic growth, providing economic education, supporting the right to organize, and fostering diversity.

Most of the manufacturing that is being deindustrialized in the old U.S. industrial centers is relocating to the U.S. Sun Belt. The AFL-CIO, in the form of CLCs, has councils capable of organizing in the following Sun Belt areas: Atlanta, southern Florida, southern California and the Silicon Valley, and Houston.

In areas where the AFL-CIO does not have capable councils, new kinds of organization could be formed that incorporate the energy of existing groups, for example, the Black Workers for Justice in North Carolina, the Los Angeles Manufacturing Action Program (LAMAP), or the Jobs with Justice Campaign, which exists nationally. Another way to maximize limited resources throughout the United States is to formalize existing regional clusters of central labor councils. By focusing organizing resources on existing clusters of councils, the National AFL-CIO creates the possibility of widening the scope of organizing by increasing the pool of activists and local unions. Accordingly, no council would have to relinquish its autonomy, but by cooperating in these regionalized efforts, each council could facilitate its own growth. The most obvious way to bolster weak councils in key organizing areas like the Sun Belt is to shift material and human resources to those areas.

The National AFL-CIO might consider long-term investments in materials and personnel in areas where there is growth and where there are capable CLCs, especially in the Sun Belt: southern Florida; Atlanta, southern California; Silicon Valley in California; and Houston.

Another glaring mismatch exists in the racial and gender makeup of the leadership bodies of central labor councils of the United States. As one CLC leader asked at the National Central Labor Council Conference held in Denver (July 1996), "Why are there almost all white people here?" Based on the AFL-CIO survey, the leadership bodies (executive boards) are 64 percent European American males, 20 percent women, 11 percent African American, 5 percent Latino, and 0.4 percent Asian. Here again, in order to facilitate the building of ties between the labor movement and those communities that are underrepresented in the leadership of CLCs, central labor councils could support the creation and affiliation of community-based labor–community organizations like the California Immigrant Workers Association, which was created by AFL-CIO Region 6 and was instrumental in the organizing of 2,000, mostly Latino, drywall workers in southern California; and the Korean Immigrant Workers Association (KIWA), which supported Latino hotel workers against Korean hotel owners in Los Angeles (Gapasin and Wial 1997).

Groups like KIWA, the Chinese Progressive Association (CPA) Workers Center in Boston, the Asian Immigrant Women Advocates (AIWA) in Oakland, and the Pilipino Workers Center (PWC) in Los Angeles address the needs of low-income immigrant workers. Each of these groups has taken up more than "labor" issues. And each group has fashioned very effective "united front" campaigns involving other sectors of the community. These types of groups, in addition to activist and organizing-oriented AFL-CIO constituency groups like the Asian Pacific American Labor Alliance (APALA), can help the labor movement build bridges to multiple communities and position CLCs to become "mobilizers" for sections of the community that normally would not interact, thus politicizing the labor movement and enhancing its power. In many ways a study of the LACFL demonstrates the strengths of embracing the Union Cities program (see chapter 1) in its entirety and also the general weaknesses of the U.S. labor movement.

Los Angeles County Federation of Labor

The Los Angeles County Federation of Labor (AFL-CIO) was founded in 1959. Today, the LACFL has 325 affiliated local unions and represents almost 800,000 unionized workers in the Greater Los Angeles Metropolitan area. The formation of the LACFL was a result of the merger of one CIO CLC and six AFL CLCs. In practice the thirty-five LACFL executive board seats were two-thirds AFL and one-third CIO. The first significant mobilization effort of the newly founded LACFL was its major role in building strike support for the nationwide basic steel strike of 1959.[2]

January 1963, with the aid of the LACFL, the Los Angeles–Orange County Organizing Committee (LAOCOC) was created with 280 union staffers dedicated to organizing. In March 1964, the LAOCOC organized an areawide organizing conference that drew 1,400 attendees. The national AFL-CIO sent Jay Lovestone, head of the department of international affairs, to address the gathering. Consequently, because neither the national AFL-CIO nor the LACFL prioritized organizing, resources were not allocated for organizing. As a result, the LAOCOC, instead of becoming a device to expand organizing, simply became a clearinghouse where unions could clear targets for their individual organizing efforts.

The war in Vietnam revealed the various factions within the LACFL. Like other central bodies in California the LACFL had contingents of delegates who opposed the Vietnam War. The national AFL-CIO, on the other hand, supported the government's policy on the war. With the active cooperation of the LACFL executive secretary-treasurer, Sigmund Arywitz, antiwar activists within the LACFL were defeated. Later, during the 1970s, the LACFL shifted more and more of its resources into the arena of electoral politics. In the late 1970s, Bill Robertson from HERE (the Hotel Employees and Restaurant Employees International Union) took over from Arywitz as the executive secretary-treasurer, and Jim Wood became the CLC's assistant COPE director, responsible for the council's political endorsements and support for candidates. Under Robertson and Wood the LACFL became almost exclusively an electoral operation. For instance, LACFL staff became the COPE contacts for different geographical areas of Los Angeles.

In 1993 Bill Robertson retired and Jim Wood was appointed the executive secretary-treasurer of the LACFL. Miguel Contreras was hired as the assistant COPE director. Shortly after being hired, he was placed on leave so he could assist Kathleen Brown in her failed attempt to win the governorship of California. Wood was elected to his post in 1994. He became ill in 1995 and died in 1996. After an inside battle with racial overtones, Contreras emerged as the new executive secretary-treasurer of the LACFL in May 1996. Contreras had been an international representative of HERE. He had also served for several years as an organizer and boycott director for the United Farm Workers union (UFW). His election coincided with the new organizing emphasis of the national AFL-CIO, and he became one of the very few members of a minority group to lead a major CLC.

Was the election of Contreras alone enough to make the LACFL a Union City? The answer is no. The organizational culture and structure of the CLC had to change. For twenty years the single-minded LACFL was dedicated to electoral politics. This affected the structure of the CLC and the perceived purpose of the LACFL. Obviously, if the direction of the LACFL is going to change, resources will have to be redirected. For instance, instead of all of the staff being directed to work in COPE, division of labor around a variety of functions has to occur. In a jurisdiction as complex as Los Angeles County, the transformation to an "organizing" CLC requires restructuring as well as a new division of labor if both organizing and politics are to become the priorities of the CLC. The transformation of a central labor council requires the support of a local union that has already transformed itself into an "organizing" union and a segment of the local community that supports union organizing (Gapasin and Wial 1998).

Local Unions

Local unions, on average, spend 3 percent or less on external organizing while focusing the largest share of their resources on servicing existing members (e.g., grievance handling and collective bargaining). Therefore, at least minimally, local unions must be transformed so that organizing becomes their main priority.

It is generally agreed that local unions must organize, but two questions commonly arise: How are local unions transformed from "servicing" to "organizing" unions? How much more transformation is needed? Specifically, should we be trying to transform local unions into organizing unions via the "internal organizing" model espoused by Banks and Metzgar (1989); or creating "organizing unions" as described by Fletcher and Hurd (1998); or to "social movement" unions as elaborated by Waterman (1993) and Johnston (1994).

In contrast to the internal organizing model, which stresses the mobilization of union members to address their own servicing needs, recent research indicates that, in order to transform a local union so that organizing efforts are expanded, organizing must become more valued by union members than servicing. Since the internal organizing model emphasizes servicing, which corresponds to the expectations of the members, the allocation of resources to servicing remains a priority. Thus, in order to change the culture of the union to one that values organizing, the objective of unions should not be to organize around grievances, but to reduce the importance of handling grievances. No research so far demonstrates that the internal organizing model increases external organizing for local unions.

The argument being postulated by many of the "organizing" local unions is that the only way to guarantee a fair deal for its members is to increase the union's share of the labor market. The obvious advantage of the market-share approach is that it appeals to economic self-interest. It is also consistent with the U.S. tradition of job-based unionism (strictly business unionism). Organizing locals offer unions a useful, short-term approach to regaining market share, but this approach cannot serve as the basis for a coherent alternative to serviced-based business unionism. Neither the internal organizing model nor the organizing approach answers the larger questions posed about the strategic direction of the U.S. labor movement. Likewise, it is my opinion that the transformation of the labor movement will require insights from those who are presently not in it. This would require that academics as well as working-class people who are not presently part of the labor movement engage in responding to the following questions: Who is identified as the constituency of organized labor? What is the mission of the labor movement? What is the relationship of organized labor to corporate America? What should that relationship be? What is the relationship of organized labor to other social movements? What should that relationship be? How do those in the labor movement deal with issues of globalization and international solidarity?

The Union Cities initiative is an attempt by the AFL-CIO to transform unions. It is not only an attempt to transform some unions into what they once were, but also a valiant effort to transform most unions into something that they have never been, namely, agents of social and economic justice.

This type of unionism incorporates broader and larger community issues into union planning and development of union policies. Broadly speaking, the initiative taken by leaders within the AFL-CIO provides a window of opportunity for the development of a new identity for the U.S. labor movement. What is suggested in the Union Cities program is an approach to unionism that positions the labor movement at the nexus of emerging and developing social movements. This approach suggests constructive and affirmative new relationships among class, popular, and democratic interests. "Social Movement Unionism" presents the possibility for a comprehensible articulation of the relationship between unionized and non-union workers, between the labor movement and other social forces (e.g., movements of minorities, immigrants, and women) and between issues of shop floor democracy and internationalism (Waterman 1993).

"Potentials" for Transformation

The real key to the transformation of the LACFL lies not only in the transformation of the national AFL-CIO, but also in a confluence of internal "potentials" for transformation. As stated previously, the transformation of the AFL-CIO nationally has been greatly influenced by the emergence of sixties and seventies radicals who were trained—on university campuses and in communities and a variety of workplaces—around broadly based social and political issues such as free speech, democracy, opposition to the Vietnam War, racial and gender justice, and environmental justice. Many of these radicals found their way into the American union movement and for the most part became dissidents in their local unions. Some persisted and were successful in bringing about reform in their local unions, and they emerged as union leaders. Some became representatives of, or even officers in, their national or international unions. Others have become high-ranking staff in unions and the national AFL-CIO. As much as this "new blood" has influenced the culture of the traditional union movement, the dominant culture of the American union movement remains that of the Cold War Warriors, who were led by George Meany and who feared communists and socialists and generally distrusted any outsiders or community "agitators."

As evidenced by the efforts to organize the unorganized and to oppose the war in Vietnam, dissident forces have existed in the LACFL since its inception. And it is clear that for the most part, Arywitz, Robertson, and Wood represented the orientation of the Cold War Warriors. Contreras, on the other hand, was recruited from the fields early on and was trained by the UFW to build union–community coalitions. He spent his early career in the union movement as a boycott director, whose job was to build community support for the cause of the UFW. His links to the UFW provided networks of friends and supporters in primarily Mexican-American communities and with other union leaders and activists, who, like him, had been trained by the UFW. The recent electoral successes of the LACFL are in part linked to Contreras's ability to bridge traditional "white" liberal Democratic Party forces with the growing Latino political machine.[3]

Still, other local union leaders and activists in Los Angeles were influenced by more radical organizations like, for example, the Centro de Accion Social Autonima-Hermandad General de Trabajadores (Center for Independent Social Action [CASA]; Juan Gomez-Quinones 1990 pp. 150–51).[4] CASA and other radical organizations not only trained young activists in the seventies to organize in communities and the workplace, but also provided an ideological orientation that included a vision of social and economic equality and justice. The key to CASA's (and other similar organizations') political efforts was a disciplined membership. Dozens of ideologically oriented young people found their way into the trade union movement in Los Angeles. They went into all of the unions, for example, United Farm Workers (UFW); United Auto Workers (UAW); United Steel Workers Association of America (USWA); International Association of Machinists (IAM); International Ladies Garment Workers Union (ILGWU); Hotel and Restaurant Employees (HERE); Communications Workers of America (CWA); Service Employees International Union (SEIU); and American Federation of State, County, and Municipal Employees (AFSCME). And, just as radicals did in past generations, they often found themselves in opposition to the incumbent leaders of the trade union movement. They found themselves at odds, especially around issues of democracy and access for minorities, immigrants, and women. For many of these radicals, the LACFL was a bastion of conservatism in the union movement and was dominated by Democratic Party politics.

Many of these radicals, who understood the importance of organizing and building alliances with community forces, built alternative movements in their local unions or created alternative organizations. One such organization was the Alliance of Asian Pacific Labor (AAPL); established in 1987, it successfully brought together most of the Asian union staff and rank-and-file leaders in Los Angeles and Orange counties. AAPL held monthly membership meetings that promoted ongoing education for union activists, built solidarity among unions, and encouraged labor–community alliances. AAPL succeeded in establishing a union movement presence within the Los Angeles Asian-American community by sending representatives to conferences, events, and meetings; distributing literature; publicizing labor activities through the Asian-American media; and promoting union consciousness. AAPL involved itself in community issues involving language rights, redistricting, voter registration, and political empowerment. Within the union movement,

AAPL worked to oppose "Japan bashing" and misdirected anti-Asian sentiment (Wong 1994, 344–45). AAPL later evolved into the Asian Pacific American Labor Alliance (APALA).

In 1991, one of the activists in AAPL, from the Service Employees International Union (SEIU), became the director of the UCLA Center for Labor Research and Education. The emphasis of the Labor Center shifted to organizing the unorganized. A conference was held on organizing new immigrants. Shortly after that, a conference for organizing Asian immigrants was sponsored by the UCLA Labor Center. At the same time a study was conducted, which revealed that none of the unions in Los Angeles County hired any Asian organizers. In part, as a consequence of the activities around immigrant organizing by the UCLA Labor Center and the organizing of Asian union activists around the country, APALA was founded on May Day 1992 in Washington, D.C.

At about the same time, the regional director of the AFL-CIO in Los Angeles persuaded the national AFL-CIO to establish the California Immigrant Workers Association (CIWA) to assist Latino immigrant workers in obtaining legalization, English instruction, and other benefits. CIWA was also an "associate membership" organization, which allowed immigrant workers to affiliate with the AFL-CIO. The organization's goal was to promote good will between the union movement and the Latino community and to build a foundation for future organizing (Wong 1994, 341–42). CIWA was instrumental in the successful unionization of 2,000 drywallers. CIWA mobilized lawyers to help fight the Immigration and Naturalization Service (INS) and got community groups like the Orange County–based Hermandad Mexicana Nacional to support the drywallers with donations of food and other necessities. It defended arrested strikers and helped pull off creative tactics like blocking the freeway in protest of the INS raids. CIWA also played a key role in researching and filing the FLSA (Fair Labor Standards Act) lawsuits, which were critical to the ultimate victory of the drywallers. The creative combination of community, legal, and workplace organizing form one of the cornerstones of social-movement unionism, but CIWA itself did not survive. Despite its success, CIWA was not seen as a priority by the AFL-CIO national leadership and CIWA's funding was terminated.

The Los Angeles Manufacturing Action Project (LAMAP) was another rich, albeit failed experience in the development of immigrant worker organizing and social movement unionism. LAMAP was created by veteran union organizers like Peter Olney in the aftermath of the

Rodney King "disruptions" in 1992 and was viewed as a community development strategy as well as a labor-organizing project.

LAMAP pioneered large-scale, multiunion labor-organizing drives that targeted whole industries rather than individual shops and that were grounded in the community. Criticizing traditional union organizing tactics, Peter Olney, LAMAP former director, says, "You can't just send a few people into town; put them up at a motel, collect authorization cards and file for a NLRB election" (Interview November 1998).

LAMAP chose the Alameda Corridor as its organizing target. This is a 120-square-mile corridor that stretches from downtown Los Angeles to the Port of Los Angeles and contains almost two-thirds of the nearly 650,000 manufacturing jobs in Los Angeles. In addition to its innovative, multiunion, industrywide approach, LAMAP designed a large-scale community component that included English as a second language (ESL) and citizenship classes and mobilized college students to volunteer in the campaign. It advocated for unions and communities, mapping out strategic plans together. Despite its day-to-day relations with unions, many unions viewed LAMAP as outside the union movement (Gallagher 1998). Some unions argued against working with LAMAP because they wanted to have total control over their organizing campaigns and did not want to share decision making with community organizations.

As a result, like CIWA, LAMAP died for lack of union support. Despite high praise from different international unions and John Sweeney himself, who acknowledged LAMAP as a "model" for organizing, LAMAP never secured stable funding from unions and eventually shut down in January 1998.

Clearly the type of organizing strategies employed by affiliates of the LACFL influence the culture of that organization. Probably none was more significant than SEIU's Justice for Janitors campaign, which successfully unionized 2,000 janitors. Clearly too, the broadly televised campaign in Los Angeles and the police riots at Century City (a section of Los Angeles) in 1990 galvanized militant sectors of the union movement. Its non-NLRB, industrywide, militant, mass-mobilization approach to recognition and collective bargaining has become a model of the AFL-CIO's "strategic organizing" approach.

Living-Wage Campaign

An example of how one union influenced the changing culture of the Los Angeles union movement comes from HERE Local 11. HERE Local 11 developed the vision of creating an independent nonprofit corporation called the Tourist Industry Development Council (TIDC), later renamed the Los Angeles Alliance for a New Economy (LAANE), to promote economic development and increase union density.

LAANE led the Los Angeles living-wage initiative with the goal of linking policy development to union organizing. It was envisioned that the living-wage issue could be a way to improve incomes and support unionization of the hotel industry's low-wage and primarily immigrant work force. LAANE understood that only a broad coalition could get a living-wage ordinance passed. "LAANE invited representatives from a number of membership-based neighborhood groups including ACORN (Association of Community Organizations for Reform Now) tenants union AGENDA (a grassroots organization based in south central Los Angeles), Communities for a Better Environment, and a number of other labor, community, and religious organizations. The coalition created a board with representation from labor, community, and religious organizations, with parallel task forces based in each of these three constituencies" (Zabin and Martin 1999, 10).

LAANE coordinated a multilevel campaign for two years. The campaign focused on policy development, coalition building, and worker education and mobilization. Ties with local universities provided interns for conducting campaign research. One research project on the potential fiscal and economic impact of the proposed ordinance that UCLA economists gave LAANE provided solid arguments to defend their position with the city council. By conferring with its own team of lawyers and with others around the country, LAANE prepared a carefully written ordinance. In addition, LAANE organized workers who would be affected by the ordinance, incorporating them into the campaign in mobilizations and as spokespersons in city-council-meeting testimonies. This was not just a campaign tactic, but rather an integral element of their central objective of building support for union organizing.

The campaign overcame concerted business opposition by means of large and frequent mobilizations in the streets and in city-council hearings, credible research, smart political maneuvering, a media strategy, and progressives in the city council. Despite a strong Republican mayor who could mobilize the business community, the Los Angeles living-wage ordinance ultimately passed on April 1, 1997, with the council voting eleven to one to override the mayor's veto (Zabin and Martin 1999, 11).

The ordinance includes a provision that any new city contract or concession agreement with a subsidy over $100,000 has to provide employees with $7.25 per hour with family health benefits or $8.50 without, twelve paid days off per year, and ten unpaid days off per year, with wages to be indexed to inflation. A year later, tenants at the Los Angeles International Airport disputed their coverage under the ordinance, so LAANE once again mobilized and successfully won an amendment to make airport coverage explicit and closed a number of other loopholes (Zabin and Martin 1999).

In addition, LAANE tried to shape the living-wage policy in a way that creates opportunities for union organizing among low-wage workers. Yet, as Madeline Janis-Aparicio, LAANE's executive director argues, living-wage requirements alone do not translate into union organizing; but if such ordinances are structured to benefit organizing, they provide leverage when combined with other policies. The living-wage effort has helped union organizing in Los Angeles in a number of ways. First, LAANE was able to negotiate a living wage and a "card-check/neutrality" agreement establishing a fair process for union recognition at a large-scale entertainment and hotel development in Hollywood, in return for city approval and tax breaks. Card check and neutrality agreements with employers allow workers to organize into unions of their choice without employer opposition. The living-wage criterion allowed the coalition to get involved in the development approval process and to raise directly the issue of wages and working conditions. It positioned the coalition so that it could offer support for the development in return for compliance with the living wage and neutrality in the event of an organizing drive. LAANE is also using this strategy in its ongoing campaign to gain card-check/neutrality at the Universal Studios entertainment complex, which is seeking approvals for expansion. As noted by Janis-Aparicio, in cities where a living-wage climate has been created, developers need the support of labor and community coalitions in order to obtain government approval. The particularly innovative element of the Hollywood deal is that the agreement covers not only the developer, but also the developer's tenants, creating a favorable organizing environment for service workers once the project is built (Zabin and Martin 1999, 12).

The living-wage ordinance has also been directly linked to a large-scale unionization drive at the Los Angeles International Airport carried out by HERE and SEIU with the support of the national AFL-CIO. Union organizers and LAANE have used the enforcement provision of the ordinance, which allows a third party to inform and educate affected workers about their rights under the living-wage law. This provision permitted them to gain access to workers at the work site and to lay some groundwork for empowering workers to defend their rights. In addition, the unionization drive has benefited from the campaign experience and leadership skills of several workers at Los Angeles International Airport, who had been involved in the living-wage effort from its inception and now serve on LAANE's board of directors (Zabin and Martin 1999).

LAANE is also working to extend a living-wage policy to Santa Monica in ways that make explicit links to union organizing. There, LAANE has created an organization called Santa Monicans Allied for Responsible Tourism (SMART) directed by a staff member who has built a base of local neighborhood supporters. Working closely with HERE Local 814, SMART has devised a strategy to promote a living-wage ordinance that would cover all employers with over fifty employees in Santa Monica's coastal zone, where the high-end tourist hotels are concentrated. In this case, the push to pass the ordinance will be part of the union campaign, so that workers more clearly take ownership of the living-wage issue and learn to see the union as their ally (Zabin and Martin 1999, 13).

Currently, LAANE is working to extend the living-wage ordinance to all private firms participating in the city's redevelopment projects, which expend the bulk of the city's business assistance moneys. At the same time, it is helping the redevelopment agency work with the developer of the Hollywood project to create a health-insurance pool for workers in the development, lowering affected employers' costs of providing insurance to their employees. LAANE's ability to pressure from the outside while offering creative solutions from the inside vastly increases its credibility and effectiveness.

LAANE's strategy is particularly powerful for the hotel industry both because the tourism industry is often supported by public money and because LAANE and HERE have developed a very close working partnership that has allowed strategic coordination and targeting. The strategy could be applied to other industries that receive some form of public spending, but so far, the only other union that has begun to work directly with LAANE is SEIU in the airport campaign. The living-wage strategy is much less effective for private-sector businesses that do not interface with government through contracts, financial assistance, or land-use planning decisions. However, the SMART strategy in Santa Monica illustrates a case where the living wage is being applied to existing private-sector firms that do not do business with local government (Zabin and Martin 1999, 13).

It is still unclear whether the living wage is an umbrella issue that can maintain an ongoing coalition. Early participants such as low-income-housing or environmental-justice groups have become less active because they are concentrating on their own issues. This centrifugal tendency has partly been avoided in LAANE's campaigns directed at large-scale real-estate-development projects, where the organization has been able to build some bridges with local neighborhood groups concerned about job access, low-income housing, and other linkage issues.

LAANE has carved out a niche in Los Angeles by focusing on "closing off the low road," and works closely with labor and community allies in this arena of economic justice. It has not yet ventured beyond this arena to "pave the high road," leaving involvement in worker training to other organizations and working only with the progressive low-wage unions that are actively organizing. However, it has used the carrot as well as the stick by partnering with government and business in strategic instances to find creative solutions to the real problems of raising standards in a low-road, competitive regional economy (Zabin and Martin 1999, 14).

LAANE has stretched the living wage issue. It has increased the number of workers whose wages have gone up by extending its coverage to more categories of workers and more public-funding streams. It has also changed the climate for organizing low-wage service workers in the tourism industry and directly aided in union campaigns. All this has changed the debate about economic development in the city of Los Angeles, many leading observers assert that LAANE is fueling a new growth with equity alliance that has changed the political landscape of the city (Zabin and Martin 1999, 14).

A direct result of the Living Wage Campaign was an ongoing coalition called Clergy and Laity United for Economic Justice (CLUE). This is a coalition made up of labor activists, community organizers and clergy. It is a coalition that continues to fight for economic justice—for instance, fighting for fair wages and healthy working conditions for workfare workers. The Living Wage effort has not only triggered similar movements in neighboring communities but also triggered the development of broader social-justice agendas and conferences like the Progressive L.A. conference held at Occidental College and attended by hundreds of activists. It also encouraged more modest networks to develop, like the Faculty/Labor Action Network (FLAN), organized by the UCLA Labor Center, which sponsors regular educational roundtables with the LACFL. The Living Wage Campaign also provided impetus for less formal labor–communities groupings and networks to develop and play a direct role in influencing the direction of the Los Angeles union movement.

Labor Council Transformation?

Another influence is the day-to-day interaction between the UCLA Labor Center and LACFL. The Labor Center and the LACFL sponsor regular educational round tables on issues critical to the Los Angeles labor movement, for example, immigration. By sponsoring a two-day training course on the AFL-CIO's Common Sense Economics program, the UCLA Labor Center was able to help the LACFL revive and reactivate a core of activists in the education committee. The UCLA Labor Center, through APALA, has organized a committee of the constituency groups called United Labor Action (ULA) for the LACFL. The ULA brings together APALA, A. Phillip Randolph Institute (APRI), Coalition of Labor Union Women (CLUW), Labor Council for Latin American Advancement (LCLAA), Jewish Labor Council (JLC), and Pride at Work (the gay and lesbian constituency group of the AFL-CIO). The UCLA Labor Center has also been useful to the LACFL by organizing conferences, doing research, providing training and assistance in planning, and facilitating the strategic planning process of the LACFL.

In an attempt to adapt itself to an organizing agenda, the LACFL created an organizing department and hired as its director, the former staff director for the Justice for Janitors Local SEIU 1877. Immigrants from Mexico and throughout Latin America with years of organizing and campaigning experience in the Latino communities have been appointed to key positions in the council. In addition, LACFL hired two people—who had formerly played important roles in LAMAP—to be the media/communications staff and the research director of the LACFL. For the position of policy director, the LACFL hired a former staff member of the Industrial Areas Foundation (IAF), a national organization founded by Saul Alinsky, which is dedicated to the economic and political empowerment of communities. In addition, the LACFL has consolidated the LAOCOC under the direct leadership of the LACFL.

On the political side, instead of relying on conventional wisdom, the LACFL focused its get-out-the-vote efforts in recent years in predominantly immigrant and minority communities where there has traditionally been low voter turnout. In Latino communities SEIU, HERE, and the UFW spearheaded a get-out-the-vote campaign that increased Latino turn out by 26 percent in the areas where they campaigned. The strategy was designed to build ties with those communities where the union's message of economic improvement could be most appreciated. On issues like the unions' opposition to Proposition 226 and the support for Governor Gray Davis, the LACFL's strategy was successful, in each case delivering over 70 percent in those targeted areas. Clearly, the developed political leverage has assisted organizing at the Los Angeles International Airport and the home health care workers campaign of SEIU.

The LACFL has clearly shifted resources to the hiring of people who could create an organizing agenda and to the formation of strategies that could intersect with community interests. But it is probably an overstatement to say that Los Angeles is a model for labor revival. Of the 85,000 new members claimed by the LACFL, 74,000 came from one successful campaign, the home health care workers campaign by SEIU. And only a handful of 325 local unions in the LACFL have adopted an organizing agenda, while the primary work of the LACFL remains electoral politics. When a major political campaign arises, everyone's priority becomes that political campaign.

The main weakness of the Los Angeles labor movement has been the inability to organize in the manufacturing sector. The 700,000-plus manufacturing workers, largely immigrant (conservatively estimated at 70 percent), are mainly untouched by unions. Existing levels of unionization in that sector are estimated at 6 percent and dropping. Boeing, the largest aerospace corporation in the area, will reduce its 7,000 unionized workers by 3,000 within the next year. And while the early part of the decade demonstrated small successes in organizing immigrants in manufacturing, for example, American Racing Wheels, there have been no similar successes lately.

Flexible production methods and the employer sanctions provision (which allows management to fire workers who do not have proper working documents) in the Immigration Reform and Control Act (1986) provide challenges to organizing that few unions are willing to take on. At the October 1999 convention of the AFL-CIO, a motion was made to call for the repeal of employer sanctions due to the adverse effects that they have on organizing. The motion was not passed and was deferred to the executive council of the AFL-CIO by the United Food and Commercial Workers (UFCW) and the International Brotherhood of Teamsters (IBT).

Another obstacle in the labor movement is that most unions are not structured so that large numbers of newcomers can be easily brought into an existing union structure. Issues of language and autonomy become problematic in most unions. And quite often, incumbent union leaders are unwilling to provide full access, let alone real political power, to newcomers.

SEIU's successful Justice for Janitors campaign in Los Angeles in 1990 was a case in point. Immigrants, many of whom were politicized in the struggles for democracy in Latin America, moved rapidly to replace the incumbent leadership. They won a majority of the seats on the union executive board. But then a power struggle ensued between the majority of the board and the incumbent leadership. As a consequence, the union was unable to conduct business. After attempts at mediation, the international SEIU opted to place the local union into trusteeship and assume control of the union.

Experiences like these indicate that organizing immigrant workers often involves direct collisions between native union members and newcomers, who are often immigrant workers. The result is that unions are often slow to organize the workers who need organization the most.

Stepping into this gap in Los Angeles and elsewhere is an independent immigrant workers' social movement. Workers' centers such as the Korean Immigrant Workers Association (KIWA), the Philipino Workers Committee (PWC), Association of Latin American Gardeners of Los Angeles (ALAGLA), Day Laborer Organizing Project, Domestic Workers Project, and the Garment Workers Coalition (GWC) are at this core of this movement.

These organizations are specifically dedicated to the organization and empowerment of immigrant workers in some of the most exploited occupations in the United States, like garment, restaurant, day labor, and high-tech-manufacturing workers. For instance, hundreds of day laborers have mobilized through the Day Laborers Organizing Project against anti-immigrant police harassment and local laws that limit their ability to solicit work. According to Victor Narro of the Coalition for Humane Immigrant Rights of Los Angeles (CHIRLA), "Immigrant workers are creating their own movement and creating their own union."

Immigrant workers face barriers on the basis of language, race, citizenship status, and immigration status, not simply as workers. The struggle of immigrants is profoundly political and cultural in nature, and the workers' centers and other immigrant worker's organizations organize on this basis, seeing community, workplace, and political organizing as inextricably tied together. Unlike most unions, they see no boundary between the democratic political issues in the community and the struggle for democratic rights on the shop floor.

Although their experience has been at the forefront of immigrant worker organizing and key to the development of social-movement unionism, these immigrant workers' centers have extremely sparse funds, and it is difficult to undertake their work on a scale large enough to have a real impact.

By themselves neither the union movement nor the immigrant organizing movement has the capacity to develop successful organizing strategies. Without a strong push by progressives from within the union movement and strong immigrant-worker organizing outside the union movement, it is unlikely that the union movement will make immigrant organizing a central focus.

In an effort to meet this challenge, the LACFL has charged its policy director, asisted by the UCLA Labor Center, with the task of creating an immigrant-workers organizing committee. The committee includes union organizers, community organizers, and independent immigrant unions. The purpose of the committee is to build bridges among the different sectors doing immigrant organizing.

The development of this committee coincided with SEIU Local 1899's contract campaign in Los Angeles. The citywide campaign to gain a fair contract for janitors sparked labor and community support from every progressive sector in Los Angeles. Students; unions; immigrant groups; youth groups; and city, state, and national politicians (including former Vice President Al Gore) rallied to the support of the striking janitors. The janitors and their supporters held mass demonstrations all over the city. The broad and militant support resulted in a contract settlement that many workers believed to be fair. Building on the momentum of the janitors' victory, the LACFL, spearheaded by the SEIU and HERE leadership, consolidated a political drive to highlight the immigrant demands for the repeal of employer sanctions, full amnesty, and workers right to organize. So far, these political efforts have resulted in a 20,000-strong demonstration for support at the Los Angeles AFL-CIO Town Hall/Immigrants Rights Conference held on June 10, 2000, and a massive effort to educate delegates to the Democratic National Convention about immigrant-rights issues. Led by a coalition of community activists and a few unions, the LACFL used the 2000 election as a device to advocate for immigrant rights and for community power while at the same time expanding the electoral base of the Democratic Party. Hopefully, union and community interaction will result in successful strategies and approaches that could be shared with the rest of the union–labor movement.

Conclusion

When the AFL-CIO conducted its survey of central labor councils in 1996, the LACFL was not one of the prime candidates to become a Union City. By all accounts the LACFL was a traditional CLC. Its primary function was to curry favor with the traditional Democratic Party forces, and for the most part it did not extend itself to organizing or to community issues. In short, the LACFL did not have either the requisites or the behaviors for being an "organizing" CLC.

The shift by the national AFL-CIO to organizing provided a catalyst that mobilized an assortment of radical forces in and about the Los Angeles labor movement. The "internal" potentials were realized when a coalition of unions supported the election of Contreras to the top spot in LACFL, but these potentials existed because of the ideological orientation of many of the activists who are now embedded in the Los Angeles labor movement. The associations, networks, and groups of these radicals are the core that provide an alternative to the dominant Cold-War-Warrior culture of traditional unionism in Los Angeles. Obviously, alternative strategies such as LAMAP and Justice for Janitors have influenced the structure of the LACFL. And the potentials of union–community alliances around such issues as the Living Wage and immigrant rights call into question the traditional ways that unions operate. However, traditional unionism still remains the dominant culture of the Los Angeles union movement. This traditional culture is characterized by an inability to "see outside the box." First, alliances with forces or issues outside the union movement are "afterthoughts," that is, they are not included in the strategic thinking of most unions. For instance, around the issue of Welfare reform, the LACFL was silent on the issue until affiliated unions became threatened by the possibility that the workfare workers would replace union workers. Even then, the issue was dealt with as a pragmatic one that affected unions, as opposed to issues that impacted the lower strata of the working class. Issues such as union jobs continue to be pitted against broad community interests such as the environment (Shuster 1999). Similarly, issues such as run-away shops and sweat shops are usually understood from a "protectionist," that is, "save-our-own-jobs" perspective rather than from the standpoint of international working-class solidarity. Issues such as affirmative action are often viewed as being divisive, and a broad-based, political agenda that is independent of the Democratic Party is still foreign to the LACFL. Similarly, the functioning of the LACFL is still bureaucratic. The real decision making remains with the key committees like the Executive Board and the COPE committee. And, as I have experienced in every other CLC, delegate meetings are usually seen as opportunities to rubber-stamp previously made decisions. CLC agendas move very rapidly without providing much opportunity to intervene. The decision-making processes of the LACFL are not readily accessible to most rank-and-file delegates, let alone rank-and-file union members.

On the other hand, debates do occur, and on occasion previously made decisions are overthrown at the delegate meetings. In order for this to occur, delegates require advance notice and they have to be organized. While still the minority, the forces that are vocal about such things as organizing have reached a critical mass. Perhaps alternative groups, like caucuses, could facilitate more democratic discussion of issues. On the other hand, more controversial issues like the defense of bilingual education are less likely to be raised on the floor of the delegates' meeting. But, because more radical union activists have become "citizens" of the union movement, many are able to have their voices heard through participation in their local union. Non-AFL-CIO people, community-based organizations, and independent unions participate in the non-decision-making committees of the LACFL. Unlike some CLCs that permit non-AFL-CIO organizations to participate in decision-making bodies, the LACFL does not.

What the leadership of the LACFL has been able to do is to balance traditional interests and the more activist transformative interests. It has done this by building on its strength, electoral politics, and by linking itself to the new political power coalition of white liberals and Latinos. Because of the huge minority, particularly Latino, population in Los Angeles, the LACFL political strategy has focused on the Latino and, to a lesser degree, the African-American communities. The rapid shift in demographics in favor of Latinos has created competition at the bottom between Latino immigrants and African Americans. The ripples of this growing tension are felt throughout local politics, for example, in school board elections.

This political pragmatism has given the leadership of the LACFL credibility among traditional and transformative local unions. This credibility has been translated into a raise in the per capita union dues paid to the LACFL by local unions and the approval to move forward on an organizing agenda. The organizing agenda has also provided radical activists, embedded in local unions, with the opportunity to create interactions that illuminate key community issues for the LACFL; for example, the fight for the democratic rights of immigrant workers. Clearly, the Union Cities project and the organizing agenda of the national AFL-CIO have created opportunities for the Los Angeles labor movement to intersect with a variety of key social movements, and, as we saw in Seattle, when that occurs, who knows what will happen?

Notes

1. From AFL-CIO survey conducted in 1996.
2. Information from author interviews and archival data provided by Carl Kesseler, senior delegate to the LACFL (June 1998).
3. It is mentioned that Contreras is a twenty-year friend of State Senator Richard Polanco, considered a key figure in Latino electoral politics.
4. Among other concepts, CASA proceeded from the conceptualization that Mexican workers, regardless of which side of the border they are born on, experience the same exploitation under capitalism and that the possibility for radical social change in the United States is linked to an international process. In community political mobilization, CASA stressed working-class interests and unity based on nationality and on selected progressive issues. They believed in effective international solidarity and in working with organized and spontaneous community mobilizations; they sought militant union leadership, rank-and -file membership, and also politically conscious but unorganized individuals.
5. These demands, which were first developed by grass-roots union and community groups, like the Labor Immigrant Organizing Network in northern California and the LACFL immigrant organizing committee, became the rallying call for immigrant rights at the AFL-CIO Los Angeles convention in 1999.

Bibliography

Banks, Andy, and Jack Metzgar. 1989. "Participating in Management: Union Organizing on a New Terrain." *Labor Research Review* 14: 1–55.
Cleeland, Nancy. 1999. *Los Angeles Times*, September.

Fletcher, Bill, Jr., and Richard Hurd. 1998. "Beyond the Organizing Model: The Transformation Process in Local Unions." In *Organizing to Win*, ed. Kate Bronfenbrenner, Sheldon Friedman, Richard Hurd, Rudolph Oswald, and Ronald Seeber. Ithaca, NY: Cornell University Press.

Gallagher, Tom. 1998. "Everybody Loved It, But . . ." *Z Magazine*, November.

Gapasin, Fernando and Howard Wial. 1998. "The Role of Central Labor Councils in Union Organizing in the 1990s." In Kate Bronfenbrenner, Sheldon Friedman, Richard W. Hurd, Randolph A. Oswald, and Ronald L. Seeber, eds., *Organizing to Win*. Ithaca, NY: Cornell University Press.

Gomez-Quinones, Juan 1990. *Chicano Politics: Reality and Promise 1940–1990*. Albuquerque, NM: University of New Mexico Press.

Johnston, Paul. 1994. *Success While Others Fail: Social Movement Unionism and the Public Workplace*. Ithaca, NY: Cornell University Press.

Olney, Peter. Interview November 1998.

Oswald, Rudolph A., and Ronald L. Seeber. *Organizing to Win*. Ithaca, NY: Cornell University Press.

Rosier, Sharolyn A. 1996. "Energized Central Labor Councils Explore New Roles." *AFL-CIO News*, August.

Shuster, Beth. 1999. *Los Angeles Times*, p. B1.

Waterman, Peter. 1993. "Social Movement Unionism: A New Model for a New World Order." *Review* 16, no. 3 (summer): 245–78.

Wong, Kent. 1994. "Building the Asian Pacific Labor Alliance." In *The State of Asian America: Activism and Resistance in the 1990s*, ed. Karin Aguilar–San Juan. Boston, MA: South End Press, pp. 344–45.

Zabin, Carol, and Isaac Martin. 1999. "Living Wage Campaigns and the Struggle for Economic Justice." http://www.phoenixfund.org/livingwage.htm.

5

Fighting for Justice Beyond the Contract

The Milwaukee County Labor Council and Sustainable Milwaukee

Stuart Eimer

In a July 1998 review of the first year of the Union Cities initiative, *America@Work* noted that though "creating the atmosphere for economic growth is a long-term goal, the Milwaukee CLC is already well along the road" (Hall 1998, 10). The article called attention to the Milwaukee County Labor Council (MCLC)–initiated Campaign for a Sustainable Milwaukee (CSM), a broad-based community coalition that has been instrumental in crafting and pursuing projects that promote economic policies to benefit a broad cross-section of the working class in Milwaukee.

In what follows, I examine both the MCLC and CSM.[1] First, I explore the reasons that CLCs are uniquely positioned to forge alliances that can craft and pursue broad-based campaigns that promise to benefit all workers in a community, be they organized or not. Second, I review the reasons behind the MCLC decision to launch CSM, and then I describe the formation of the campaign. Next, I examine several MCLC–CSM projects that advance broadly defined interests, paying particular attention to how they address the needs of Milwaukee's minority community. Finally, I discuss the broader implications of the MCLC experience, focusing on both the successes and the problems that CSM has generated.

Research for this study was conducted in a variety of ways. Information pertaining to the MCLC was gathered through a number of structured interviews with the secretary treasurer in 1996 and with the president in 1999. Data concerning CSM were generated via participant observation and interviews. From September 1993 until October 1994, I worked as a project assistant for the Center on Wisconsin Strategy, a research institute that provided technical assistance to CSM. I was present at most monthly meetings, many subcommittee meetings, and the Community Congress. Interviews were conducted with the executive director of CSM in 1996 and 1999, and with CSM staff members in 1999 and 2000. Primary documents and secondary sources concerning both organizations were also utilized where appropriate.

AFL-CIO CLCs

While the constitutionally stated objectives of CLCs vary from body to body, their general function is to provide interunion communication, mutual aid, and political coordination. At present, their objectives, as outlined in the *Rules Governing AFL-CIO Local Central Bodies* (AFL-CIO 1991), are:

(a) To assist in furthering the appropriate objects and policies of the AFL-CIO, or of organizations affiliated with the AFL-CIO (provided such objects or policies are not inconsistent with the objects or policies of the AFL-CIO).

(b) To serve as a means of exchanging information among affiliated bodies on matters of common interest.

(c) To provide aid, cooperation, and assistance to affiliated local unions and other affiliated bodies in their common and individual endeavors.

(d) To propose, support, and promote legislation favorable to and oppose legislation detrimental to the interests of workers and organized labor.

(e) To encourage workers to register and vote, to exercise their full rights and responsibilities of citizenship, and to perform their rightful part in the political life of the local, state, and national communities.

(f) To engage in such other activities as are consistent with the objects and principles set forth in the Constitution of the AFL-CIO and the policies of the AFL-CIO.

Simply stated, the CLCs are charged with the crucial task of being the AFL-CIO's coordinating arm at the local level.

CLCs gain their capacity to coordinate by connecting disparate unions, much as a hub connects spokes on a wheel. In any given community, CLCs are the primary institutions that link organized workers be they skilled or unskilled, blue collar or white collar, private sector or public sector. Competent CLCs can exploit these links to generate and mobilize local solidarity, compelling affiliated local unions to support one each other in the pursuit of their respective collective bargaining interests.

By helping local unions secure their own narrowly defined economic interests, CLCs help facilitate effective "business unionism." As Hoxie described it, such unionism is

> essentially trade conscious, rather than class-conscious. . . . [I]t expresses the viewpoints and interests of the workers in a craft or industry rather than those in the working class a whole. It aims chiefly at more, here and now, for the organized workers of the craft or industry, in terms mainly of higher wages, shorter hours, and better working conditions, regardless of the welfare of the workers outside the particular organic group, regardless in general of political and social considerations, except so far as these bear directly upon its own economic ends. (Hoxie 1920, 45)

Given the decentralized and fragmented industrial-relations systems in the United States, such unionism is in many ways an eminently rational strategy for securing the short-term material interests of union members.

That said, business unionism will get you only so far. There is a vast array of issues that affect workers, ranging from labor law to housing policies, that cannot adequately be addressed by a labor movement that concerns itself only with taking care of its affiliate's business. Well aware of this, CLCs have often played a leading role in moving labor beyond "business unionism" to voice and pursue legislative and political interests that are not addressed in collective bargaining agreements (Burke, 1899; Lorwin 1933; Fink 1978). As one CIO leader explained it when writing about the CIO's labor councils,

> workers and Labor Union members have many problems affecting their lives in addition to wages, hours and working conditions, and related

matters involving the employer. These are the wide range of the citizens in the community. The CIO Council becomes the voice of the Labor movement about housing, public and personal health, child care, education, public and private welfare, city and community planning, recreating, and a large number of things which are the concern of the worker as citizen where he lives. (Silvey 1948)

Effective CLCs can unite their affiliate local unions in order to craft and pursue general goals like those stated by Silvey. This process is facilitated by the fact that the CLC stands above its affiliated locals, enabling it to take a wider view of social relations in a given locale, a view that local unions are often blind to because of their emphasis on their own collective bargaining agreements. From this "supra-local" perspective, the CLC is better able to spot or develop campaigns that will benefit workers even though the campaigns are not linked to their contracts. It is via the CLC that local unions can transcend their particularistic interests to become involved as a "labor movement" in broader struggles such as communitywide movements for social justice or political campaigns. As opposed to "business unionism," this sort of activity has sometimes been referred to as "social movement unionism," defined here as an "effort to raise the living standards of the working class as whole, rather than to protect individually defined interests of union members" (Seidman 1994, 2).

When engaging in social-movement unionism, CLCs inevitably encounter nonlabor organizations that have similar interests. Building bridges to these organizations can provide labor with allies in short-term struggles around particular issues. In some cases, these temporary alliances may provide the basis for more stable coalitions that can craft and pursue longer-range goals. This has been the case in Milwaukee where the MCLC has been able to move beyond temporary, ad hoc alliances to forge a durable coalition that, in its own words, is "committed to creating and retaining family-supporting jobs, to building healthy communities, and restored natural environments, to racial and gender justice, to responsible business practices, and to accountability in how tax dollars are used in economic development" (CSM 1998a, 3).

Economic Context

Like labor councils in many industrial cities, the MCLC has witnessed significant changes in its city's population and industrial base. In 1990,

Milwaukee's population stood at 628,000, down from 717,000 in 1970 (USDC 1992, 36). As the overall population has declined, the movement of whites to the suburbs has corresponded with a growth in the minority population. From 1940 to 1990, the African-American population grew from 1 percent to 30 percent, while the number of whites living in the city declined by 250,000 (CSM 1995, 5). The Latino community in 1990 accounted for about 6 percent of the population, while Asian Americans accounted for 2 percent and Native Americans 1 percent (USDC 1992, 36).

As in many of America's industrial cities, the changing ethnic composition of the city corresponded with a decline in the city's industrial base. Manufacturing, which had accounted for between 40 and 50 percent of the labor force for most of the century, had declined steadily and now accounts for approximately 20 percent of all employment (CSM 1995, 5). In raw numbers, that amounted to the loss of over 50,000 manufacturing jobs between 1979 and 1986 alone (White 1986).

As industrial jobs left town for other locales (e.g., the suburbs, the South, or overseas), they were replaced by low-wage service-sector employment. In 1994, Milwaukee ranked third in the country, behind Miami and Los Angeles, in the creation of such low-wage jobs (Levine 1994). In 1990 these service-sector jobs paid only a fraction of what the remaining industrial jobs did, averaging a mere $13,457 year, compared to $21,363 in manufacturing (DILHR 1990).

The changing composition of Milwaukee's economy has been especially hard for people of color in the central city. As entry-level manufacturing jobs that paid decent wages disappeared, unemployment levels and poverty levels increased. By the mid-1990s, unemployment levels for young black and Hispanic men exceeded 50 percent, and 38 percent of Milwaukee's children lived in poverty (CSM 1995, 7).

The changing economy also impacted on organized labor. Survey research found that union density had dropped from 34 percent in 1980 to 24 percent in 1984 (White 1986). Ten years later, union density stood at just 18.6 percent for the Milwaukee–Racine area (Bureau of the Census 1994). These losses trimmed the size of the MCLC from the 120,000 members it had at its founding in 1959, to approximately 85,000 members in 1996 (interview with Bruce Colburn, January 31, 1996).

Campaign for Sustainable Milwaukee

The MCLC, like most of the American labor movement, did little to address the declining economic situation it found itself embedded within.

As Bruce Colburn, former secretary-treasurer of the MCLC, put it, labor had grown comfortable, and was coasting. When it did act, it was usually in an ad hoc defensive fashion, attempting to stop a plant closing or to fight against legislation like NAFTA. After a string of losing battles, the decision was made to forge a proactive economic program that would enable labor in Milwaukee to do more than react to crisis after crisis. As Colburn stated, "We knew what we were opposed to in this economy, but we weren't always sure what we were for" (interview with Bruce Colburn, February 1955).

To answer this question, the MCLC took the lead in launching the Campaign for a Sustainable Milwaukee (CSM). In fall 1993, it sponsored a meeting that brought together labor leaders, housing activists, environmentalists, community organizers, religious leaders, third-party activists, and government officials. That the MCLC invited such a broad array of actors from the community is worth noting. It signified the belief that these groups had a common interest in developing the capacity to voice their concerns about matters that were usually addressed as single issues. Moreover, it signaled an effort by labor to develop a broad-based coalition that could mount a proactive campaign for the community at large. This stood in marked contrast to past efforts in which labor tended to seek community allies when it needed help fighting a battle.

CSM formed four task forces in areas deemed critical to Milwaukee's future: jobs and training, environment and transportation, capital and credit, and education. Each task force consisted of people who had expertise in the particular area. They were asked to generate an analysis, recommendations, and specific policy suggestions for their respective areas. The goal was a final report that would be ratified at a large public meeting in fall 1994.

The plan was developed over the next thirteen months, with each task force reporting on its progress to a monthly meeting of fifty to a hundred people. This process facilitated a dialogue among communities that, although often on the same side, were often too busy to communicate with one another. Union members learned about the problems surrounding mortgage redlining in Milwaukee; housing activists listened to environmentalists' concerns about abandoned industrial sites; and environmentalists learned about labor's trouble holding on to jobs that paid a living wage. Although they addressed separate issues, the reports all suggested that working people in Milwaukee were not participating in the decisions that generated each particular problem.

In October 1994, the final report was presented at a Community Congress meeting that attracted over two hundred people from throughout the city. The MCLC's Colburn cochaired the meeting along with Gwendolynne Moore, an African-American state senator from an inner-city district. The congress brought together representatives from dozens of community organizations, sixteen local unions, and all levels of government. During the congress, general presentations were made on each of the report's recommendations. Small groups then mulled over the particulars, suggested changes, and prioritized their goals. At the end of the day, attendees at a general plenary session voted to endorse the report, pending minor changes.

While the report addressed a variety of topics, it was the section on jobs and training that drew the most attention, as local papers published articles detailing CSM's proposal for family supporting jobs (Norman 1994). The proposal articulated a comprehensive development strategy for the metro-economy. Its recommendations focused on Milwaukee's potential to become a "prime location for advanced manufacturing" and were guided by the general principle "that public policies should exert upward pressure on community standards for acceptable business conduct, reserve economic development resources for assisting companies in achieving those standards, and insure democratic accountability in the use of public resources" (CSM 1994).[2]

Having issued their recommendations, CSM began the task of ensuring that the report did not become just another tome collecting dust in offices around the city. It developed an executive committee, chaired by the secretary-treasurer of the MCLC, which comprised community and labor leaders as well elected officials. Organizationally, it developed a variety of task forces charged with pursuing the campaign's stated goals.

Living Wages and the Workers' Rights Board

In March 1995, CSM launched its campaign for a living wage. Using an ordinance enacted in Baltimore as its model, CSM began a campaign to require firms contracting with the city, county, and school board to pay a minimum wage of $7.70 an hour. According to Bill Dempsey, CSM director at the time, CSM poured energy into this campaign because CSM leaders thought the campaign would "have the most impact on the local economy, involve the most people, develop leadership, and build a strong, diverse coalition" (interview with Bill Dempsey, January 31, 1996). Moreover, they believed that they could win, and victory was deemed important for the fledgling coalition.

Over the next two years, CSM coordinated grass-roots activities aimed at pressuring the respective governing bodies to enact living-wage measures. The issue was framed as one that would have particular impact for central-city residents. As one member of the task force put it,

> If you work full time, you shouldn't be forced to live in poverty. Over 85 percent of central city households have at least one wage earner; but that person is paid sub-poverty level wages. Our top priority must be raising wages in Milwaukee's central city. (CSM 1998b)

While it did not always get the wage levels it sought, CSM did force all three bodies to enact legislation. At the city level, contractors were required to pay $6.05, while at the school board and county board, the minimum pay was set at $7.70.

With these victories under their belts, the MCLC and CSM then sought to address the problem of low-wage work in the private sector. In winter 1996, a Workers Rights Board (WRB) was established to protect the rights of workers, whether they were organized or not. Comprising labor, community, and religious leaders, the WRB provides a "forum to give voice to the injustices workers face on the job and in the community" (MCLC–WRB pamphlet, n.d.). Through public hearings, the WRB attempts to use "moral and public pressure to encourage fair behavior by employers" (MCLC–WRB pamphlet).

To date, hearings have been held on a variety of matters including organizing, labor abuses in the fast-food industry, and welfare reform. In the latter case, the board listened to testimony from welfare mothers, union leaders, and progressive elected officials in front of a crowd of 500. The event functioned to highlight problems with welfare reform that had dire consequences for central-city residents, while also bringing union and community people together in a common space to forge a common agenda.

Job Access and the Central City Workers Center

Beyond issue-centered campaigns like that for the living wage and those targeted by the Workers Rights Board, the MCLC and CSM have sought to address the plight of low-wage workers in Milwaukee via the Milwaukee Jobs Initiative (MJI). Working with members of the business community, they secured a $5.1 million economic development grant from the Casey Foundation and $2.63 million in local matching grants. These funds were targeted for investment in a broad range of training and economic development projects (MJI 1997). The goal of these projects is to

> improve access to jobs for disadvantaged, young adult job seekers (aged 18 to 35) with particular outreach to disadvantaged men; and to mount a reform of public and private jobs-related services and systems, in order to improve the long term functioning of the labor market for this population and consequently, enhance the well being of disadvantaged children, families and communities. (CSM 1995, 2)

To accomplish this, the MJI developed three sectoral initiatives in manufacturing, printing, and construction designed to provide people with the specific forms of training needed to secure jobs at firms with a stated need for workers.

The construction component of the MJI had it roots in efforts by CSM, the MCLC, and the Milwaukee Building Trades and Construction Council to secure a project agreement for a new convention center. In this campaign, the building trades desire for a project agreement was merged with the interest that CSM had in ensuring that minority and female workers could secure work in the construction industry. As Colburn summarized it in a letter published in the *Milwaukee Journal Sentinel*,

> A fair project agreement is in the interest not only of building trades union members, but also of the Milwaukee area community. . . . This community wants all of the people of this area to benefit from this new center. A fair project agreement will lock in strong, specific work-force participation by minorities and women. It will make sure that these new workers become a part of tested training programs that will provide long-term family supporting employment in the construction industry. (Colburn 1996)

After a year-long campaign that featured one of the largest rallies in Milwaukee history, the joint labor–community alliance won a project agreement for the building trades that also benefited women and minorities by specifying that 25 percent of the workers would be minorities, and 5 percent, female. Shortly after this victory, a similar agreement was reached for construction of the new Milwaukee Brewers' stadium.

In both of these struggles, victory was credited to the cooperation between labor and community organizations. As the *Milwaukee Labor Press* noted,

> Without the help of community groups labor would not have gotten a project agreement on the Midwest Express Center and Miller Park. Community groups helped turn it around, and labor in turn helped them get language in the agreement that said 25 percent of the workers on the project must be minorities and 5 percent must be female. (MLP 1998a, 1)

With the project agreements in place, a newfound demand for minority workers emerged in a city with no institutional mechanism for filling this demand. To address this situation, CSM stepped in with funds secured through the MJI to create the Central City Workers Center (CCWC). The stated mission of the CCWC is to provide "aggressive outreach, recruitment, training, placement and tracking services to residents interested in construction jobs and other family supporting careers" (CSM Milwaukee@Work, n.d.). CCWC outreach targets forty-six central-city census tracts, and is interesting in that it seeks to enlist people as members, as opposed to just delivering services. To join, a worker needs either to pay dues or to volunteer at the Workers' Center.

In exchange for membership, workers gain access to a broad array of programs. There are classes offered by the local technical college that educate and train workers for placement in jobs and apprenticeship programs. Other services provide legal assistance in such matters as recovering a driver's license, something that is crucial for construction workers who must have access to various job sites. The CCWC also helps cultivate "softer skills" via things like the Skilled Trades Collaborative, a network of tradespeople of color who provide mentoring for members of the Workers Center.

When combined, the various programs function as a quasi–central-city union and hiring hall, which contractors can contact knowing that it is a source of reliable, trained workers. By the end of 1998, the CCWC had placed almost two hundred people, mostly African-American men, in the construction industry at an average wage of $13.47 (interview with Bill Dempsey, February 3, 1999).[3]

Central City Transit

MCLC figures suggest that over the past twenty years 70 percent of the job growth in the Milwaukee area has been in the surrounding suburbs (MLP 1998b, 8). CSM figures suggest that nearly half of all African

Americans in Milwaukee do not have cars (CSM *v.* Thompson 1998). Given the absence of adequate mass transit, these figures create a situation in which many central-city residents are unable to tap into the economic growth in Milwaukee's suburbs. CSM's Central City Transit Task Force has sought to address this problem by expanding access to affordable mass transit and ensuring that federal transportation money designated for the region be "spent on a balanced transportation plan which includes buses and central city light rail" (CSM 1998a).

To date, this effort has centered on how $241 million in federal dollars will be spent. CSM developed its own proposal, which centered on improved bus routes and a light rail system, as opposed to increased highway construction. A broad range of tactics has been employed to advance this proposal, from press conferences and sit-ins to a civil right lawsuit against the state of Wisconsin. The lawsuit was filed on behalf of seven African-American individuals and twelve organizations, including the MCLC, 9–5's Poverty Network Initiative, the Amalgamated Transit Union Local 998, Citizens for a Better Environment, and a Latino community organization called Esparanza Unida. The lawsuit argues that African-American residents

> are segregated and clustered in the central north side sections of the city without mass transit options to access the vast majority of emerging employment opportunities located in suburban areas. Thus, respondents' [WI officials] use of federal funds will have a severely disparate impact upon complainants on account of their race. Unless respondents implement a well balanced and comprehensive transportation plan for the East-West Corridor, which is the transportation spine of the Milwaukee metropolitan area, minority citizens will continue to suffer inferior employment opportunities and access to other recreational, educational and commercial amenities. (CSM *v.* Thompson 1998)

While the lawsuit itself has not been resolved, its very existence caused the U.S. Department of Transportation to delay the release of $214 million in federal transit money to the Milwaukee area while the complaints were investigated. According to Nick Rudelich, the legislative director for Amalgamated Transit Union Local 998 who was involved in the founding of CSM, holding up the money gave "more leverage to those who filed the discrimination complaints" as they continued to push their demands (Sandler 2000, 1).

CSM/MCLC Joint Organizing

One of the main goals of the Union Cities program was to urge CLCs to promote organizing by getting one-half of the locals in their community to develop an organizing plan and to shift resources into organizing. Given that CLCs have no formal power over their affiliates, this can be a difficult challenge. By fall 1998, few unions in Milwaukee were involved in new organizing, and as a result little organizing was occurring. A variety of reasons were posited for the lack of organizing, ranging from a simple lack of commitment and experience among affiliates, to the fact that many local leaders were white males with little connection to potential targets that had high concentrations of minorities and women (CSM 1998b).

To address this situation, the MCLC, the CSM, and the State Federation of labor crafted an organizing plan and set out to raise money from foundations and religious organizations to finance a joint organizing project that could help build labor's organizing capacity. By 1999, the "Organize Milwaukee" project had been funded at levels that permitted four organizers to be hired and housed within CSM. These organizers perform two major functions. First, they work closely with the MCLC and its affiliates, helping to coordinate Solidarity Action Teams, which turn out for pickets, rallies, and other events where membership mobilization is important. Second, they provide technical and organizational support to locals that do not have the resources to hire organizers or that simply need help building their organizing capacity.

Over the last year, the second type of activity has taken a variety of interesting forms. On several occasions, CSM organizers have enlisted members of the American Federation of State, County, and Municipal Employees (AFSCME), SEIU, and other unions to make house visits for other unions. On one occasion, during a steelworkers' campaign at a foundry where the majority of the workers were Hispanic, this involved recruiting translators from both the labor movement and the community to accompany organizers on house visits. The campaign was successful, and CSM is now supporting the union as it fight for a first contract (phone interview with Christy Nordstrum, May 2, 2000).

In some instances, CSM organizers have staffed and run campaigns from start to finish. A prime example of this was the Amalgamated Transit Union (ATU) drive to organize Laidlaw, a company that contracts with Milwaukee

County to provide transportation for the elderly and disabled. CSM organizers built a strong committee within the firm, coordinated house visits, and helped put political pressure on County Board members. These efforts resulted in an organizing victory as well as ongoing campaign to force the County Board to adopt a Labor Peace Ordinance, which will require firms receiving contracts with the county for more than $250,000 to remain neutral during any organizing campaigns that might be directed at them (phone interview with Christy Nordstrum, May 2, 2000).

Regardless of the outcome of a particular campaign, CSM's capacity to mobilize both labor and the community in support of organizing has many intangible benefits. Christy Nordstrum, one of the CSM organizers, suggests that it is ability "to mobilize broader community support, religious support, political support, that gives workers who are trying to organize the real sense that they aren't alone in this" (phone interview with Christy Nordsturm, May 2, 2000). Moreover, she reports that CSM's visibility and capacity make it hard for companies to claim that workers are being manipulated by a far-off union bureaucracy that cares only about collecting dues money. When workers look out and see community and religious leaders working with an organization that is mobilizing in the community year round, the employer's charges become suspect (phone interview with Christy Nordstrum, May 2, 2000).

Conclusion

Six years after the Community Congress, the MCLC and CSM had made significant strides toward proactively addressing Milwaukee's economic problems. With an alternative economic development strategy in hand, CSM worked to institute policies and build institutions that can implement their plans. In doing so CSM attracted support from dozens of organizations, some of which are simply paper endorsers and some of which actively participate in the task forces that are of most concern to them. It has also involved thousands of people in its projects.

What has enabled the MCLC to move from ad hoc alliances to a stable coalition? In large part it seems to be due to the councils' willingness to participate in projects that benefit both union and nonunion workers alike. The MCLC explicitly defines its mission as "fighting for economic and social justice in the workplace and in the community" and considers its mission to be that of "raising the living and working conditions for everybody in the community" (interview with John

Goldstein, February 3, 1999). More important than a mission statement, however, is the fact that the MCLC has put its leadership, resources, and capacity where its mouth is. Through action, it has demonstrated its willingness to craft and pursue projects that address a broad array of concerns beyond the collective-bargaining interests of its affiliates.

The MCLC's pursuit of these goals, however, has not been without problems. There have been tensions within the council over its work on central-city issues. For unions with members who tend to live in the suburbs, it is not always clear why they should get involved in projects that address problems in the central city, and they wonder why more attention is not paid to the suburbs. John Goldstein, the president of the MCLC, suggests that these complaints are valid to the extent that the MCLC does not have the power it could have in the suburbs, the place where much of the job growth has been. Even so, he argues that the MCLC must use its power in the city and the county, where it has the ability to exercise real influence and to affect change.

There are also those in the labor council who do not agree with the militant grass-roots tactics employed by the MCLC and CSM. As Goldstein explained it, there is a tension between people who think change needs to come from the bottom up and those who think it should come from the top down. Some unions are simply more comfortable trying to become friends with elected officials who can grant favors than with mobilizing members at the grass roots in order to exercise power (interview with John Goldstein, February 3, 1999).

Disagreements over strategies and tactics are to be expected in CLCs. As local federations, they are home to a broad array of local unions, all of which have their own organizational cultures and short-term interests. Being attentive to these differences, while also trying to forge a labor movement that can pursue more general interests, is no easy task, which is no doubt part of the reason CLCs are often dormant organizations. The degree to which the MCLC leadership has managed to develop a critical mass in the council that is committed to broader movements for social justice and that is interested in building stable coalitions with nonlabor organizations, stands as testament to the possibilities of the AFL-CIO's Union Cities program.

Notes

1. For a broader analysis, see Stuart Eimer, "From 'Business Unionism' to 'Social Movement Unionism': The Case of the AFL-CIO Milwaukee County Labor

Council." *Labor Studies Journal* 24, no. 2, summer 1999, 63–81.

2. The demands are worth noting because they represent an overt intervention in the regional economy. They included the creation of: an early warning system to retain jobs that are in danger of being lost; industry training partnerships to design systems that both promote incumbent worker training and ensure a highly skilled future labor workforce; community-based training to deliver skills to people who are often neglected by public-sector training efforts; industrial extension programs to help Milwaukee-area companies adopt new technologies and processes; community-standards legislation to hold government contractors and recipients of public subsidies accountable to standards of socially responsible business conduct as a condition of receipt of public assistance and clawback legislation to recover public funds from firms that violate community performance mandates; public policies to support community and labor organizing; community job banks and service credits to make job searches easier and to facilitate the trading of services; ESOPS and responsible financial institutions to empower workers in their own firms; creation of incentives for pension and religious institutions to use their capital for investment in their community; targeting of sectors for investment so that public dollars flow into industries that provide the best potential for growth in family-supporting jobs; an expanded Earned Income Tax Credit; a raised and indexed minimum wage; and an established minimum level of benefits for all (CSM, 1994).

3. It should be noted that during the summer of 1999 a review of Sustainable Milwaukee records for June 1999 found that fewer people were placed in the construction industry than claimed. CSM had claimed that sixty-five people were placed in June while auditors found only nineteen placements. This led to the suspension of the original contract and the creation of an interim contract with CSM while the matter was reviewed. No challenges of the previous placement numbers were lodged (Spivak and Bice 1999, 2). The contract with CSM was ultimately renewed.

Bibliography

AFL-CIO. 1991. "Rules Governing AFL-CIO Local Central Bodies." Washington, DC.

AFL-CIO. 1996. Web page.

AFL-CIO. 1997. Web page.

AFL-CIO. 1997. "The Road to Union City," *America@Work*. March, pp. 15–17.

Burke, William Maxwell. 1899. *History and Functions of Central Labor Unions*, vol. 12, ed. T. F. o. P. S. o. C. University. New York: Macmillan.

Colburn, Bruce. 1996. "Project Accord Will Benefit Everyone," in *Milwaukee Journal Sentinel*, May 12.

CSM (Campaign for a Sustainable Milwaukee). 1994. "Rebuilding Milwaukee From the Ground Up." Paper presented at Community Congress, October 22.

———. 1995. Annie E. Casey Foundation Jobs Initiative: Making Connections. Application for a Planning Grant.

———. 1998a. Milwaukee@Work: 1997–1998 Annual Report on the Campaign for a Sustainable Milwaukee.

———. 1998b. Organize Milwaukee Proposal.

———. N.d. Milwaukee@Work: Construction and Apprenticeship Training Programs.

CSM *v.* Thompson. 1998c. *Campaign for a Sustainable Milwaukee et al. v. Governor Tommy Thompson et al.*

DILHR (Department of Industry, Labor, and Human Resources). 1990. *Employment, Wages, and Taxes Due Covered by Wisconsin's U.C. Law.*

Fink, Gary. 1978. "The Rejection of Voluntarism." In *Labor and American Politics*, ed. Charles Rehmus et al. Ann Arbor: University of Michigan Press.

Hall, Mike. 1998. "One Year Down the Road to Union City." In *America@Work.* July, pp. 8–11.

Hoxie, Robert Franklin. 1920. *Trade Unionism in the United States.* New York: Appleton.

Levine, Mark. 1994. "The Crisis of Low Wages in Milwaukee: Wage Polarization in the Metropolitan Labor Market, 1970–1990." Center for Economic Development Briefing Paper No. 3, November.

Lorwin, Lewis. 1933. *The American Federation of Labor.* Washington, DC: Brookings Institution.

MCLC–WRB (Milwaukee County Labor Council, Workers Rights Board). N.d. "Milwaukee Area Workers' Rights Board." Pamphlet.

MJI (Milwaukee Jobs Initiative). 1997. "Connecting Central City Resident to Family Supporting Jobs." Pamphlet.

MLP (*Milwaukee Labor Press*). 1997. "Hope for Good Jobs Comes with Central City Workers Center," June 26, pp. 1, 10.

———. 1998a. "Workers' Rights Board Hears W-2 Horror Stories." January 29, pp. 8–9.

———. 1998b. "Center City Workers Center Is Getting the Job Done Right." June 25, pp. 1, 17.

Norman, Jack, 1994. "Activists Work on Economic Plan with Jobs in Mind," *Milwaukee Journal*, September 23.

Sandler, Larry. 2000. "Cash Infusion Anticipated for Downtown Transportation $241 Million in Federal Funds Could Arrive Next Week, Barrett Says," *Milwaukee Journal Sentinel*, January 14, 2000, p. 1.

Seidman, Gay. 1994. *Manufacturing Militance: Workers' Movements in Brazil and South Africa, 1970–1985.* Berkeley: University of California Press.

Silvey, Ted. 1948. "Industrial Union Councils: What They Are—How They Work," *Telephone Organizer*, February, p. 5.

Spivak, Casey, and Dan Bice. 1999. "Sustainable Milwaukee Head Leaving as Audit Faults Agency Work," *Milwaukee Journal Sentinel*, August 17.

USDC (U.S. Department of Commerce). 1992. *Statistical Abstract of the United States, 1992.* Washington, DC: U.S. Government Printing Office.

———. Bureau of the Census. 1994. *County and City Data Book.* Washington, DC.

White, Sammis, and Philip Schneider. 1986. "The Declining Strength of Unions in Milwaukee." Urban Research Center. Milwaukee: University of Wisconsin.

6

The Political Awakening of a Central Labor Council

Wisconsin South Central Federation of Labor

Roland Zullo

The touchstone of political power for any interest group lies in its ability to stuff the ballot box—which is why every measure of political access, from preelection issue framing to effective post-election lobbying, depends on political unity. In a free democracy, of course, deciding to vote and choosing to support a candidate are ultimately private matters, allowing individuals to exit from the process and still benefit from the activities of others who are working to achieve common causes. This "collective action" problem exists for all interest groups, but is more formidable for organized labor. The reason is that unions are mobilized first to achieve *economic* gains directly from employers and second to secure broader *political* gains through the electoral process (Wallihan 1985, 164). Resources to support negotiating, administering labor agreements, financing strikes, and so forth—functions aimed at achieving distributive gains through the private relationship with employers—take priority over political action. Unions therefore have strong incentives to pursue narrow economic interests over universal ones, leading to the segmentation of labor and dissention on political strategy (Form 1995). Adding to the disunity, political participation is based on the voluntaristic model: Individual union members can legally refrain from financing the political activities of their unions; local unions can elect to refrain from participating in regional coalitions; national unions can reject the political endorsements of the AFL-CIO. Consequently, political activity is not adequately financed due to the constraints on local and state bodies to compel contributions from affiliates (Draper 1989, chap. 3).

This chapter is about an effort by a labor coalition to defy these institutional impediments, establish multiunion coalitions, and exert control over a political region. While several large labor and nonlabor organizations were necessary partners, clearly a central labor council stood at the vortex of political mobilization activities. In the span of six years, the South Central Federation of Labor (SCFL), a council located in Wisconsin, and allied organizations have transformed a modest political outreach program into a system for winning marginal contests. The aim is not to trumpet the achievements of SCFL, but to describe obstacles in revitalizing labor's political capacity at the local level and the prospective role of central labor councils to overcome them.

For several reasons, SCFL is an appropriate case for a detailed investigation. First, as described in the next section, the effort to build political capacity began prior to the devastating 1994 election when Republicans assumed control of Congress and also before the call by the federal AFL-CIO to reinvigorate political education. Thus, the origin for these activities is largely independent of events at the federal level: This was an initiative by union leaders acting on developments within a local region. Second, over the past several election cycles SCFL has experimented with numerous operational strategies to create an effective political outreach program. This offers a chance to describe the role of new resources, particularly computers, and how they can be integrated with traditional methods of political-outreach. Descriptions of the mechanics of union political outreach are scarce and based on a former era (Kroll 1951; Wartenberg 1951), so an update is due. A third advantage of this case is that union leaders have invited empirical tests of their tactics since the 1996 elections. The findings from this research are mixed: sometimes supporting leaders' assumptions about union members, yet occasionally contradicting the conventional beliefs about union-member political behavior.

SCFL Background

Prior to 1994, political outreach by SCFL was limited to an occasional distribution of literature in a targeted local election. The geographically concentrated mailings usually consisted of a brief statement on SCFL letterhead expressing support for a candidate. The outreach was financed with money raised through the annual "Bean Feed," a casual fund-raising dinner at which political speeches are prohibited; yet politicians do attend and mingle with affiliated members of the local federation. The Bean Feed would raise about $2,000 annually through the sale of food alone, and occasionally resources from the national AFL-CIO supplemented this money in presidential elections.

All this changed in late spring of 1994, when the director of COPE (Committee on Political Education) from the Wisconsin Education Association Council (WEAC)[1] and an aide for Walter Kunicki, who was then speaker of the state assembly and one of the most influential Democrats in the state of Wisconsin, contacted the president of the South Central Federation of Labor. The purpose of the meeting was to address a threat to the majority position of assembly Democrats. Governor Tommy Thompson, a Republican, had been offering administrative positions to assembly Democrats in selected districts throughout Wisconsin. This was not a gesture aimed at cross-party conciliation, but rather an artful method of removing incumbents from targeted swing districts, allowing for the contest and takeover of seats by Republicans. Over the years Republicans gradually won assembly districts, and in the fall of 1994 they gained control of the majority. Three of the conquered swing districts were in suburban and rural Dane County,[2] a region that encompasses the political territory covered by SCFL.

The South Central Federation of Labor is a mid-sized labor council located in Madison.[3] Madison has historically elected progressive political leaders to the assembly, typically Democrats. Indeed, in the 1998 election the Republican Party did not even field candidates in Assembly Districts 77 and 78, which occupy central Madison. Just as predictable, the largely rural districts beyond Dane County have a strong tradition of voting for conservative candidates. Swing districts tend to occupy those geographic areas that straddle the left-leaning urban center and right-leaning rural towns and suburbs. The growth in suburban population at the perimeter of the city, coupled with the expansion of municipalities just beyond the city, has created considerable ambiguity over the political direction of the districts just outside of central Madison. What began at that spring meeting was a battle to gain control over four state assembly districts—three lost to the Republicans and one open seat that had been previously held by a Republican. What has developed since then is a political-outreach system for influencing local races, and even upward to congressional elections.

Building a Local Political Coalition

Marshalling Funds

Inadequate funding places serious constraints on any political outreach program. Costs are incurred in the operation of telephone banks, the provision of food and beverages, the preparation of outreach material, postage, and so forth. To finance the outreach in 1994, the coalition prepared a budget and calculated a per capita cost of $1.31 to run the campaign. Letters were sent to union leaders describing what was at stake, the general plan, and the cost of the program. The response was impressive: nearly all the affiliates with SCFL contributed, and even unions that were not particularly active provided money. Unions that declined did so largely because of their own tight budgets or because they considered the contributions from the union parent body sufficient. Larger unions that have a history of political activism, such as AFSCME (American Federation of State, County, and Municipal Employees) and WEAC, contributed more than their share of funds.

Convincing affiliates to support a political program financially was easier after the Republican sweep of Congress in fall 1994. Using the same per capita appeal process, the coalition was able to collect over $25,000 to finance the spring 1995 campaign. Some of the largest costs are related to the production and postage for mailed outreach material. Another large expense is the hiring of staff to manage the outreach process. In 1994, paid staff was not necessary because the coalition targeted only four state assembly districts. Yet, as the coalition began to target elections and the membership lists expanded, the outreach program became more complex. Tactics now involve a mix of mailings and telephone and face-to-face contacts, which vary across political levels and districts. By 1995 effective coordination required a point-person to be responsible for implementing the coalition plan. The person that the coalition hired, an employee of Wisconsin Citizen Action, had both a high interest in politics and the computer skills necessary to manage the member database.

Another important qualification was that the coordinator came from a nonunion coalition partner. This was significant, as it implied an absence of favoritism during the outreach process. Equally notable: As a precondition for participation, the largest unions insisted that the president of SCFL chair the coalition. Had an area union dominated the administration and coordination of the outreach, it would have raised concerns over the fair allocation of collective resources by other coalition partners. Establishing an administrative apparatus that was perceived by coalition affiliates as unbiased solved this collective-action problem. Key, then, to marshalling broad financial participation is the creation of a system that is dedicated to winning elections and minimizes the opportunity for any one union to use collective funds to advance a specific agenda.

Variation in the political agendas among coalition partners is unavoidable and presents a serious obstacle to affiliate mobilization. To accommodate the unique political aims of affiliates, the coalition has adopted flexible rules that permit various levels of participation. This is most evident in the established conventions for dealing with disagreements in the endorsement process. If a relatively small number of coalition partners disagree with a supermajority, then SCFL will simply pull the names of the members of those organizations off the lists to remove them from outreach for that specific race. This allows any affiliate to make endorsements that depart from the coalition, but still participate in coalition activity for races where they agree. If there are deep divisions over the endorsement of a candidate, the coalition will simply refrain from targeting and financially supporting the race. In such cases, an affiliate can still endorse and promote the denied candidate, but resources for that candidate do not come from the coalition budget. Rather, the supporting affiliate must use funds that are beyond their contribution to the coalition effort. By providing an outlet for affiliates that disagree with the coalition, these rules focus coalition attention toward races and issues where there is broad agreement. From the perspective of the affiliate, participation with the coalition does not require the subordination of political strategy to the majority: they can choose to accept coalition-sponsored outreach in some instances and decline in others.

Mobilizing Volunteers

Local political outreach requires a network of reliable volunteers to staff telephone banks, assemble mailings, perform door-to-door canvassing, conduct literature drops, and so on. In 1994, the labor coalition managed to recruit around four hundred volunteers. The two largest area unions, Madison

Teachers and AFSCME, supplied the most manpower. It is not surprising that these are both public-sector unions: Compared to unions that represent workers in the private sector, public unions have a stronger tradition of political activism because the relationship between elections and collective bargaining policy is more direct. However, using direct appeals, the coalition was able to recruit a broad cross-section of activists including representatives from the building trades, industrial unions, and the service sector. Member volunteers from nonaffiliated unions such as WEAC and the Teamsters, as well as members from the largest nonunion coalition partner, Wisconsin Citizen Action, also participated. The volunteer list is stored at SCFL and, prior to each election cycle, must be updated to account for attrition and the recruitment of new activists. As affiliate participation in the political coalition has expanded, so has the number of volunteers. The present list stands at around seven hundred and fifty volunteers.

During the first campaign, much of the work assigned to volunteers was related to sorting, stuffing envelopes, and labeling literature to be mailed to member's homes. In 1996, the coalition debated over the feasibility of this practice after discovering it was cheaper and easier to contract these tasks to a unionized printer and mailer. The primary reason it was cheaper was that the vendor could secure less expensive carrier route rates by processing the outreach materials in a specific order and bundling them into packets. Coalition leaders concluded that it would be too difficult to coordinate these tasks with volunteers, so they contracted the mailing tasks and assigned members to phone banking and house visits.

One of the most difficult outreach functions to staff is the member identification (ID) telephone bank, where volunteers are asked to call coalition members and attempt to assess their level of support for the labor-endorsed candidate. Because member lists are imperfect and calling is performed during evening hours, angry responses are common, and the potential for an unpleasant experience is high. Even under optimal conditions, it is grinding telephone survey work that requires volunteers to find out how members will act in the privacy of the voting booth. Despite these difficulties, union leaders perceive the information as crucial. During the survey, respondents are first asked to state a candidate preference. After the reply, they are asked whether they could be persuaded to vote for the opposing (i.e., labor-endorsed) candidate. Those members who answer in the affirmative to the second question are considered "leaning," and COPE officials consider these members as prime targets for political outreach.

In 1994 the ID process was conducted by paid staff from the national AFSCME headquarters in Washington, D.C. This removed the chore from the local coalition, but the release came at a cost: The assessment by the national AFSCME staff was largely restricted to the early phase of the election campaign and did not allow for the tracking of membership preferences toward the end of the cycle. While it is valuable to know where a member stands on a candidate two months prior to an election, more useful information is where a union member stands on election day. Critical decisions are made in the final days before the election, particularly relating to the allocation of get-out-the-vote (GOTV) resources. Having to rely on an international union for periodic updates on member preferences was cumbersome owing to all the other demands placed on the international.

Consequently, by 1995 the member ID function was brought in-house. The coalition engages in various steps to encourage volunteers to participate in the telephone ID process. To lower the travel burden, telephone banks are set up in several locations in the city, and volunteers are invited to work from any of the locations. Routinely, AFSCME in the west side of Madison and Madison Teachers in the east side of Madison assemble telephone banks. In the past, WEAC in south Madison also had an open telephone bank. The coalition will also purchase food for volunteers, and occasionally it provides child-care assistance.

Volunteers are also needed to accomplish activities for building support for the COPE-endorsed candidates, including activities such as literature drops, and workplace postings. In the earlier campaigns, most of outreach methods did not require member-to-member contact. Door-to-door visits were attempted in the most vulnerable political districts, but the effectiveness of this tactic was debated. It is an outreach method that works best when population and union-member density is high and therefore is less feasible in the suburban and rural targeted areas. In 1998, the coalition sought to increase the level of the personal contact between volunteers and members in two ways. First, volunteers were assigned as liaisons in the workplace and given the responsibility to take the political message to fellow employees. A national AFL-CIO representative facilitated this strategy by coordinating volunteer outreach tactics and conducting literature distributions at the plant gate. The second form of outreach was via the telephone: volunteers were asked to call persons in their local from a coalition telephone bank. The belief was that a call from someone who was familiar with union leaders and work conditions was more persuasive than a volunteer stranger. The relationship between voter turnout and these tactics are reported on later in this chapter.

In the final days before the election, the phone banks are used to conduct get-out-the-vote (GOTV) contacts. Persuading volunteers to make GOTV calls is relatively easy because the interaction is much less invasive than the member-ID contacts. A typical call will remind members to vote, and often messages are left on voice machines. A more intrusive GOTV tactic, termed "knock and drag," involves traveling to members' homes and providing transportation to the polls. This method is much more time intensive and is used sparingly.

To increase the precision of the GOTV contacts, volunteers are assigned as poll watchers. Poll watchers work in pairs, and their role is to monitor the polling place on election day, looking for identified supporters of COPE candidates, and striking these members off a list when they show up to vote. At certain times during the day, poll watchers report to a central office those persons on the list that could not be identified as voters, and these persons receive a telephone call or a house visit. As the coalition became proficient with computerized membership lists, call-in voter information was stored in a digital database, and new lists were generated containing the names of those in the district who had not yet voted. These lists are provided to the next shift of poll watchers and to the GOTV telephone banks. This activity grows more intense toward the evening and terminates when the polls close.

Internalizing the Mailing Lists

The effective allocation of volunteer and financial resources depends on an accurate list of the members from coalition affiliates. The key pieces of information needed are the names and addresses of members, their phone numbers, their organizational affiliations, and their political districts. Until 1995, SCFL relied on a list provided by the national AFL-CIO; this list is a compilation of membership lists submitted by national unions. The coalition found the data on the list incomplete, inaccurate, and dated. Much of the problem is due to the unavoidable lag time in creating the list. Data originate as submissions from union locals to the national unions, and then the national union often modifies the information before sending it to the AFL-CIO. It was discouraging to volunteers, as well as a waste of resources, to attempt to contact persons who did not belong to the union, had moved, or were deceased.

Consequently, SCFL and allied organizations internalized this activity. Prior to the spring election of 1995, SCFL developed a master list from local affiliates. The data came from two sources: (1) the mailing list for *Union Labor News*, the publication produced by SCFL and (2) data supplied by locals and nonlabor organizations that did not subscribe to *Union Labor News.* The first required permission from the affiliated union to use the mailing list for *Union Labor News* for political outreach. The second required unions that did not subscribe to *Union Labor News* to submit a list of members. In most cases leaders complied, particularly after they were reassured that the list was to be used only for COPE purposes. Some of these lists were in digital form, and were relatively easy to standardize and append to the master list. Other information was in paper form and had to be input by hand, requiring many volunteer hours. Digital membership information at the local level clearly improves the efficiency of the list-compilation process.

Thus, one role for SCFL is to coordinate the collection of fresh member data and to maintain it locally. Leaders have found it is easier to assemble a member database for each major political cycle rather than try to maintain a list over time. Currently, SCFL compiles a new list for each of the fall elections and uses these data for the subsequent spring local elections. Every summer membership data are collected, beginning with the larger locals and working toward the smaller ones. Once a master list is prepared, other data are added, such as voting histories, phone numbers, and political districts. The process does require an up-front expenditure of resources; however, it is believed that the more precise data help the coalition conserve on other outreach costs and more efficiently allocate volunteer energy. Local data can be rapidly manipulated to deal with election contingencies and upgraded with the inclusion of new coalition affiliates, and lists can be strategically generated for a variety of purposes and races.

Once the database is compiled, it must be accessed during the election cycle for various outreach activities. These tasks require someone with database management skills who can efficiently generate output. As the COPE plan became more complex, it was important to give someone the task of generating lists, mailing labels, and so forth. The coalition experimented with different database-management options. A large area union involved in the coalition, WEAC, was the first vendor to manage the lists. The key problem with WEAC was that because of the demands placed on their organization by membership, they were unable to offer SCFL prompt service. At considerable expense, SCFL tried to contract this work to a commercial vendor in 1996. The chief problem with this strategy was that the commercial vendor lacked familiarity with the data. Coalition leaders would receive output that was inconsistent with their understanding of the membership: for example, some large unions had incomplete lists, and others were overstated. Because of these difficulties, SCFL has brought the operation in-house, and now hires an activist-consultant or delegates database-management duties to the coalition coordinator.

Categorizing Members and Crafting a Message

One pearl of conventional wisdom is that persuasion techniques are most effective for union members that are identified as "leaning" for or against a candidate. This rests on the assumption that members' response to political outreach varies, based on their political attitudes and voting behavior. Indeed, the purpose of the member-ID process (described above) is to identify "leaners," because it is believed that they will be most responsive to union outreach material. Early in the ID process, respondents are classified as supporting the COPE candidate, opposing the COPE candidate, or leaning for or against the COPE candidate. Once members are categorized, the data are supplemented with voter turnout information gathered through public voter files. Theoretically this provides the coalition with two vital pieces of information: whether someone will support the COPE candidate and the likelihood the member will vote. Resources and outreach strategy then flow from this categorization.

Table 6.1 outlines member dimensions and outreach tactics. Proportionately, the greatest level of resources is directed at members who have a history of voting and who are identified as leaning toward the labor candidate. These members receive several persuasion and GOTV appeals. Resources are also directed at members who express support for the COPE candidate to reinforce their preference and encourage them to vote. For members who are identified as opponents of the COPE-endorsed candidate, conventional wisdom is to ignore them. This action is based on the belief that the opinion of such members is stubborn and that information directed at them will have the undesirable effect of stimulating voter turnout for the opposition. Unexpectedly, the research performed in 1996 suggested that this practice might have harmed the ability for the coalition to influence the political behavior of union members.

Table 6.1

Union Member Dimensions and COPE Information Tactics

| | Tactics | |
Member identification	Voters	Nonvoters
Support COPE candidate	Reinforce, GOTV	Reinforce, register, GOTV
Leaning for or against COPE	Persuade, GOTV	Persuade, register, GOTV
Oppose COPE candidate	Ignore	Ignore

A second pearl of conventional wisdom holds that a precise, targeted political message is more persuasive than a broad, inclusive one. Thus crafting a unified political agenda among diverse and often competing groups is problematic: as the coalition grows, the political demands of the members associated with the coalition become more disparate. It then becomes difficult for coalition leaders to reach agreement on a compelling common theme. Leaders initially conceptualized a diverse strategy, creating a tailored message that would target specific types of members. Public-sector workers, for example, would receive political material that targeted their concerns (e.g., privatization); the trades, their issues (e.g., project labor agreements); and so on. This proved prohibitively costly because professionally produced material is much less expensive when it is ordered in large volume. The logical alternative was to design a set of materials that addressed several issues that would have universal appeal.

In 1994, the coalition sent four mailings to members in each of the four targeted state assembly districts. The material featured a cartoon format for graphics, and the text covered a range of issues. Since then, prior to drafting the outreach, coalition leaders have tried to pare down the list by surveying a cross-section of union members to identify the "hot" issues. The survey also has an important role in the consensus-building process. Establishing objective measures of what members think is important makes it easier to mediate personal differences among leaders and come to terms on a short list of campaign issues. Once the list of issues is decided, the coalition drafts material that compares the candidates on the identified issues. The emphasis on comparing candidate positions on issues, rather than simply endorsing them, was prompted by research sponsored by the national AFL-CIO that suggested members want political material that helps them make informed decisions (Hart and Associates, Inc. 1995).

What has evolved is a sequence of mailings that begin with general statements about issues and become more specific and comparative as the election nears. The comparative literature places the candidate side by side on four to six issues, usually economic, along with the official positions of the candidates. Issue positions are garnered from newspaper citations, position papers, interviews, and voting records. Citations are provided to add legitimacy. The eventual selection of issues is intended to arouse interest by a broad cross-section of union members. Typically the building trades get an issue, the public sector, the industrial unions, and so forth, but the literature also includes generic issues such a living wage. By establishing outreach that has something for all members of the labor movement, the aim is to reduce disagreement among coalition partners.

Measuring Success: Political Outcomes and Findings

Making the Difference in Marginal Races

The 1994 fall campaign yielded no political victory: All four targeted state assembly districts were lost. Yet the experience created such a sense of solidarity and purpose that the coalition leaders decided to continue. The consensus was that the conservative threat at the state level was not going to dissipate, a sentiment augmented by the Republican takeover of Congress. Arguably, the loss of political friends at the national level added urgency to the mission of establishing a friendlier political environment locally.

The first sign that the coalition was making progress was the 1995 spring school-board elections. Conservative school-board member, Nancy Mistel, a visible opponent to the Madison Teachers union, was up for reelection. Highly favored, Mistel won the election by only a narrow margin and afterward publicly blamed the labor coalition and the teachers for the close call. Leaders knew they were having an impact. In 1997 one of the three school-board seats was taken from the conservatives, marking the beginning of a trend that led to the eventual dominance of the school board by progressive leaders. Labor-endorsed candidates won two of three open school-board seats in the spring 1998 election. School Superintendent Cheryl Wilhoyte, a long-time adversary of Madison Teachers, resigned over the school-board turnover and accepted a position with the Edison Project, a firm specializing in the private management of public schools. In the spring 2000 elections, labor took two of two targeted seats.

County elections during the spring election of 1996 offered the first, and perhaps greatest, victory for the coalition. Conservatives have traditionally held about half of the seats on the Dane County board. In 1996, sixteen of the twenty-six endorsed seats were won, shifting control away from conservatives. Moreover, two of the endorsed candidates who did lose lost by as few as ten votes. After that election, progressives controlled the Dane County board. In the spring 1997 race, the endorsed candidate for County Executive, Kathleen Falk, won convincingly over a conservative rival. Labor suffered a setback after the spring 2000 races, winning only three of eleven targeted races and ten of nineteen of their endorsements. Control has now shifted back to conservatives.

As the successes at the school-board level illustrate, the coalition has stronger influence over those races that draw from the voting populations of central Madison. For example, progressives continue to dominate the Madison city council. In the Madison mayoral race of 1997, the COPE-endorsed candidate for mayor, Sue Bauman, won the election by fifty-five votes.

At the state level, the coalition has managed to protect the seats of labor-friendly incumbents and win back one of the four original contested assembly seats. In the fall of 1996, four state assembly seats in Dane County were targeted. One district was held by Democratic incumbent Dave Travis, but perceived as vulnerable, so the coalition provided resources to protect against a loss. Republican incumbent Rudy Silbaugh held the third seat, but was challenged by Tom Hebl, a Democrat. Late polling indicated the race was close, motivating coalition leaders to devote considerable resources to supporting Hebl, including a heavy deployment of poll watchers and telephone volunteers. Hebl won the election, taking back one of the original contested assembly districts. Between 1996 and 1998 Hebl registered a 100 percent voting record on labor issues, was supported again by the coalition in 1998 and reelected. Also in 1998, attempting to capitalize on name recognition, Nancy Mistel vacated the school-board seat and ran against COPE-endorsed candidate Jon Erpenbach. Mistel lost and since then has not reentered local politics.

It is more difficult for a local coalition to influence an election as political races reach the federal level. In 1996 the coalition targeted the second congressional district, supporting former Madison mayor Paul Soglin over incumbent Scott Klug, a Republican. Klug won convincingly, but vacated the seat two years later. The coalition targeted two

Table 6.2

Chronology of Elections, Coalition Targets, and Outcomes

Election	Targeted races	Political outcome
Fall 1994	Four state assembly seats	No victories
Spring 1995	School board, city council	No school board wins, but political opponent publicly declares labor responsible for a close call. City Council remains progressive.
Spring 1996	County board, school board	Labor wins 16 of 26 endorsed seats on the Dane County Board
Fall 1996	Four state assembly districts	One district taken, one district protected
Spring 1997	Madison mayoral	COPE-endorsed mayor wins by 55 votes
	Dane County executive	County executive wins
Spring 1998	School board	One of three school board seats taken
	School board	Two of three open seats; school board is 6 to 1 progressive incumbents
Fall 1998	One senate seat	State senate win
	Two state assembly seats	One assembly seat retained
Spring 2000	Eleven county board	Three county board wins
	Two school board	Two school board wins

federal elections in the fall of 1998. Progressive Tammy Baldwin was running against Jo Musser for the second congressional district seat vacated by Scott Klug. Russ Feingold, an incumbent senator, was in a close statewide contest against a Republican from the first congressional district, Mark Neumann. Both labor-endorsed candidates won, Baldwin by a convincing margin and Feingold by fewer than 3,000 votes. Table 6.2 provides a chronology of the races and outcomes:

As it became evident that the coalition was having some impact on marginal contests, a broader cross-section of unions and other progressive groups joined. The boost in financial support coupled with greater economies permitted the coalition to expand outreach capacity. This growth has earned the coalition the recognition of candidates. Now candidates frequently contact SCFL for assistance in conducting literature drops, making telephone calls, and so forth. To reinforce the connection between labor and electoral success, volunteers dispatched for a candidate are instructed to identify their relationship with the coalition.

Political candidates, even conservative ones, schedule interviews with coalition leaders well in advance of elections. These interviews allow labor leaders to ask candidates specific questions on issues, forcing politicians to commit to policy matters as a precondition for an endorsement. Even a political candidate who is quite sure an endorsement is not forthcoming will tend to support a policy that is important to the coalition to minimize labor opposition in the race. This phenomenon has yielded dividends for labor and the community. Perhaps the best example was the passage of a living-wage ordinance for Dane County and the city of Madison in March 1999. The living-wage initiative began in 1996, paralleling the growth in political capacity of the coalition. The vote on the measure at the county board drew considerable conservative support, a tally of thirty-three to four, with two authors of the ordinance absent during the vote. Madison City Council also passed the ordinance, in part because of the support from conservatives who agreed to the measure during the preelection interview.

The 1996 and 1998 Research

In 1996 the coalition sent a series of information and persuasion mailings to the homes of union members. To measure the effectiveness of the program, a field experiment was conducted that compared the political attitudes and preferences of union members who were exposed to different levels of the literature. More specifically, a random sample of respondents was divided into three groups: (1) a control group that would receive no outreach, (2) a group that would receive the first two pieces of union literature, (3) a group that would receive the full sequence of three literature pieces. To eliminate "noise" from the experiment, the complete sample was excluded from other planned outreach tactics. Respondents were surveyed twice: first in late August, before any outreach was sent, and then a second time just prior to the November election. Measures from both surveys and public voter turnout data were used to assess the impact of mailings on attitudes, choice of candidate, and voter turnout.

In 1998 the research was smaller in scope, the goal was limited to testing the efficacy of GOTV tactics. The sample, drawn from within the SCFL region, consisted of union members identified as "drop-off" voters (i.e., members who vote in presidential elections but do not vote in off-year or local elections). These members were classified into four groups: (1) those who were to receive face-to-face contact, (2) those who would get a telephone call from someone in their union, (3) those who would get a telephone call from a volunteer at SCFL, and (4) a control group that received no contact. Public voter-turnout data were collected, and voting rates were compared with turnout type.

Results and Implications

Two findings lend some evidence that literature sent to homes influenced union members' perception of candidates. First, receipt of the literature was linked to an effect that was generally in the direction that labor expected: Union-member perceptions of the COPE-endorsed candidates saw an improvement, while ratings of candidates opposed by COPE were suppressed. Second, union members who voted were influenced more by the literature than were nonvoters. We speculate that this is probably because voters are more serious consumers of campaign material. Nonvoters are more likely to discard the literature sent to their homes than to spend time reading it. Predicted candidate ratings are shown in Table 6.3.

Two implications emerge from these findings. The most obvious is that it does seem possible to influence the general attitudes that union members have toward candidates through educational material distributed by mail. Second, if labor unions wanted to reduce the cost of the outreach by "weeding out" unresponsive members before the election cycle, they could focus on voting history. Whether or not a person votes appears to be a reliable indicator of responsiveness to union-sponsored outreach. Voting histories are public data that can be obtained through municipal records. With some training, union volunteers can access these records and begin to collect voter-turnout data well before the beginning of the political cycle.

Despite these favorable findings, perhaps the most important outcome from the 1996 study was an appreciation for the limited effectiveness of a direct-mail approach. An intriguing result was that the two direct-mail pieces sent earlier in the political campaign appeared to have a greater

Table 6.3

Predicted Ratings for Political Candidates in Wisconsin's Second Congressional District and Mail Outreach, 1996 Election

	All respondents		Voters only	
	COPE-endorsed candidate	COPE-opposed candidate	COPE-endorsed candidate	COPE-opposed candidate
Control group (no outreach)	45.6	56.5	43.9	56.5
First two pieces of literature	55.5	54.8	56.7	54.0
Three pieces of literature	47.8	52.3	49.8	52.6

Note: Values are between zero and 100. Higher values reflect more positive feelings toward a political candidate.

impact on attitudes than the third piece. One explanation for this finding is that the content and delivery of the third piece was not well understood or appreciated by union members. While plausible, this contradicts the testimony of activists we interviewed: Most described the member response to the third piece as favorable. A second and more believable explanation is that the third piece was sent too close to the election to have any effect. The third piece arrived at members' homes about one week before the election. Perhaps recipients made up their minds by that time or the literature was not digested because it was "lost" within the blizzard of other direct-mail campaigns.

If correct, then it implies that it is best to begin educating members early in the election cycle. Labor should not rely on a last-minute "blitz" just before the election to change the minds of voters. These results suggest that it is more effective to educate members early before they have established firm opinions based on other competing information sources. By distributing outreach materials early, the union can distinguish its message more clearly from other political positions.

Even more surprising was the finding that union members who stated a strong preference for the COPE-*opposed* candidate two months before the election were more likely to be persuaded toward the COPE-endorsed candidate than any other group, including those who were identified as "leaning" toward either candidate. There are two possible explanations for this seemingly illogical outcome. First, persons who tell us that they are "strong" for the wrong candidate (or any candidate for that matter) are more serious about politics, and therefore, are more responsive consumers of political information. Perhaps this group was more likely to read the information sent to their households. Second, the member-ID process itself is flawed, and it fails to identify "leaners" as coalition leaders believed. Maybe many of the persons who tell us that they are "not strong" or "persuadable" (i.e., leaners) have actually made up their minds: They just refuse to reveal their preferences to a stranger over the telephone. These two possible explanations are not mutually exclusive. In any event, those respondents who identified themselves as strongly favoring the opposing candidate were just as likely (if not more likely) to be persuaded to move toward the COPE-endorsed candidate. This finding was registered from two separate measures.

This poses a critical issue for the practice of identifying members, implying that the policy of excluding some members from outreach may have actually harmed labors' ability to support COPE-endorsed candidates; this implies further that labor should not limit the universe of members slated for outreach, but instead strive to include all persons sympathetic to labor, regardless of political philosophy. In the very least, a redesign of the member-ID process seems to be called for, because the ID process used to date does not appear to be an effective method of distinguishing between members who will be persuaded by union-sponsored outreach and those who will not. In the absence of a redesign, it is advisable to move the member-ID process to later in the campaign cycle after the persuasion forms of outreach have been distributed and to use the ID information for only GOTV activities.

Strategically, the research appears to be demonstrating that persuasion and GOTV activities can be considered distinct political-mobilization tasks. Thus, it may be possible to enhance the economic efficiency of the process by classifying union members according to their voting histories and then targeting voters with persuasion tactics and nonvoters with GOTV tactics. Over election cycles, as nonvoters become "hardcore" voters, they receive less GOTV and more persuasion material.

Another revealing limitation of the union outreach, however, was that the mail campaign did not affect members' choice of candidates. The data yielded little evidence that the mailings caused union members to change their votes from the COPE-opposed candidate to the COPE-endorsed candidate. This finding suggests that it is much easier to change a union member's perception of a political figure than to persuading him to vote for that candidate. Voters do not enter the political cycle as blank slates, but rather carry with them longstanding political predispositions built from their life experiences. For union leaders, this implies that information alone will not move significant numbers of union members to the COPE candidates, much more comprehensive strategies are needed, strategies that raise workers' consciousness of the relationship between political platforms and the well-being of the trade union movement.

The mail outreach also did not have an impact on the likelihood that members would vote. Leaders perceived this result as double-edged. On the one hand, it says that the mail campaign did not boost voting for members who preferred the COPE-endorsed candidate: a negative outcome. On the other hand, the mail campaign did not stimulate voter turnout among members who favored the COPE-opposed candidate either. This latter finding is important because the concern in 1996 was that mail sent to the homes of members who favored the COPE-opposed candidate would stimulate turnout for the opposition. There was no evidence of this, suggesting, first, that persuasion pieces can be safely mailed to all members and, second, that other forms of GOTV persuasion, such as telephone calls and face-to-face appeals, are needed to increase voter turnout.

One obvious limitation of the direct-mail campaign is that it lacks human interaction; probably the chief reason for the weak impact of the 1996 outreach on voter behavior. Indeed, evidence in both the 1996 and 1998 projects indicated that human interaction is a necessary component to effective outreach. In 1996, several unions, including most notably the UAW, was significantly more successful in persuading members to vote for the COPE-endorsed candidate. Post-research interviews revealed that the UAW has institutionalized a steward-to-member communication system in the factory. This process allows the UAW to disseminate information rapidly: from union leaders, to shop stewards, to rank and file through face-to-face contact within the workplace.

The 1998 GOTV research indicated a direct correlation between the level of personal contact and the likelihood the "drop-off" voters would to go to the polls. Those who had face-to-face contacts with members in the workplace had the highest voting rates. The second most effective form of contact was member-to-member telephone calls between persons in the same union, followed by volunteer-to-member contacts. The results from 1998 are in Table 6.4.

Historically, there are two methods for increasing the level of personal contact used by labor. The first is workplace centered, similar to the UAW model, in which an active steward system is called upon to promulgate persuasion and GOTV materials at the worksite. The second is community centered, in which volunteers are assigned a geographic area to canvass and

Table 6.4

Voting Rates and Member Contact Type, 1998 Elections

Type of contact	Estimated probability of voting (%)
Face-to-face contact at work	80.0
Member-to-member telephone call	69.6
Volunteer-to-member phone call	65.8
Omitted group voting rate	60.7
Overall sample	65.6

are responsible for delivering persuasion material at some point during the election cycle and for performing GOTV appeals on election day.

Union-member volunteers who are uncomfortable with the role of advocating a specific candidate can be assigned the less intrusive task of appealing to another member's obligation to participate in the political process. An evaluation of nonvoters from the 1996 data indicated that most preferred the COPE-endorsed candidate. When we examined the union nonvoters from the 1996 sample, it was evident that the majority (about 70 percent) favored the COPE-endorsed candidate. Thus, just getting nonvoters out to the polls will, on average, improve the chances for a COPE victory. One strategy, particularly if resources are limited, is to forgo persuasion techniques and concentrate on voter-registration drives: Offer shared rides to the polls, make contact via the telephone to remind members of an upcoming election, and make face-to-face appeals in the workplace or in the community.

Central Labor Councils and Local Political Activism

If there is one grand lesson, it is that successful coalition activity is an organic process that requires planning, budgeting, strategizing, and an abundance of shoe leather. Operationally, the process of mobilizing workers for political goals is comparable to the mobilization that takes place by unions to achieve benefits through employers. There is, however, at least one important difference. From the perspective of a union member, responding to a political appeal by voting for a candidate is a low-risk action, compared to the potential consequences for participating in a union organizing drive or a strike. Political mobilization should therefore be easier, except for the collateral problem that the perceived potential for gain is lower as well. Obtaining benefits from the employer is direct and tangible compared with the residual gain a member enjoys by influencing social policy. Building worker solidarity around issues emerging from the work relationship, such as compensation and employer fairness, tends to be easier than unifying citizens around public policy themes. The relevancy of political action is therefore far more difficult for union members to appreciate. Hence the critical role of political education: to raise member awareness of the connection between their lives and the general strength of the labor movement as expressed through public policy.

Initially, coalition leaders affiliated with SCFL tried to educate members efficiently by using "professional" techniques. The temptation is understandable. It is relatively easy to hire firms to conduct member surveys, create literature, and mail information to members. A far more challenging task is to establish a system for conducting interactive outreach: convincing union leaders to join a coalition, organizing the work of volunteers, localizing operations, and engaging the membership. The view of coalition leaders, which is supported by the election results and research findings, is that intense personal contact is needed to build an identity between union membership and political activism. Any successful mobilization effort involves the creation of energy and enthusiasm, and experiences so far raise doubts that arm's-length political education tactics alone can accomplish this feat. Technology can enhance the political outreach process, as this case illustrates, but the role of technology is supportive to traditional member-to-member political mobilization tactics.

Essentially, what labor unions must do is transition from economic to political mobilization with each election cycle. Because central labor councils are regional federations, they are uniquely positioned for facilitating these periodic transitions. The SCFL example demonstrates that, by pooling resources and achieving economies of scale, labor councils can coordinate and localize many of the functions necessary for member-to-member outreach. By reducing dependency on state and federal bodies, regional leaders can assemble a more flexible and effective system for educating union members on political issues and influencing local elections. Key is whether labor leaders can construct a system that accommodates the unique political demands of affiliates without undermining the common goal: to steer resources toward winning elections for the broader labor movement. On this point, trust between coalition leaders and the central labor council staff that administers collective resources appears critical. Once such a system is institutionalized, the labor council provides organizational consistency over subsequent election cycles as it is in an advantageous position to experiment with various outreach methods; gradually refine coalition tactics; and, by becoming more efficacious, build coalition membership.

Notes

1. WEAC is the National Education Association affiliate in Wisconsin and is not a member of the AFL-CIO.

2. In 1990, Republican Rudy Silbaugh won an open seat, District 46, which is located in Eastern Dane County, was vacated by Democrat Tom Loftus. Republican Eugene Hahn was elected to District 47 in 1990, a seat previously held by Robert Thompson, a conservative Democrat. Thompson received an appointment by Governor Tommy Thompson. In western Dane County Joe Wineke, a Democrat, vacated the District 79 seat that was subsequently taken by Republican Richard Skindrud in a 1993 special election.

3. The South Central Federation of Labor has approximately seventy-five local union affiliates, or about 80 to 90 percent of area unions, covering about 32,000 members.

Bibliography

Cavanaugh, Jim. 2000. President of the South Central Federation of Labor; various interviews held between February and April.

Draper, Alan. 1989. *A Rope of Sand: The AFL-CIO Committee on Political Education, 1955–1967.* New York: Praeger.

Form, William. 1995. *Segmented Labor, Fractured Politics: Labor Politics in American Life.* New York: Plenum.

Hardman, J.B.S., and Maurice F. Neufeld, eds. 1951. *The House of Labor: Internal Operations of American Unions.* Westport, CT: Greenwood.

Hart and Associates, Inc. 1995. A Nationwide Survey Among Union Members and the General Public on Politics and Legislation. Report to the AFL-CIO, May.

Kroll, Jack. 1951. "The CIO-PAC and How It Works." In J.B.S. Hardman and Maurice F. Neufeld, eds., *The House of Labor: Internal Operations of American Unions.* Westport, CT: Greenwood, 116–25.

Wallihan, James. 1985. *Union Government and Organization in the United States.* Washington, DC: Bureau of National Affairs.

Wartenberg, George. 1951. "Political Action in a Congressional District." In J.B.S. Hardman and Maurice F. Neufeld, eds., *The House of Labor: Internal Operations of American Unions.* Westport CT: Greenwood, 126–33.

7

Building Political Power and Community Coalitions

The Role of Central Labor Councils in the Living-Wage Movement

Stephanie Luce

At its 1997 convention, the national AFL-CIO passed a resolution declaring itself committed to getting local governments to pass living-wage ordinances. Since then, a number of state federations have also endorsed this goal, urging their central labor councils (CLCs) to pursue local living-wage campaigns.

To what degree have CLCs taken up the challenge to engage in living-wage campaigns, and to what extent has the living-wage movement helped the labor movement rebuild itself? This article evaluates the progress that CLCs have made in meeting these challenges. I will address the following regarding the role of CLCs in the living-wage movement: where CLCs have been involved in campaigns, what their goals are for supporting the campaigns, how effectively the campaigns have met those goals, the types of coalitions they have built or worked in during the campaigns, and what occurs with the CLCs and organizing around living wages after the laws are passed.

To answer these questions, I worked with my colleague Doug Kandt to interview CLC and non–CLC living wage activists from campaigns across the country. Altogether, we conducted over thirty interviews with people representing approximately forty past or ongoing campaigns. Their stories help illustrate the potential of the living-wage movement for the growth of the labor movement.

What Are Living Wage Ordinances?

Living-wage ordinances vary in form, but the basic idea is that they are legislation that requires firms that receive public money in the form of service contracts or subsidies to pay their workers a higher hourly wage. In most cases, the ordinances require these firms to pay the wage necessary to bring a worker with a family of four up to the federal poverty line, although some ordinances have higher and lower wage levels, and some also mandate benefits.

Since the first living-wage campaign was won in Baltimore in 1994, approximately forty other municipalities have passed such laws, and the rate at which ordinances are passing is increasing.[1] The ordinances exist mostly in cities, but they have also passed in seven counties and one school board. There are ordinances in large cities like Boston, Los Angeles, and Chicago, but also in smaller cities like Ypsilanti, Michigan, and Somerville, Massachusetts. They exist in wealthier cities, like Madison, Wisconsin, and in poor ones, like Detroit. There are laws in cities in the northeast, midwest, west, and south, and while most of the ordinances that have passed so far have been in urban areas, some of the counties with ordinances have rural portions. And while certain states have often had state minimum wages higher than the federal level, a handful of ballot initiatives and state laws have recently passed under "living-wage" rhetoric.

There appears to be no sign that the movement is slowing. Campaigns are currently under way in at least fifty cities, and university students have taken up the challenge of running on-campus campaigns for requiring that all university employees be paid a living wage. The list of these ongoing campaigns is too long to provide here, but they include cities and counties over the United States, as well as universities such as Harvard, Johns Hopkins, and the University of Virginia.

How Are CLCs Involved?

What has been the role of CLCs in this movement? Given that labor activists tend to wear multiple hats, it is not always clear which campaigns should be considered CLC campaigns, but to date, CLCs have played a leading role in the successful campaigns in approximately seventeen of the forty campaigns.[2] They have played a substantial role in an additional nine of the forty past campaigns,[3] and CLCs are currently active in numerous ongoing campaigns, including those in Berkeley, the Port of Oakland, and San Francisco, California; Cleveland, Ohio; Albuquerque, New Mexico; Knoxville, Tennessee; Omaha, Nebraska; Rochester, New York; Greensboro, North Carolina; Charleston, South Carolina; and others.

What does it mean for a CLC to be involved in a campaign? A number of labor councils, such as the South Central Federation of Labor in Wisconsin, the South Bay Labor Council in California, and the Metro Detroit AFL-CIO have funded staff to work specifically on the campaigns. Metro Detroit, for example, hired one person to work full-time for several months to coordinate the living-wage campaign with its get-out-the-vote efforts, and another person to work one day a week to do outreach to churches. In other cities, CLCs have offered financial support to fund mailings and brochures, assistance with lobbying the city council and mayor, and help with turnout for events. For example, in Somerville, Massachusetts, the CLC planned a StreetHeat action before a Board of Aldermen meeting (interview with Frank Borges 1999). In Tucson, the living-wage campaign paired up interfaith council and labor council members to conduct "Living Wage Walks" in communities, where organizers talked to community members about the living wage and where people were asked to "step up and tell their stories to legislators." The Chicago Federation of Labor had its Union Summer interns work on the living-wage campaign in that city.

In addition, in a few cases CLCs have used their position to get assistance from the national AFL-CIO for their campaigns. The South Florida AFL-CIO got Linda Chavez-Thompson to testify at a city council meeting, and to write an op-ed piece in Spanish in the newspaper the Monday before the vote, asking people to call the mayor in support of the ordinance (interview with Mike Ozegovich 1999). John Sweeney has written letters and op-ed articles for campaigns in California and Florida and has testified in front of the New York city council in favor of its ordinance (interview with Christine Silvia 1999).

Why Are CLCs Involved?

CLC leaders gave a variety of reasons for getting involved in living-wage campaigns. The most common response was that the campaigns were "the right thing to do" (interview with Fred Veigel 1999). One after another, labor leaders told us that they did not get involved in the effort for the sake of the labor council, but for the dignity of working people. Tony Romano of the Greater Boston labor council remarked, "Organized labor doesn't just look out for organized labor. We make much more than the people affected by this; these were not union people, but they still have to make a living" (interview with Tony Romano 1999). Southern Arizona labor council president Ian Robertson adds, "I'm tired of being called a labor boss, and that we're only interested in collecting dues. Here was an opportunity for labor to be a community partner" (interview with Ian Robertson 1999).

Inspired in part by the national AFL-CIO's new emphasis on community economics, some CLC leaders are working to understand their local economies better, which is leading to an increased awareness of poverty. For example, Tommy Crenshaw, president of the Greater Charleston, South Carolina, CLC, recently conducted a study of working families in the South and found that "most of our families are two to three paychecks from total poverty. . . . [I]n most of our families, the husband and wife both work, [and] a lot of people are working overtime and second jobs." Crenshaw has worked to start a living-wage campaign because "We want to get to where people don't have to do this to survive" (Cook 1999).

Beyond doing the right thing, many CLC leaders noted other goals for pursuing the campaigns. In line with the AFL-CIO's Union Cities program, labor leaders saw the living-wage movement as a way to build political power and community coalitions. St. Paul activist Bernie Hess, of the United Food and Commercial Workers Union, said that "It dawned on the Trades and Labor Assembly that this was good for the community, and for getting into the community. . . . It was a chance to create coalitions." This was important for building the labor movement, because it helped "break down stereotypes" of the labor movement as monolithic, and "humanized people's perceptions of labor" (interview with Bernie Hess 1999). Several interviewees stressed the need to work in coalitions to change the community's image of labor and to establish a group that could be mobilized on various issues.

CLCs also hoped to use the campaigns to strengthen their political clout. In many of the cities, COPE (Committee on Political Education) used the living-wage as a plank in endorsement decisions. Interviewees remarked that the issue was a good catapult for talking to city councils, and two cities noted that they thought this could be valuable in resisting privatization efforts or making city council members look at contracting out in a new light. While most living-wage ordinances are passed by city councils, in Detroit the CLC chose to run their campaign as a ballot initiative, specifically to help turn out voters to elect their slate of endorsed candidates.

Finally, a number of CLCs mentioned that the campaigns could help with organizing. In some cases this was a specific concern, as it was in Chicago, where the CLC was asked by SEIU to get involved because their members could benefit directly from the ordinance. In other cities, the plan was indirect: "by working on living-wage campaigns that will benefit the working poor, the labor movement can improve its image and perhaps "cause people not covered by contracts to think about organizing" (Robertson interview 1999). Simply raising the issue may create a more favorable climate for new organizing. In an interview Judy Goff of the Alameda CLC noted, "We believe the living wage supports organizing, because it points out the great gap between the minimum wage and a livable wage" (1999).

Outcomes of the Campaigns

Have the campaigns been successful in meeting the goals of the CLCs? Specifically, are living-wage campaigns or ordinances helping raise the wages of low-income, nonunionized workers; build new alliances between labor and community organizations; build political power for labor; protect public-sector jobs from outsourcing; and organize workers into unions?

Winning Higher Wages for Low-Income Workers

In terms of "doing the right thing," labor activists at least feel positive about their role in the living wage movement. AFSCME (American Federation of State, County, and Municipal Employees) Council 96 organizer Erik Peterson had these thoughts about the Duluth, Minnesota, campaign: "It was a proud moment for many of us in the labor movement sticking up for economic justice," and Tim Leahy of the Chicago Federation of Labor says that the ordinance "had reverberations among workers" (interviews with Erik Peterson 1999; Tim Leahy 1999). Most of the CLC leaders who had pursued the ordinances because they wanted to help low-wage workers stated that they felt that the campaigns were a success.

But are the ordinances really successful in helping these workers? Unfortunately, it is not clear how many workers have actually received the higher wages mandated by the laws. Various research has shown that implementation is a serious problem in at least some of the cities with living-wage ordinances and that not all of the eligible workers are getting the living wage.[4] Some CLC leaders are recognizing the need to take implementation seriously so that their goals of raising wages for workers are realized. Andrea Cole of the Greater New Haven Labor Council agrees that labor needs to be involved: "The Comptroller's Office is responsible for implementation and tracking. We don't know anything. We basically dropped the ball. It was a big mistake, not being involved" (interview with Andrea Cole 1999). However, the majority of interviewees noted that the CLC has not played a role in the implementation of the laws. Even where the living-wage coalition was involved in writing the ordinance and regulations, almost all have left the monitoring of employers up to the city. This is in part due to resource and staffing shortages and in part to the difficulty of keeping up interest in the issue after the laws are passed. The result is that many workers are not actually receiving living wages even though the laws are enacted.

There are some exceptions, however. Most notably, the Los Angeles County Federation of Labor has supported the LA Living Wage Coalition in its efforts to educate workers about the ordinance, to lobby the city council to close loopholes and expand the law, and to push the city to improve its implementation process.

Another exception is found in Oakland, California. In an interview in 1999, Judy Goff of the Alameda, California, CLC remarked on the Oakland and Hayward ordinances, "We're getting the impression that we need to go back and get into the process again to ensure that it's being implemented." Following that, the East Bay Alliance for a Sustainable Economy (EBASE), an organization formed in large part out of the living-wage campaigns in the area, took up the fight for implementation. Since then, they have issued a report on the status of implementation in Oakland and have made living-wage implementation a core function of their organization. According to staff member Howard Greenwich, EBASE has now started a campaign to ensure that workers at the Oakland Coliseum are covered under the ordinance (Greenwich 1999).

In Chicago, living-wage advocates pushed the city to create a Living Wage Implementation Task Force comprising union, CLC, and city representatives who meet monthly to address problems in implementing the law. When the city ruled that certain home health-care workers were not covered by the ordinance, the union representatives on the task force pressured the city to change the ruling, resulting in raises from $5.30 to $7.60 an hour and more than $30,000 in back pay for over five hundred workers. According to Keith Kelleher of SEIU Local 880 and ACORN (Association of Community Organizations for Reform Now), "The Task Force was key to our getting that raise" (interview with Keith Kelleher 1999). The bottom line is that CLCs cannot be assured that they have accomplished their goal of assisting low-wage workers if they do not take part in the implementation of the law.

Building Community Coalitions

Building ties with the community and other organizations is perhaps where participating in the living-wage movement has seen the greatest success for the labor movement. Over half of the respondents said that the campaign had led to their working in coalition with groups they had never worked with before. Ian Robertson explains: "Absolutely [the living-wage campaign] helped us gain allies, and start dialogue with groups we never otherwise would have. Come on, I work in a mine, and now I'm sitting down with people from Earth First!" (Robertson interview 1999). The South Florida AFL-CIO worked in a large coalition of groups, 90 percent of which they had never worked with before (Ozegovich interview 1999). Harold Meyerson writes in the *LA Weekly* (1999) that the Los Angeles County Federation of Labor and its head, Miguel Contreras, are now "working with community-based organizations that the more hidebound, pre–John Sweeney labor movement would not have touched."

In each city the coalitions look different, but almost all are diverse. For example, the Cambridge coalition consisted of the Eviction Free Zone, Carpenters Local 40, and the National Lawyers Guild. The Duluth campaign was supported by fifty-seven groups, including active participation from the Minnesota Senior Federation, AFSCME, Green Party, Low-Income People Organizing for Power, and the Catholic diocese and other churches. Interviewees listed hundreds of other participating organizations, including groups such as Jobs with Justice, Students Against Sweatshops, American Friends Service Committee, Childcare Services, ACORN, the African-American Economic Justice Project, the NAACP, AARP, Citizen Action, NOW, the Grey Panthers, and a number of interfaith groups. New relationships have also been established with academics, small business owners, and elected representatives.

How real are these coalitions? While some community activists still have reservations about the politics of their local labor councils, many make positive remarks about their new alliances. Bill Appel from Metro Justice in Rochester, New York, commented in an interview that the national AFL-CIO is one of the few shining lights of hope in today's political environment. While Metro Justice has existed for about thirty years, it had never worked with the labor council and most of its affiliates until the change in national and local labor leadership. Now, Metro Justice is working "even with the more conservative unions" in the area. Bill is highly optimistic about the potential of the Rochester campaign, initiated by the CLC, to create new alliances. Tom Hucker of Progressive Montgomery in Montgomery County, Maryland, also had praise for the CLCs' involvement in the campaign there (interview with Tom Hucker 1999).

Perhaps the best measure of the strength of the coalitions is to look at the ability of the groups to last and move on to new joint projects. In almost every case, the CLCs stated that the living-wage coalitions were still in existence and had plans to work together again. In some cities, the coalitions have already succeeded in passing successive legislation, as in Milwaukee, where the group passed an ordinance at the city, county, and school-board levels over three years. Others are working on other legislative campaigns, such as "Right to Organize" ordinances. A few of the cities used the campaigns to help build new organizations, such as a labor–clergy alliance in Madison, Wisconsin, and the East Bay Alliance for a Sustainable Economy in Oakland, California. Many of the CLC leaders feel excited about their new relationships and expect to continue working together. As Ian Robertson said, "The momentum is there, the ball is rolling, we don't want to let it stop" (Robertson interview 1999).

Building Political Power

In terms of building political power, Detroit's campaign was most closely linked with political activities as it was explicitly designed to get out the vote for the CLC's endorsed candidates. The ordinance itself passed with 80 percent of voters voting in favor. David Reynolds points out that, given that the ballot itself was five pages long, with the living-wage proposal at the end, the fact that 120,000 people voted on the initiative "shows that we got the message out"[5] (interview with David Reynolds 1999).

In other cities, CLCs are trying to use the campaigns as one part of a larger strategy to build political power and improve (or clarify) relations with elected officials. According to John Goldstein from Milwaukee, "Politicians who we pushed to support the resolution could no longer claim they were labor supporters [if they didn't support it]. It helped clear the air" (interview with John Goldstein 1999). In San Jose, the South Bay CLC made the living-wage ordinance an issue in the city council elections when it endorsed Cindy Chavez, the CLC political director, against a Chamber of Commerce candidate. After Chavez won, South Bay CLC president Amy Dean remarked that "Linking the living wage campaign to the candidate was key to victory" (Moberg 1999). In Somerville, Massachusetts, the CLC used the ordinance as leverage for endorsements. According to Frank Borges, "The Labor Council said they would not endorse any candidates until the Living Wage was passed—and we actually bypassed the primaries without endorsing anyone, because it [the living-wage ordinance] wasn't passed yet" (Borges interview 1999).

However, other campaigns have not had as much success in using the issue as leverage in campaigns. For example, in Madison, Wisconsin, mayoral candidates were challenged to come out in favor of the proposal in order to receive endorsements from the CLC and Progressive Dane, the local New Party chapter. Most of the mayoral candidates did endorse the proposal, including the victorious candidate. However, once in office the new mayor stalled on passing the law and eventually worked to oppose it. This has been a common problem for several living-wage coalitions that are able to get endorsed candidates to support the law during their campaign but find that those candidates are either lukewarm or even on the opposition once they are in office. This was the case in Montgomery County, Maryland, where two candidates who had been backed by the CLC and Progressive Montgomery, the New Party chapter spearheading the campaign, reversed their support and voted against the proposal. In response, the labor council was still able to politicize the issue by running a full-page advertisement in a local paper with the headline, "BETRAYAL." The ad called on the two council members to resign. As Eric Huebeck writes in *Labor Watch,* "It is highly unusual for the AFL-CIO, at any level, to allow a confrontation with the Democratic Party to spill out into the public arena," which may suggest that CLCs are beginning to develop more political independence.

Other CLCs have also talked of punishing those officials who did not support the living-wage ordinance. Frank Borges of SEIU in Somerville,

Massachusetts, says "One board [of aldermen] member played both sides, telling us he was for it, and business he was against it. We punished him. He had won the primaries for the mayor's race and was expected to win, but labor got behind the campaign for a candidate who was a key sponsor of the Living Wage bill, and she won" (Borges interview 1999). In Boston, the lone dissenter on the ordinance vote, Thomas Keane, was targeted as "enemy number one" (Jonas 1999) by labor in the next round of elections. However, Keane easily won the election over the labor council–endorsed challenger.

Fighting Outsourcing and Privatization

Have any of these victories translated into success in slowing down or reversing the trend in city outsourcing and privatization? In almost all of the campaigns, interviewees said that the living-wage ordinance has had either no impact or an unknown outcome. Some of these respondents seemed unconcerned with the threat of privatization in their community, while others noted that it was a problem but that they were not sure that the living-wage ordinance would have an effect. In a few cases, living-wage activists are putting greater emphasis on the issue. As will be discussed later, implementation of the Los Angeles ordinance resulted in a few contracts being brought back "in-house" in that city. In Duluth, Erik Peterson claims that the campaign "did raise the issue of privatization, and gave language to nonlabor groups to talk about this issue. It's not just about self-interested public unions, but other groups can ask, why do away with good jobs?" (Peterson interview 1999.) However, the Duluth ordinance does not cover service contracts, so there is no direct connection between the law and the issue. In St. Paul, Bernie Hess is trying to convince AFSCME to use the living-wage ordinance and coalition to fight the mayor's attempts to privatize the water and other services (Hess interview 1999).

Organizing Workers

Have the campaigns helped with new organizing? Although the living-wage movement has had an impact on building coalitions and helping the image of labor, this has not yet translated into a lot of new organizing opportunities. Only a few CLCs could point out specific organizing drives that resulted from the living-wage campaigns. Most respondents said that there wasn't much of an effort to use the campaigns for this purpose, but rather that the coalitions are now attempting to get new legislation passed that would assist organizing more directly, such as a Right to Organize resolution or card-check neutrality agreements for economic development assistance.

Some interviewees noted that they would have liked to use the living-wage movement to assist with organizing, but there are difficulties for CLCs in doing this. For example, John Goldstein of the Milwaukee CLC says, "We weren't in a position to connect it [to organizing]. Had we had more unions involved in organizing some of these services—school bus drivers, for example, are all unorganized, but were affected by the ordinance—it could have been a great tie-in. But no one was organizing them" (Goldstein interview 1999). Fred Veigel of Ypsilanti echoes this point: "I don't think it will lead to new organizing here. Maybe in large cities if someone stays on top of it, but not in small towns. Unions are not after these kinds of companies, with two to three people working on the contract cleaning City Hall, for example. No one wants to go after that. They won't put their money, effort or time into something unless it's large numbers" (Veigel interview 1999). Most labor councils feel constrained in what they can do to promote organizing, given that they are only voluntary federations and not unions themselves.

On the other hand, a few CLCs have managed to use the campaigns to spur new organizing. The campaigns can assist organizing by generally improving labor's image and educating workers about unions, as well as by creating a chance to get organizing leads during the campaign itself; for example, in Chicago, the campaign helped SEIU find leads for new organizing among home-health-care workers (Swope 1998). Keith Kelleher of SEIU says, "You can bet that every time we do an action around living wages we get calls." Local 880 has won two elections so far, representing approximately 800 workers, as a direct result of contacts developed during the living-wage campaign (Kelleher interview 1999).

In addition, in a few places the campaigns have encouraged more cooperation between unions, which has helped resolve jurisdictional disputes. In Los Angeles, for example, HERE and SEIU have worked together with the CLC to build a large-scale organizing drive at the airport.

The campaigns can also assist organizing by inserting union-friendly language into the laws. CLCs have worked with labor lawyers to think creatively about ways to incorporate union-friendly language into the ordinances themselves. For example, the San Jose ordinance contains a requirement for "third-tier review" of contract bids. This process requires the city council to consider the bidder's history as an employer and the working-condition commitments in evaluating the bid. Specifically, all proposals must include information on compensated days off provided to employees, the number of employees that would be retained to staff the contract, and provisions for "labor peace." The labor peace clause allows the city council to deny a contract to any firm with a poor labor-relations record, in order to help assure that the services provided will not be disrupted due to a labor dispute. The recently passed Hartford ordinance also contains a labor peace clause, which essentially requires any publicly funded development project to allow workers to be represented by a union in exchange for a no-strike agreement. Jill Hurst of SEIU explains that the clause is desirable for labor because "it forces [employers] into negotiations with us" (interview with Jill Hurst 1999).

Another strategy is to have a "union opt-out clause," such as the one in the Los Angeles city ordinance. This is language that allows the employer to not pay the living wage if there is a collective bargaining agreement (CBA) in place and if the union and employer both agree to let that agreement supercede the living-wage ordinance. Some organizers believe this clause gives unions leverage in organizing, because some employers may agree to card-check, which allows the union to bypass the National Labor Relations Board election process, or they may agree to be neutral in an organizing drive, in exchange for a CBA that provides less than the living-wage amount.

These types of clauses are controversial among union organizers: some argue that the labor peace agreements may actually hurt companies where there are organizing drives going on. The fear is that the clause could backfire and that the city council could deny contracts to firms where there is a lot of labor activity. Others note that the labor peace language is useful, but that people must not think that this can replace actual organizing. As SEIU organizer Keith Kelleher states, "You can't have labor peace if you don't have labor war," suggesting that real gains can not be won without workers engaging in organizing struggles on the ground, no matter how strong the ordinance language is (Kelleher interview 1999).

Furthermore, the "union opt-out" clause is seen by some as a tool that may build the labor movement at the expense of workers. Supporters of the clause claim that organizers would never use the clause unless it was in the workers' interest. For example, the workers may agree to lower wages in exchange for better health coverage or job security. However, accepting a lower wage violates the arguments made during the living-wage campaign that say that the living wage is the basic minimum necessary for workers to survive. In either case, there is a handful of ordinances that do contain these kinds of clauses designed to assist union organizing.

In a few cities, the living-wage coalitions have worked to go beyond the living-wage laws to get agreements with the city over specific development projects. For example, in Oakland, the living-wage campaign helped lead to new organizing at the Port of Oakland, which is being dredged in order to renew and expand it. The CLC has worked with their community allies from the living-wage campaign to win a project labor agreement to build the new development with union jobs. Part of this agreement included hiring halls and an apprenticeship program to prioritize hiring from the community (Goff interview 1999; Business Wire 1999).

Finally, the campaigns can lead to new organizing through struggles over implementation, where the union is able to use the ordinance as leverage with companies. In Los Angeles, the Labor Council helped coordinate the effort to use the living wage as leverage for new organizing. After the city ordinance was passed, the Living Wage Coalition met with union representatives to work out the details of how to translate living-wage organizing into union organizing. The coalition hired a researcher to monitor all contracts coming up for bid and to notify the unions about the companies making bids according to a system devised by the unions and CLC that would help alleviate jurisdictional disputes. The unions can then approach employers and offer them assistance in lobbying for their bid in exchange for card-check and neutrality in an organizing drive.

In one case, the Living Wage Coalition and HERE were successful in getting the city council to deny a bid for concessions in the new terminal of the Ontario Airport[6] to antiunion Host Marriott and instead award it to a company that had signed a neutrality agreement, CA-1. The union has since won an election and a contract with CA-1. In addition, the coalition was able to persuade the council to hold up the approval of a concession contract at Los Angeles International Airport for Host Marriott until the company wrote a letter to the Department of Airports, assuring that they would comply with the living-wage ordinance and not harass union organizers who talked to workers. Host Marriott eventually agreed to comply with the ordinance, even before submitting its bid for a renewal and expansion of its lease, and in exchange, the Living Wage

Coalition endorsed its bid for a revision and expansion of its lease (Uchitelle 1999). The endorsement is powerful because LACFL executive secretary-treasurer Miguel Contreras is one of five appointees on the city Airport Commission.

Organizing around the ordinance also led to coalition members discovering that janitors at the city library were not being paid the living wage and that the workers had a variety of grievances with their employer. With the coalition's assistance, these workers asked the city to enforce the living-wage ordinance. When the employer refused to comply, the city took away the contract and brought the work back "in-house," returning the workers to the SEIU bargaining unit. The workers joined the union and received the living wage.

Barriers to CLC Involvement in the Living Wage Movement

Despite the growing number of CLCs involved in campaigns, most of the six hundred labor councils, and even many of the more than a hundred and fifty Union Cities are still not involved in campaigns. There are a number of reasons this is so. First, many people believe that the living-wage movement will not necessarily help the labor movement. Some say that if the low-wage workers receive higher wages through the ordinances, they will have less incentive to want a union. According to Bernie Hess, of UFCW in St. Paul, "the perception by the labor bureaucracy was that [the living wage ordinance] would lessen their power" (Hess interview 1999).

As mentioned previously, many of the contracts covered by the ordinances are not prime targets for the CLC's affiliates because of the type of job or the number of workers covered. Others may believe that the labor council should not waste limited resources on a campaign that will not directly benefit existing members, on the small chance that some new workers will organize. In addition, there are cities where there is little contracting out or where there are more pressing issues, and the CLC just has not found a living-wage campaign to be the most useful strategy to pursue.

In addition, some CLCs are hesitant to get involved in campaigns where the mayor or influential council members oppose the issue. Tim Leahy of the Chicago Federation of Labor (CFL) said that they wanted to distance themselves from the living-wage coalition that was "personalizing [the living wage campaign] against Mayor Daley" and "digging themselves in a hole" (Leahy interview 1999). While Leahy believes that the CFL was responsible for getting the city to consider the living-wage proposal, Keith Kelleher says that joint campaign of the CFL and the living-wage coalition sealed the victory and that the CFL was on board with the campaign because of overwhelming support from its affiliates (Kelleher interview 1999).

But what about those places where there are ongoing campaigns, where the CLC has not been involved? Most of the community activists whom we interviewed about this issue were not willing to be quoted publicly about the weaknesses of their local CLCs. One activist said that the CLC was a "dinosaur central" that did not really do anything. Others remarked that their CLCs were "pretty conservative" or "the more traditional type of union leadership." A number of activists claimed that the labor councils were mostly interested in state legislative issues, not local organizing.

Even in some of the cities where the CLC was involved in the campaign, there were a few criticisms of their level and type of participation. Some of the labor council leaders prefer to try to push through the living-wage proposal by "talking with their friends" on the city council or in the mayor's office. This is a natural response for those labor leaders who have not had much or any experience in building grass-roots community campaigns, but even in some places where the CLC leadership is fairly progressive, the temptation to avoid the hard work of a two-year organizing effort is great when CLCs know they have connections in the city administration. Of course, it is not only labor leaders who are tempted to pass the ordinances this way, but CLCs, with their histories of COPE endorsements and lobbying are especially prone to top-down legislative approaches.

Some of the new CLC leaders recognize this and have made efforts to at least combine their lobbying with real community organizing. For example, Alameda County CLC Executive Secretary-Treasurer Judy Goff acknowledges that the fast time frame of the Hayward campaign hurt their ability to do community outreach. She comments, "To maximize success, a living-wage campaign should not be rushed" (Goff interview 1999). CLC members in the living-wage working group in Sonoma County, California, realize this as well. While the group believe that they have the votes to get ordinances passed in several places, they have decided to wait to find staff so that they can "organize municipal/city wide coalitions," among other things (interview with Martin Bennett 1999).

It must be noted that this way of thinking is a dramatic change for many in the labor movement, as union organizing tends to operate in a very short time frame. Because living-wage campaigns are more like community organizing than union organizing, many from the labor movement have had to adjust their ideas about how the campaigns should run. As Russ Davis of Massachusetts Jobs with Justice comments, "Community organizers tend to think in terms of years: union organizers tend to think in terms of weeks" (R. Davis 1999). However, the lessons learned in living-wage campaigns may an analogy for unionists who rush through organizing campaigns to win an election, only to find that they don't have enough support built to last through the fight for a first contract. It appears that the living-wage movement is helping some union leaders to see the benefits of longer-term community organizing-type campaigns.

Conclusion

So, how would we assess the participation and contribution of CLCs in the living-wage movement? CLC involvement in the campaigns must be judged according to how effective CLCs are in getting the ordinances passed, as well as how successful living-wage campaigns are for meeting the goals of the CLCs and the labor movement.

In terms of involvement in the movement, although the numbers are not yet overwhelming, CLCs *are* rising to the challenge to get living-wage ordinances passed by local governments. CLC involvement in the movement has increased since the first campaign in 1994, when the labor movement was hesitant to get involved in living-wage campaigns. In fact, a 1998 article in the *American Spectator* describes the living-wage movement's success in raising the minimum wage where unions or the Democratic Party have failed to do so. The author, Daniel McGroarty (1999), writes that it is not "John Sweeney's AFL-CIO" that has run this successful stealth campaign against a generally conservative political establishment, but the New Party and ACORN. But unlike the early days, recent campaigns are just as likely to be initiated by a CLC as by a community organization. Of the fourteen ordinances passed in 1999, approximately ten had significant involvement from a CLC. CLCs are also increasing their commitment to the campaigns in terms of resources. For example, a growing number of CLCs are funding staff people to run campaigns. This involvement alone is a tremendous change for the labor movement. It is highly unlikely that a decade ago these community campaigns would have had the general support of the AFL-

CIO, state federations, and dozens of CLCs around the country. Although the transition to a new labor politics is uneven, the degree to which the labor movement has opened up to working with other groups must not be understated.

But how successful are the campaigns in meeting the other goals of the CLCs and the labor movement in general? According to the AFL-CIO Executive Council, the role of labor councils is to:

- Build a strong local movement of working people *through mobilization and education* to support working families' issues in their communities,
- Build a strong *political voice* for working families by engaging them and their communities in the political process,
- Build a united and effective *public voice* for working families by fostering strong and diverse unions that participate actively and positively in their communities around a common agenda. (AFL-CIO Executive Council 1999, emphasis in original)

Given this mission, the living-wage movement appears to offer promise in meeting each of these goals, to different degrees. Many of the CLC leaders seem to believe that the campaigns helped somewhat in educating workers about wage equality and about the labor movement itself, although this effect seems moderate. In fact, the two facets seem interrelated: Where there was greater mobilization, there was more education. For example, in Duluth, where the campaign canvassed approximately one-fourth to one-third of the city, a city poll showed that the ordinance had 70 to 80 percent support. On the other hand, Dave Slaney in Cambridge remarks that because there was never enough opposition to the campaign to make it controversial, general public knowledge about the issue is low (interview with Dave Dlaney 1999). This point simply echoes what was mentioned earlier—that it can be much easier to just push a living-wage ordinance through a city council than to organize a real campaign. Where the CLCs are taking the time to do the latter, the results are stronger.

In terms of building a political voice, the CLCs have been able to use the living-wage issue as leverage in political endorsements. However, CLCs need to be better prepared to deal with those officials who go back on promises made to get an endorsement. Even some of the city councilors who vote in favor of the proposals attempt to win exemptions for firms in their districts, or controversial industries. As Fred Veigel notes, "If you want a tough ordinance you have to put it on the ballot—

if you want to get it the way labor wants it. Otherwise, when you get into the city council, even if you are friends, there are always these negotiations—exempt this, change that." Rarely does labor have enough clout to get the strongest ordinance passed through council. This is also a consideration after the law is passed: Certain living-wage allies who voted for the law may be more reluctant to fight hard on implementation when it means confronting a particular employer.

In short, without the power to hold candidates accountable, the labor movement has no political independence and is tied to "politics-as-usual": supporting candidates you think will win and hold power in the city rather than supporting those who most closely represent a labor platform. For example, in Los Angeles, the CLC endorsed Richard Riordan's reelection for mayor even after he opposed the living-wage proposal (and had taken numerous stands against workers and unions). Although they later reversed their decision, they still voted to take no stance in a race between Riordan and his opponent, Tom Hayden, a firm backer of the living-wage ordinance.

Similarly, the San Francisco Labor Council backed mayoral candidate Willie Brown for reelection, over his opponent Tom Ammiano, the main sponsor of the living-wage proposal. While the living wage should not be the litmus test for any candidate endorsement, Brown refused to support any specific proposal and worked to stall adoption of an ordinance. Despite this and other questionable items on Brown's record, such as his silence on hospital privatization, the labor council took an unprecedented step by endorsing him very early in the campaign. The result of all of this was that, rather than using the issue to build political clout, the CLC may have hurt itself. According to an article in the *SF Weekly,* numerous rank-and-file unionists actively defied their leadership in supporting the Ammiano campaign (L. Davis 1999). One union member quoted in the article noted the dissatisfaction with the Brown endorsement: "It came down to leadership saying this is where we are, and folks saying this isn't right. It's machine politics and it's not fair. I know of a lot of folks who outwardly had to pitch for the mayor because the Labor Council put us up to it, but really just didn't want to perpetuate that machine." In both of these cases, it appears that the CLC preferred to endorse the candidate with a better chance of winning rather than the living-wage supporter, on the hopes that the endorsement would pay off in future political negotiations.

Without real political independence, it seems unlikely that the living-wage movement can make a major contribution to changing labor's political voice. Without new strategies to improve accountability of leaders on key issues, the best the living-wage movement can offer is to solidify political relationships, turn out voters and as John Goldstein puts it, "clear the air"—sort allies from enemies (Goldstein interview 1999). Building real political power will require more than an ordinance or community campaign: It will require new alternatives for labor in the political arena, such as campaign finance reform, new political parties, and/or proportional representation. CLC leaders must confront this reality if they truly want to translate living-wage victories into a lasting political gain.

Finally, what is the potential for the living-wage movement to help with organizing? The campaigns to date have shown that translating living-wage campaigns into union organizing is not easy, especially in cities where the covered contracts are spread out or do not cover a lot of workers. It is especially difficult for CLCs to find ways to assist their affiliates with organizing: As Fred Veigel points out, they can't force anyone to do anything.

CLCs can still use living-wage campaigns to support new organizing indirectly, by improving the image of the labor movement locally and getting low-wage workers to think about unions as a solution to improving working conditions. But to directly assist organizing, perhaps the best success has been in cases where the labor council has been able to play a coordinating role in large-scale efforts to organizing on a workplace-wide basis, such as with the airports in Los Angeles, or occupation- or industry-wide, such as the temporary-worker project in the Silicon Valley. In these cases, the CLC can help affiliates to conduct research on the local economy, settle jurisdictional disputes between unions, raise funds to hire organizers, lobby political representatives, and coordinate citywide actions to support, for example, fights for recognition or contracts. Although living-wage ordinances have similarities, they do differ greatly from city to city. The laws can be written to target specific employers or industries where there is a greater potential for organizing or where the labor movement has a strategic interest. For example, in cities where there is a heavy reliance on tax abatements and subsidies to redevelop the downtown, the CLC can work with its affiliates to ensure that these types of assistance are covered by the laws and then lay out an organizing plan.

While CLCs cannot force any union to do the actual organizing, they do not need to sit back and wait until their affiliates are ready to go. Rather, labor-council leaders can use living-wage campaigns to build coalitions, political power, an atmosphere that supports unionization, and tools that can be used as leverage in new organizing.

Notes

The author is grateful to Mark Brenner and Dan Clawson for comments on earlier drafts of this article, and to the many CLC leaders and living-wage activists who agreed to be interviewed for this chapter. The research was funded in part by the Political Economy Research Institute at the University of Massachusetts–Amherst.

1. Since the Baltimore ordinance, two ordinances were passed in 1995, five in 1996, eight in 1997, ten in 1998, and fourteen in 1999.

2. These are: Detroit, Ypsilanti, and Ypsilanti Township, Michigan; Miami-Dade County, Florida; Tucson, Arizona; Los Angeles County, Oakland, San Jose, and Santa Clara County, California; Hudson County, New Jersey; Buffalo, New York; Kankakee County, Illinois; and Dane County, Madison, and Milwaukee City, County, and School Board, Wisconsin.

3. These include Hayward, Pasadena, and Los Angeles, California; Hartford, Connecticut; San Antonio, Texas; Chicago and Cook County, Illinois; Duluth, Minnesota; and Boston, Massachusetts.

4. See, for example, Sander and Lokey, 1998; Luce, 1999; and Niedt et al., 1999.

5. The other two contractor–living-wage ordinances that have been run as ballot initiatives in St. Paul, Minnesota, and Missoula, Montana, were not successful. Neither of these was a CLC-run campaign.

6. The city of Los Angeles owns several airports, including one in the city of Ontario, California.

Bibliography

AFL-CIO Executive Council. 1999. "Building a New Labor Movement in Our Communities: The New Alliance." Pamphlet, August.

Business Wire. 1999. "Precedent-Setting Project Labor Agreement Approved by Port of Oakland Board Commissioners." August 11. http://businesswire.com.

Cook, Dan. 1999. "When the Minimum Wage Isn't Enough: Can the Living Wage Movement Jumpstart SC Progressives?" *Free Times,* July 14–20.

Davis, Lisa. 1999. "Breaking Ranks: Union Leaders Endorsed Willie Brown, but the Rank and File Has Other Ideas." *San Francisco Weekly,* November 10.

Davis, Russ. 1999. "Labor and Community Organizing: Jobs with Justice." Presentation at the Labor Center, University of Massachusetts, Amherst, November 23.

Huebeck, Eric. 1999. "The Living Wage Campaign." *Labor Watch.* Washington, DC: Capital Research Center, October.

Jonas, Michael. 1999. "Labor Group Endorses Newcomer to Replace Seat Vacated by Keane." *Boston Globe,* August 15, p. 2.

Luce, Stephanie. 1999. "The Role of Secondary Associations in Local Policy Implementation: An Assessment of Living Wage Ordinances." Doctoral diss., University of Wisconsin–Madison.

McGroarty, Daniel. 1999. "The Year of the Living Wage: Political Activists Succeed Where Unions Have Failed." *American Spectator,* May 32(5): 52–53.

Meyerson, Harold. 1999. "The New Unionism Finds a Home." *LA Weekly*, October 8, p. 15.

Moberg, David. 1999. "Unions Push Personal Politics in Lieu of Cash Contributions." *Boston Globe,* October 10, A28.

Niedt, Christopher, Greg Ruiters, Dana Wise, and Erica Schoenberger. 1999. The Effects of the Living Wage in Baltimore. Economic Policy Institute, working paper no. 119.

Sander, Richard, and Sean Lokey. 1998. "The Los Angeles Living Wage in Operation: The First Eighteen Months." Report presented to the Los Angeles City Council, November 16.

Swope, Christoper. 1998. "The Living Wage Wars." *Governing Magazine*, December, p. 23.

Uchitelle, Louis. 1999. "Minimum Wages are Being Set, City by City." The *New York Times*, November 19, C1, C19.

Interviews

Appel, Bill. Metro Justice, Rochester, New York. November 1999.

Bennett, Martin. Sonoma County CLC. November 1999.

Borges, Frank. SEIU Local 285, Somerville, Massachusetts. October 1999.

Chapin, Perry. South Central Iowa Federation of Labor. October 1999.

Cole, Andrea. Greater New Haven Labor Council. November 1999.

Coley, Tom. Triad CLC, Greensboro, North Carolina. October 1999.

Earhardt, Ray. Southerners for Economic Justice, North Carolina. November 1999.

Ellis, Sean. Metro Detroit AFL-CIO. October 1999.

Gillette, Richard. Clergy and Laity United for Economic Justice. January 1998.

Goff, Judy. Alameda County (CA) CLC. September 1999.

Goldstein, John. Milwaukee CLC. November 1999.

Greenwich, Howard. East Bay Alliance for a Sustainable Economy. December 1999.

Hess, Bernie. UFCW, St. Paul Trades and Labor Assembly. October 1999.

Hucker, Tom. Progressive Montgomery, Montgomery County. November 1999.

Hurst, Jill. SEIU Connecticut State Council. November 1999.

Janis-Aparicio, Madeline. Los Angeles Living Wage Coalition. April 1997.

Johnson, Dick. Minneapolis CLC. November 1999.

Johnson, Tammy. Progressive Milwaukee. April 1997 and 1998.

Kaczarowski, John. Buffalo CLC. November 1999.

Kelleher, Keith. SEIU Local 880 and ACORN, Chicago, Illinois. December 1999.

Leahy, Tim. Chicago Federation of Labor. October and November 1999.

Ozegovich, Mike. South Florida AFL-CIO. September 1999.

Peterson, Erik. AFSCME Council 96, Duluth, Minnesota. October 1999.

Reynolds, David. Metro Detroit AFL-CIO. October 1999.

Robertson, Ian. Southern Arizona Labor Council. October 1999.

Romano, Tony. Greater Boston Labor Council. October 1999.

Salvatore, Bob. San Antonio CLC. September 1999.

Schroeder, Kathryn. South Central Federation of Labor, Wisconsin. September 1999.

Shaw, Jack. Hudson County CLC. November 1999.

Silvia, Christine. AFL-CIO Policy Department. November 1999.

Slaney, Dave. USWA, Cambridge, Massachusetts. November 1999.

Veigel, Fred. Huron County CLC. September 1999.

III

Voices from the Field

8

Building Organizing Capacity

The King County Labor Council

Jonathan Rosenblum

On the face of it, it seemed an unlikely duo: Barbara Judd, a tax expert and Microsoft temporary worker, talking about developing tax-assistance software at Microsoft's swank suburban campus; and Harry Lucia, a truck driver, describing how his blue-collar compatriots haul forty-foot cargo containers on and off the piers at the Port of Seattle, Washington. Both represented the growing army of "contingent" workers in the U.S. economy, and on June 24, 1999, they sat in front of the local Jobs With Justice (JWJ) Workers Rights Board panel, describing their common struggle in seeking a voice at work in the new global economy. Judd told the Workers Rights Board how she and workers at the Microsoft tax project decided to organize earlier in the year because of a lack of job security and disparate wage and benefit packages. Hired through four different "temporary" agencies, her seventeen colleagues included MBAs, certified financial planners, attorneys, and CPAs. "This is our dilemma," she said. "Everyone wants the product of our labor. No one wants to take responsibility for us as employees. We asked our agencies for reclassification and pay adjustments, and they said, 'We can't help you, Microsoft makes all the rules.' We asked corporate Microsoft and they respond, 'Talk to your agency, we are not your employer'"(Video 1999). When they organized with WashTech, an affiliate of the Communications Workers of America, the same thing happened. Microsoft denied its status as employer, claiming that the role fell to the myriad of personnel agencies that pay one-third of all Microsoft workers. And the temp agencies' lawyers maintained that Judd and her colleagues did not form "an appropriate bargaining unit."

"God bless you, sister," truck driver Lucia said. "We're just like you, we're contract employees." Lucia described how he and about seven hundred port truck drivers haul containers from the piers to railroad yards and warehouses in Seattle and Tacoma. Thanks to deregulation and union busting, the drivers are no longer considered regular employees paid by the hour. Instead, the dozens of trucking firms that manage the movement of containers call them "independent owner-operators" and pay them by the trip. Lucia told how the drivers, many of whom are recent immigrants, would wait in line for three hours—unpaid—to pick up their load. He described how they were denied health benefits; how they had no job security from one day to the next; and how, when they organized with Teamsters Local 174 and demanded bargaining rights, the trucking firms—just like the temporary hiring agencies at Microsoft—denied any responsibility as employers. "We are trying through the Teamsters to organize ourselves so that we too can demand the pay that we ought to be getting and get out of this downward spiral," Lucia said. "The steamship lines—they're the ones that tell these people what we can make. We have no say" (Video 1999).

The stories that Lucia and Judd told to the Workers Rights Board frame not just the structural changes in today's economy, but also the organizing challenges that face the labor movement. If organized labor is to rebuild working-class power, it must restore and solidify bargaining clout in its traditional base, and it must build worker organization in emerging and traditionally nonunion industries. Recognizing this, the new leadership of the AFL-CIO has established an organizing department, expanded its Organizing Institute recruitment and training center, and created a $20 million organizing fund (AFL-CIO Web A 1999). A portion of the organizing budget has been dedicated to determining whether central labor councils (CLC), in tandem with local and international union support, can significantly ramp up both the quantity and quality of organizing activity. In select cities, the organizing department has established cooperative organizing campaigns involving the CLC and local unions. One such project was established in Seattle, which historically has enjoyed an active labor movement, from the citywide general strike in 1919 to more recent organizing around the World Trade Organization. Now two years old, the organizing project, Seattle Union Now (SUN), offers some early lessons about the strengths and limitations of a CLC-based organizing model.

The Twin Challenges in Seattle

Labor's slide has been amply measured and documented. Nationally, union density—the percentage of nonsupervisory workers belonging to a union—fell from 35 percent in 1955 to just around 14 percent at the close of the 1990s (Census 1980; BLS 1999). Two primary factors drove this: First, corporations launched a concerted offensive against workers and their institutions. And second, most unions focused on defensive battles to the exclusion of reaching out to the unorganized masses. Especially in the last twenty-five years, companies broke up industrywide agreements, contracted out and exported union jobs, took advantage of new technologies to downsize employee payrolls, and forced concessions at the bargaining table. With few exceptions, unions fought defensive battles to maintain collective bargaining agreements and to mitigate the worst of the rollbacks and job cuts. Broad sectors of union leadership were content to focus on the political arena without a strong emphasis on mobilizing from the shop floor level. And they accepted labor's marginal role in deciding the major social and economic questions of the day. As a result, both union and nonunion workers took huge hits. Tracking the fall between 1978 and 1995, the period of maximum union busting and corporate profit taking, was a 12 percent decline nationally in workers' buying power and a commensurate loss in health care and retirement benefits (AFL-CIO Web B 1999). Seattle was no different from the nation as a whole. Between the 1950s and 1998, union density fell from 55 percent to 21 percent (Lynch 1999; Bureau of Labor Statistics 2000). The 1980s, especially, saw union busting in a range of traditionally organized industries. Taking a cue from the Reagan administration, Seattle's downtown hotels and restaurants broke the master union contract agreement in 1984 and succeeded in decertifying many bargaining units. In 1986, Lockheed Shipyard, once a Seattle union stronghold, locked out more than nine hundred workers and broke the union. In trucking, deregulation provided transportation executives with an opportunity to break Teamster power in the Port of Seattle cartage industry, which went from 90 percent union to less than 30 percent, with a concurrent loss of bargaining power and a decline in wage and benefits standards (King County Labor Council et al. 1999; interview with Bob Hasegawa, secretary-treasurer, Teamsters Local 174, spring 1999). Paralleling the loss of union density in traditionally organized sectors of the economy has been the growth of the technology sector, with notable players including Microsoft, amazon.com, AT&T Wireless, and the venture-capital firms that crowd around and gamble on the fortunes of hundreds of start-up companies. Seattle's technology sector has been devoid of unions during its meteoric twenty-year rise. For many in the industry, the excitement of being in a cutting-edge industry, the satisfaction of making good money, and the allure of bonuses and stock options made the idea of unionization seem archaic, if not downright bizarre. But as the industry has matured, technology executives, driven by keen attention to stock valuation, have shaped the workplace into the more familiar American picture of haves and have-nots. Today in many technology development firms more than half the workers are in "contingent" positions—jobs with no future security and often lacking benefits and advancement opportunities.

"New Voices" and the CLCs

By the late 1980s, on shop floors and in communities throughout the country, a growing number of (relatively) young, discontented workers and new leaders were arguing for—and acting upon—a broader, more aggressive response to attacks on workers' rights and standards of living. Within some international unions, this spirit of resistance manifested itself in innovative organizing efforts—such as the Service Employees' Justice for Janitors campaign—or in militant contract struggles, such as the Mine Workers' eleven-month strike against Pittston Coal in 1989–1990. Notably, both campaigns refused to play by the establishment's rules. The SEIU janitors' campaign rejected the increasingly unfair and unproductive National Labor Relations Board process and substituted direct action aimed at building owners. Pittston miners and their supporters challenged the company with widespread civil disobedience. Both of these campaigns recognized that workers win better pay, job security, and dignity through direct action and even extra-legal tactics.

When the New Voices slate won the National AFL-CIO leadership in 1995, it pledged to support such efforts to reverse labor's course. The more aggressive, unapologetically pro-worker spirit of John Sweeney,

Richard Trumka, and Linda Chavez-Thompson stood in stark contrast to the Kirkland administration, which only lethargically had resisted the North American Free Trade Agreement (NAFTA) and the rise of Newt Gingrich in the early 1990s. The New Voices leadership recognized the potential for CLCs to help rebuild labor activism, and launched the Union Cities initiative, which emphasizes the CLCs' key role in supporting the rebuilding of local union member activism and in promoting new organizing. One of the goals of the Union Cities project is to encourage unions to shift 30 percent of their resources into organizing, to activate local union members for campaigns, to hire staff dedicated to organizing, and to take on larger, more ambitious organizing targets.

New Voices in the CLCs

In the spring of 1993, the executive secretary of the King County Labor Council, Rick Bender, was elected to head the Washington State Labor Council, AFL-CIO. His place was taken by Ron Judd (no relation to Barbara Judd). A Kentucky native and outdoors enthusiast, Judd had moved to Washington state in 1978 to work as a mountaineering guide on Mt. Rainier. When winter came, he took up electrical work at Seattle's Todd Shipyard and became active in the International Brotherhood of Electrical Workers (IBEW) and the Metal Trades Council. As the Todd workers' chief shop steward, Judd promoted labor's fight back against a lockout by Lockheed, and after serving on staff with IBEW Local 46, Judd was elected in 1990 to head the Seattle–King County Building and Construction Trades Council. Under his leadership, the Building Trades piloted new internal education and mobilization training programs and began to look more seriously at organizing. In early 1993, Judd turned down an offer from Washington's new governor, Mike Lowry, to become head of the state Department of Ecology, opting instead to run for King County Labor Council (KCLC) executive secretary.

Judd brought to the KCLC a spirit for coalition work, risk-taking, and militancy, which dovetailed nicely with other changes the Seattle labor movement was undergoing. A series of large strikes in 1989 had prompted unions to begin coming together to support one other in organizing, bargaining and strike support, politics, and broader economic development campaigns. In 1993, local unions and community organizations had joined together to form a Seattle-area chapter of Jobs With Justice, which became a mobilizing arm in support of labor and community struggles. This solidarity in action served as a platform for the council's Union Cities initiative and for what developed into the joint AFL-CIO and KCLC organizing project, Seattle Union Now.

New Leadership, New Militancy

On May 27, 1993, Jobs With Justice and several international unions coordinated a national day of action to protest the ineffectiveness of labor laws in protecting workers' rights. Demonstrations were held at twenty-six National Labor Relations Board (NLRB) offices around the country. In Seattle, organizers from the service employees' and steel-workers' unions coordinated the action in which two hundred labor and community activists, including the newly elected CLC leader, protested at Seattle's Federal Building. Judd told the NLRB regional director, "We want you to take the message back loud and clear that we are dead set on changing the labor laws in this country. We will not stop until it happens and we will do whatever it takes to make it happen" (Scanner 1993). Chanting and singing, eighteen protesters sat in front of the building's elevators and were arrested. First in line to be handcuffed was Judd. His participation in the action sent a message to affiliate unions and CLC delegates about the need for direct action and provided a direction for those frustrated with the NLRB. His arrest created legitimacy for more aggressive, confrontational tactics in labor struggles. The civil disobedience garnered widespread publicity, and at the June meeting of the King County Labor Council Judd urged delegates to get involved in demonstrations, to give money to support the arrestees, and to build the Jobs With Justice chapter. With increasing support from the CLC, the new activists joined a contract fight being waged by Alaska Airlines flight attendants. Bargaining, which had proceeded anemically for two years, had finally reached an impasse. Union members launched a campaign of job actions they called CHAOS—Create Havoc Around Our System. The company threatened to replace workers permanently. To support the flight attendants, more than five hundred labor and community activists marched with them to Alaska Airlines' corporate headquarters near Seattle's airport. Some twenty-five activists staged a sit-in at Alaska Airlines' headquarters and were arrested.

As the conflict continued, it became linked to the national struggle over "replacement workers" when the company "permanently replaced" seventeen flight attendants, allegedly for engaging in a sick-out. Concurrently, Congress was considering legislation banning the use of "permanent replacements." The bill was being blocked by a handful of senators, including Washington State Republican Senator Slade Gorton. When the airline fired the flight attendants, JWJ, the KCLC, and the Washington State Labor Council turned their attention to Senator Gorton, staging protests at his public appearances throughout the state and holding an interfaith candlelight vigil outside his Seattle home. When Gorton opened a new campaign office south of Seattle, a hundred activists—including some of the fired flight attendants—showed up at the welcoming party, complete with a cake iced with the words, "Workplace fairness now!" The workers' gift was firmly declined by the rattled senator and his panicked staff, who barred the door to their open house.

These demonstrations raised the standard for creative, militant, non-violent labor protest in Seattle and succeeded in uniting two key constituencies of the labor community: moderates and progressives. More moderate trade unionists, who focused on labor's role in politics, were drawn to the fight because they saw Gorton as an arch-enemy to unions in all industries. And progressives joined, eager to bring creative street heat and heightened militancy to a highly public contract fight. Six months after the first CHAOS action, the flight attendants won a new contract—and hundreds of labor activists shared in the victory.

The passage of the North American Free Trade Agreement gave impetus for more actions and increased militancy. In March 1994, labor was still licking its wounds from the NAFTA political battle when an international trade conference convened in Seattle. As business executives from the United States, Canada, and Mexico prepared to sit down to a "Free Trader of the Year" awards banquet, some two hundred labor and community activists flooded into the conference center, chanting, "No justice, no dinner!" A lone security guard stood in front of an escalator leading to the banquet hall. "You can't come through here," he told the picketers. "How much do you make an hour?" one protester retorted. "They can't be paying you enough to stop us—we're coming through." Eyeing the mass of picketers, the guard made a quick calculation. "You have a point there," he said, and stepped aside (interview with Dave Schmitz 1999).

The protesters surged up the escalators, swarmed into the dining hall, and announced their willingness to be arrested. As a handful of Seattle police and private security guards looked on helplessly, demonstrators danced in a conga line around the banquet tables. The dinner was canceled. The militancy of the action—a precursor to the 1999 World Trade

Organization protests—succeeded without any arrests because, as one participant noted, "so many were willing to be arrested." The action was about more than disrupting a dinner. "As long as we keep making noise, business and the politicians won't forget about the workers and the importance of preserving jobs, " said Machinists Lodge 751 Steward Jim Hutchins (*Aero Mechanic* 1994).

New Militancy, New Organizing

In his first year at the helm of the King County Labor Council, one of Judd's priorities was to bring the resurgent energy around street heat into the arena of new union organizing. A number of unions, such as the Building Trades, the Service Employees, the Steelworkers and the Teamsters unions, had recently begun shifting more resources into organizing. Moreover, several relatively young, energetic organizing directors and rank-and-file activists were pushing for more organizing and more interunion cooperation.

In the past, the Washington State Labor Council had convened an organizing committee, which had served primarily as an information clearinghouse. At the urging of organizers and activists, the King County Labor Council called a meeting to determine how to better promote and coordinate organizing among unions. The new organizing committee, including more than fifty organizers from two dozen different unions, assembled a plan in early 1994 to create a KCLC organizing program to be staffed by a full-time organizer. Key unions in this effort included the Steelworkers, Machinists, United Food and Commercial Workers, Carpenters, Service Employees, Teamsters, International Brotherhood of Electrical Workers, and Office and Professional Employees.

The purpose of the organizing program was to coordinate activities among unions, share information and lessons, and get unions to support one another on large and important organizing targets. To fund the organizing program, the KCLC organizing committee called for a five-cent per capita assessment from local unions. In a council vote in late 1994, the organizing assessment won majority support, but by the narrowest of margins failed to gain the necessary two-thirds. Some dissenting unions were skeptical of the national push for organizing, while others saw the need but felt the responsibility lay within the individual affiliates, not with the CLC.

Despite the defeat, the committee went back to the drawing board without the designated staff resources, but with a renewed intent to collaborate on organizing. "We didn't see the vote as a failure. On the contrary, it was clear there was widespread support for organizing initiatives," said Dave Schmitz, organizing director for UFCW Local 1001. "We just had to come up with a stronger plan and involve more locals. We needed to develop the same urgency and fighting spirit about organizing that we had at actions such as the NAFTA banquet," he said (Schmitz interview 1999).

The rise of the New Voices slate in the national AFL-CIO during the summer of 1995 gave hope to local activists that the call for new organizing and militancy would now be echoed from the national leadership of the labor movement. "I didn't know much about Sweeney but I knew Trumka from hearing him speak at National Rainbow conventions," recalled Norma Kelsey, an office worker and president of OPEIU Local 8 in Seattle. "Trumka's ideas were the same ideas that the local leadership here valued and were putting into action. The New Voices leadership gave us support and encouragement. After years of feeling like we didn't have a vibrant national movement, we came into a new light. It felt like a renaissance age for labor" (interview with Kelsey 1999).

As fortune would have it, one of the first public expressions of this new spirit sprang from strike action by the Seattle area's bedrock of organized labor, the Boeing Machinists. In October, 1995, Machinists struck Boeing over a new contract. The major issue was job security. In their first joint appearance as the newly elected AFL-CIO leadership, Sweeney, Trumka, and Chavez-Thompson came to Seattle and led 6,000 Machinists and supporters in a march and rally. The King County Labor Council, along with leaders from surrounding CLCs, formed a labor–community coalition in support of the striking Machinists. The council's labor agency, the social service arm of labor, coordinated food, monetary and holiday gift donations to the strikers. And Jobs With Justice led rallies, a prayer vigil, and a petition drive in support of the Machinists, augmented by an interactive strike-support Web site. After sixty-nine days on the picket line, Boeing Machinists won an agreement with improved job security language. More than the actual contract language itself, the public and the strikers saw the fight cast in a larger context. "It shows the company and the United States—*corporate* United States—that when the unions stick together, we have some power," Machinist Joan Williams declared at the ratification victory party (KOMO TV 11 P.M., December 12, 1995).

A little more than a year later, labor activists were handed another opportunity to develop greater unity through street heat. In February 1997, eighteen musicians, members of the American Federation of Musicians Local 76, struck the prestigious Fifth Avenue Theatre in downtown Seattle for a new contract. Management responded by "permanently replacing" the workers. It was opening night of the Disney show, "Beauty and the Beast," and the spotlight was on the theater as more than a thousand labor and community supporters jammed Fifth Avenue, blocking traffic and forcing a halt to the show. Every evening, a brass band of musicians played outside the venue while crowds of up to two thousand supporters picketed, danced, and held up traffic.

Violinist Libby Poole-Pressley describes rounding the street corner to the theatre early one evening as the crowd began to build: "I was floored. Here were hundreds of people helping us out in a stunning show of labor and community solidarity. To us striking musicians, it felt like magic to have the power of that many people behind us" (*Labor's Voice* 1998). After thirteen days on strike, the musicians won a stunning contract victory that the area labor movement embraced as a textbook lesson in militant direct action.

New Organizing and Union Cities

Throughout 1997, while the labor council continued to provide support to striking workers, the KCLC organizing committee accelerated efforts to bring the same strategic focus to bear on large-scale organizing targets. The resource question, which had run into a dead end with the 1994 per capita vote, resurfaced as a result of two new developments at the national level. First, the new AFL-CIO organizing department had committed to supporting local and regional organizing efforts. Representatives from the national organizing department began visiting Seattle to discuss large-scale campaign plans with organizing committee members and local union leaders. And second, the launch of the Union Cities effort, which sought to bring together union organizations at all levels "in a common effort to educate and motivate union members, defend the right of workers to join unions, organize thousands of new members and create a powerful new political voice that speaks for working families" (AFL-CIO 1997). While not promising significant national subsidies for organizing, Union Cities gave political and programmatic support to those calling for a shift of local resources to organizing.

To launch Union Cities, the AFL-CIO leadership announced a series of

"Organizing for Change, Changing to Organize" conferences in spring 1997, to be held in thirteen different cities. Seattle was the site of the first conference, drawing together more than seven hundred labor activists and community and religious allies on March 26. President Sweeney challenged the gathering to "join in a national organizing campaign to rebuild our membership and rekindle our movement" and then led activists in a march to support the United Farm Workers' strawberry campaign (*Labor's Voice* 1997).

To meet this challenge, forty-nine elected union leaders and staff came together at the Boeing Machinists union hall in Seattle for a full-day Union Cities planning session on July 22, 1997. The organizers reviewed some sobering facts: While the 21 percent union density in the Seattle area remained well above the national average, the labor movement was not organizing anywhere near the level necessary to grow, much less tread water over time (Bureau of National Affairs 1997). Out of about 562,000 private-sector, nonconstruction workers in King County, fewer than one thousand had participated in a union representation election in the previous twelve months (Rosenblum 1997). A small number of unions were growing significantly, but overall union growth through new organizing was statistically inconsequential—the 21 percent density figure being rescued only by a temporary hiring-up of machinists at Boeing. With the economy projected to add 27,000 jobs a year through 2007, the labor movement would need to increase its organizing efforts tenfold in order to achieve the 3 percent growth outlined in Union Cities (Anne E. Casey Foundation 1997).

Meeting participants identified a number of roadblocks to organizing:

- Low membership involvement in the local union's day-to-day activities
- The "servicing" model of unionism, which relegates members to a passive role within the organizations
- The crisis-management nature of union life, which makes it hard to plan and execute ambitious, long-term organizing strategies
- The lack of significant resources to carry out ambitious organizing
- Difficulty in getting union leadership and members to "think outside the box" and consider innovative approaches
- Labor laws that stifle organizing

Overcoming these obstacles, the participants agreed, would require pooling resources and experiences to support new organizing.

Following the day-long meeting, seven different committees of organizers and activists distilled the session's ideas into a coherent plan, and on September 3 the council's full delegate body adopted the King County Labor Council Union Cities Organizing Plan. The plan established staff and KCLC delegate responsibilities for carrying out Union Cities work. It set forth work plans for boosting organizing and mobilizing, launching a broad-based union member educational program, and initiating outreach to build a more diverse delegate body and KCLC executive board. The plan also challenged KCLC affiliates to adopt resolutions committing more resources toward organizing and greater membership involvement. To coordinate implementation of Union Cities, the council hired a full-time organizer. In essence, the organizing committee's 1994 goal of creating a CLC-funded organizing position had been achieved.

Union Cities and the Cooperative Organizing Project

As the Union Cities project moved forward, the KCLC organizing committee advanced its internal discussions, along with talks with national AFL-CIO staff, on large-scale organizing efforts. First the council and the Hotel Employees and Restaurant Employees International Union (HERE) explored the prospect of an ambitious organizing drive among hospitality workers. The local HERE branch had not organized significantly in many years as downtown union density in hotels had fallen from 50 to 20 percent. The KCLC and HERE collaborated on research and development of a comprehensive campaign plan that included community outreach, economic leverage, and multiunion support actions. Some fifty-seven organizers and activists, including more than forty outside of HERE, contributed their insights and expertise to the plan.

The process of planning out a single campaign inspired Organizing Committee members to look at creating an umbrella structure that would support several different campaigns simultaneously. During the fall and winter of 1997–1998, the organizing committee conducted a comprehensive review of affiliate campaign prospects and surveyed unions on their existing organizing resources and future needs. Several unions identified large-scale campaigns that they intended to launch in 1998–1999. Through the survey, the committee identified the primary needs as increasing capacity to mobilize members in support of organizing; researching organizing targets and industries; and training and developing staff and volunteer organizers (King County Labor Council 1998).

Committee members sought to create a central body of staff organizers that would work toward three principal objectives:

1. The organizing center would assist unions in planning campaigns and building increased capacity to organize.
2. With the coordination of the center, unions would commit to support one another in campaigns by mobilizing for actions and by contributing staff and members to make house visits and participate in other campaign activities.
3. The center would coordinate a communitywide campaign that would articulate workers' demands for the right to organize, reestablishing the right to organize as a civil right.

Working with Andy Levin, AFL-CIO assistant director of organizing, the committee drafted a "statement of commitment" that outlined the structure and staffing of the new central organizing body and the criteria by which local campaigns would access its resources (AFL-CIO 1998).

The document envisioned that unions would become "core unions" once they were approved by an executive committee consisting of AFL-CIO and KCLC leadership. To be a core union, an organization had to have organizing targets, a campaign plan, sufficient trained staff, and rank-and-file volunteer organizers. The union had to commit to train 15 percent of its members in organizing and mobilizing within two years. It had to have a detailed internal mobilization program; sign up 5 percent of its members on "member pledge forms," which committed them to participating in a given number of actions a year; and commit to mobilize its members to support other organizing campaigns. Additionally, unions were encouraged to try innovative organizing strategies that did not rely on the National Labor Relations Act, to organize in new sectors, and to take on large-scale campaigns (AFL-CIO 1998).

Core unions would work with staff at the organizing center to boost membership involvement and to advance their campaigns. The center's staff would include six organizers and an office manager hired by the AFL-CIO and the KCLC's Union Cities organizer. The staff would include organizers who specialized in mobilization, community outreach, research, internal and external communications, and training. The "statement of commitment" described the AFL-CIO staff roles as capacity building, not as filling the gaps in an affiliate's campaign (AFL-CIO 1998).

The SUN Comes Out in Seattle

In spring 1998, the final editing changes were made to the "statement of commitment," the project was officially named "Seattle Union Now: Our Voices at Work," and a director was hired. On May 14, 1998, President Sweeney came to Seattle to launch Seattle Union Now (SUN). Along with Judd and leaders from the five initial "core unions," Sweeney signed the SUN Statement of Commitment. The five core unions and campaigns were:

1. Service Employees District 925, which that month had launched a campaign to organize childcare teachers throughout King County;
2. Teamsters Local 174, which was in the process of kicking off a campaign to organize truck drivers at the Ports of Seattle and Tacoma;
3. The International Alliance of Theatrical and Stage Employees Local 15, which planned to build on its base of stagehand and theater work;
4. The International Longshore and Warehouse Union, whose Inlandboatmen's Union affiliate planned to organize local tug and barge workers;
5. The Hotel Employees and Restaurant Employees union, which intended to build on its base of 3,000 members in the Seattle area.

Of these five campaigns, two were already were in full swing. On May 1, SEIU District 925 launched its child care teacher organizing campaign with a march and rally led by the AFL-CIO secretary-treasurer, Rich Trumka, and the AFL-CIO Women's Department director Karen Nussbaum. The union announced its intent to reach out to the 6,000 child care teachers in King County, whose pay averaged $7 an hour, and to organize them into a regional master contract. The campaign envisioned a nontraditional approach to organizing. Teachers would petition their managers to recognize their union voluntarily, avoiding the lengthy delays of the NLRB election process. The carrot for employers was a union commitment to work jointly with employers and parents to secure increased public funding. As Mary Mosteller, a child care teacher, described it, "Parents cannot afford high rates and centers cannot afford to improve pay and benefits on their own." The alliance of teachers, directors, and parents would provide the clout to raise standards in the industry, she explained (*Labor's Voice* 1998).

Meanwhile, Teamsters Local 174 was launching its campaign to organize some seven hundred truck drivers at the Ports of Seattle and Tacoma. On May 31, the union convened a campaign kick-off rally at the cavernous hall of Local 19, International Longshore and Warehouse Union. More than two hundred owner-operator drivers showed up and pledged to unite for uniform pay and benefit standards on the waterfront. Truckers also heard solidarity messages from other waterfront unions, from the King County Labor Council, and from U.S. Congressman Jim McDermott (Democrat of Washington State).

As with the child care workers, the truck drivers mapped out a nontraditional campaign. Because most of the drivers were considered independent contractors, they could not utilize the National Labor Relations Act to gain recognition. Instead, they intended to build political support and launch direct actions in order to bring the port economic powers to the bargaining table.

In both of these campaigns, along with the other core union efforts, the local union was expected to run its field operations, such as worker contacts and building the worker organizing committee. SUN assisted the unions in building their internal mobilization capacities and supported the campaign with research and with media, political, and community outreach. The SUN communications organizer, Gretchen Donart, trained child care teachers and organizers on media relations. KCLC Union Cities organizer Verlene Wilder led a lobbying effort to get additional child care funding through a county ordinance. For the truckers' campaign, a SUN research organizer, Julie Farb, developed an ambitious research agenda, while other staff worked with the union to reach out to immigrant communities.

The SUN project also tried to capitalize on public displays of solidarity and organizing success in order to embolden unions to increase their organizing efforts. In July 1998, the King County labor council honored employers who had signed voluntary union-recognition agreements in recent months. A packed meeting of the council—plus a dozen local elected officials—honored two theater managers who had recognized the stagehands union, the president of a local truck driving company, and several directors of child care centers. "It was an incredible night. Imagine, a standing ovation inside the Seattle Labor Temple—for *employers*," said Kim Cook, organizing director for SEIU District 925. "It was an amazing opportunity to celebrate employers who do the right thing. We seldom get the chance to do that. Labor is more used to staging boycotts and organizing picket lines. And here we were encouraging people to patronize businesses because they had done the right thing when it came to workers' rights" (interview with Kim Cook, December 1999).

Revising and Refocusing the Project

SUN's goal was to bring several more campaigns into the fold by the end of 1998, but as the fall progressed, several union organizing efforts remained technically outside SUN's orbit. These included the Communication Workers' budding WashTech union; SEIU's regional health care organizing campaign; and the Building Trades' exploration of a multicraft, industrywide organizing drive. Organizers from these and other unions often said they "weren't ready yet" to join SUN as "core unions." Chief among the reasons given was that unions felt they could not promise to meet the criteria for inclusion, in particular the numerical goals for educating and mobilizing rank-and-file members. It became clear that the criteria for admission to SUN, conceived in order to help drive more ambitious and thoughtful campaign planning, was actually an impediment. Accordingly, in November and December, SUN staff and leadership met with core unions and decided to replace the exclusive participation model with a more flexible model under which the project would engage a broader range of unions and recognize the different levels of internal membership development and campaign planning.

SUN leadership and the core unions rewrote the original statement of commitment. The principles of capacity building and multiunion efforts remained intact, but the unions, the KCLC, and the AFL-CIO agreed this would come about without the formal admission process. The new document gave priority to unions that had ambitious, sensibly funded and staffed campaigns; that involved rank-and-file union members; and that committed to work with SUN and other unions on an ongoing basis. It pointedly omitted the numerical criteria, instead stating that priority would be given to unions that were "prepared to mobilize for and support other unions in their organizing work" and to campaigns that "support and reinforce our overall Right-to-Organize campaign." Decisions about which campaigns would receive more assistance would be decided by the SUN director, in consultation with the SUN executive committee (Seattle Union Now 1999). In January 1999, the change was made official as President Sweeney and Executive Secretary Ron Judd of KCLC signed the revised statement of commitment.

SUN staff immediately began working with other unions. During the winter, Building Trades union workers from all crafts, along with many workers from outside the construction trades, donned boots and hard hats on Saturday mornings and trudged out in the Seattle rain to talk with workers at nonunion job sites. Amid cozier surroundings, union members began meeting with clergy and lay activists to discuss how to support SEIU's Catholic health care campaign.

In February 1999, the King County Labor Council convened a day-long "Right to Organize" conference. The goal of the conference was twofold. First, it aimed to refocus unions on opportunities to organize together; and second, it aimed to have the unions, along with community allies, sketch out common capacity-building goals and objectives, given the broader mission of SUN. Some eighty union organizers and members turned out for the planning session, along with close to twenty community and religious allies. As with the Union Cities planning process, the group broke into areas of focus, and in the month following each group developed a comprehensive set of benchmarks on which unions would work together. The result of this meeting was the King County Labor Council's Right to Organize Plan, which was adopted unanimously by the delegates on March 17 (see Table 8.1).

The plan committed the council and its unions to support organizing campaigns in four major areas: mobilizing, community and religious outreach, political accountability, and organizing contingent worker.

In the arena of mobilizing, unions agreed to bolster their capacity to mobilize for one other and committed to develop a rapid-response team of activists, trained and prepared to engage in direct action on very short notice in defense of organizing workers. On community and religious outreach, organizers recognized that typically outreach consisted of emergency appeals for support once a campaign was underway and facing employer opposition. To move away from "911 calls," or "the rent-a-caller routine," unions committed to building lasting relationships with community and religious allies through a comprehensive outreach program. And they committed to support efforts by Jobs With Justice to strengthen its Workers Rights Board.

With many organizing campaigns dependent on the active support of elected officials, the organizers agreed to educate politicians early on in campaigns and to ask for their explicit involvement at various stages. The actions could include writing letters, walking picket lines, making house visits, attending organizing committee meetings, or joining workers

---

Table 8.1

King County Labor Council Right to Organize

Overall goals

1. Establish and develop the Right to Organize as a commonly recognized civil right.
2. Develop workers' power by mass union organizing in King County.

We will accomplish our goals by:

Mobilizing thousands of union members and community allies in defense of workers rights.

Winning broad public awareness of the obstacles workers face and broad public support for Right to Organize initiatives, with street heat actions, media campaigns and other activities that shine a light on injustice.

Holding employers and their allies accountable when they resist workers' efforts to organize, and bolstering and supporting those employers and their allies that respect and honor workers' Right to Organize. We will do this through our political work, through legislation and litigation, and through public campaigns.

Challenging ourselves to undertake larger, more ambitious organizing campaigns that build worker power.

Source: KCLC 1999.

---

in public actions. The organizers committed to track the involvement of elected officials and to utilize their record of involvement in the council's political endorsement process.

Finally, unions recognized the need to collaborate more directly in the area of organizing contingent workers. Increasingly, unions were organizing independent contractors, contract workers, seasonal or casual workers, and involuntary part-time workers. With so many of these campaigns falling outside the traditional rubric of organizing, unions saw a need to develop common approaches on campaigns involving contingent workers. The result of the right to organize planning process was a contingent-worker-organizing task force.

SUN in Action

It was expected that the SUN project would drive the work in the Right to Organize Plan, and in 1999 SUN staff worked with eighteen different affiliate unions on fourteen different organizing campaigns, ranging from initial research efforts to first contract fights. Much of the work was not specific to an individual campaign, but rather focused on union membership education and mobilizing, and on solidifying relationships with community, religious, and policy-making allies.

For instance, increasingly unions found themselves organizing immigrant workers, most notably among the port truck drivers and in the region's booming construction industry. These efforts challenged unions to educate current members about the need to organize workers of all nationalities and to deal with the nation's anti-immigrant laws. On May 19, the U.S. Immigration and Naturalization Service (INS) raided a construction site one block north of the Seattle Labor Temple. A SWAT team of armed and bulletproof-vested INS officials stormed the property and detained nine Mexican and five Canadian construction workers, several of whom had been involved in a previous organizing drive. Union organizers heard about the raid and rushed to the site; three were detained when they protested the INS action. "It was because of my skin color," Jimmy Matta, a Carpenters union organizer, said. "The first people they targeted were Latinos" (*Seattle Press* 1999).

That night, Joe Watling spoke before a packed meeting of more than a hundred and fifty King County Labor Council delegates and guests. "It took months to put together a crew with all the construction going on in this area," he said. "We were like family—it didn't matter what language you spoke or the color of your skin. We were united. Today the INS came and took away my family."

The following month, union members and community allies rallied outside the Seattle INS office as part of the AFL-CIO's week of activities highlighting workers' right to organize. Mary Tran-Thien, a SUN community organizer, worked with immigrant rights groups to educate union members about the discriminatory impacts of immigration law, and initiated an outreach effort to educate community allies about workers' rights. And the King County Labor Council supported community-sponsored lobbying to have Seattle and King County declared an "immigrant safety zone," which would limit local government cooperation with INS law enforcement.

Other SUN work was more explicitly campaign-driven. In August, frustration boiled over and tempers exploded at the Port of Seattle, where truck drivers had long endured three-hour lines and falling pay. The previous month Canadian drivers struck the Port of Vancouver, B.C., over pay and union recognition. On August 17, Seattle and Tacoma drivers parked their vehicles in solidarity and also as a means of advancing their own union recognition demands. "We're sticking together to make a better life. We need health care, good wages. Nobody's making a living now," said truck driver Yetbarek Tesfay, an Eritrean (Ethiopian) immigrant who emerged as one of the strike's leaders (International Brotherhood of Teamsters 1999).

With the Teamsters, SUN formed a solidarity committee of waterfront and railroad unions, coordinated media outreach work; and developed presentations to local, state, federal, and port elected officials. SUN staff also played an active role in picket-line organization and direct-action tactics. Fortuitously, the strike occurred as the union and SUN neared completion of an extensive "white paper" detailing the drivers' conditions and the economics of the ports. Campaign organizers rushed the paper into publication, and it became a widely quoted document in the media and in political circles. For two weeks, drivers picketed port terminals in Seattle and Tacoma, staged a brief sit-in at the Burlington-Northern railroad yard, and broadcast their plight extensively through the general media and industry press. Combined with smaller solidarity actions by Longshoremen and other port unions, the strike crippled the movement of containers for several days before trucking companies and shipping lines rebounded with an aggressive, and ultimately successful, back-to-work push. The strike was broken, but the campaign moved forward with renewed militancy and public awareness.

Central Labor Body Organizing

The experiences of the King County Labor Council since 1993, and more specifically the role of SUN since mid-1998, suggest three basic roles that a central organization can play in promoting organizing. A strong CLC can *support* affiliate organizing drives, *coordinate* organizing among several affiliates, or *initiate* organizing drives. Often the relationship between the central labor body and an affiliate will cover more than one of these categories. The specific relationship between a CLC and an affiliate is subject to many variables, notably local organizing history and existing relationships between affiliates and the central body.

Supporting Organizing

Supporting organizing is the most common—and to many, the most natural—of the three basic roles of the CLC. As a supporter, the central labor body mobilizes labor and community allies or draws on its political connections for campaign backing. In this role, the central body's role follows from developments in the field campaign. The supporter role is successful to the degree that the affiliate has a realistic campaign plan, ample trained staff, and a functioning worker organizing committee. Campaigns that lack the basic field elements necessary for success cannot rely on "shortcuts"—external support or political leverage—to overcome an employer's antiunion campaign.

A prime example of the way the KCLC provided support for organizing is SEIU District 925's child care teacher campaign. While SEIU District 925 staff has been responsible for the core work of contacting workers, building organizing committees, and developing workplace actions, SUN's role has been to assist at the grass-roots level with specific projects such as mobilizing other union members for rallies, providing training for media outreach, and giving research assistance. The KCLC also supported the child care campaign by honoring employers who had voluntarily recognized the union at a labor council delegate meeting, and by encouraging union families to patronize those centers. Finally, SUN staff worked closely with District 925 to develop and lobby for a local ordinance that, once enacted, provides additional county funds to child care centers that had collective bargaining agreements.

Coordinating Organizing

CLCs that enjoy close relationships with affiliate unions may be asked to help coordinate organizing campaigns. In contrast to the support role, a CLC that is playing a coordinating role will be involved in developing and implementing strategies, often including elements of the field campaign. The coordination can take two forms: facilitating multiunion activities or helping to coordinate particular aspects of an affiliate's campaign.

The multiunion coordinating role of the CLC works best when the individual affiliates ask the central body to convene and facilitate multiunion activity. In late 1999, several local unions found themselves in organizing and bargaining struggles against Providence Health Care, the largest health provider in Washington state. The unions—including two Service Employees International (SEIU) locals, two United Food and Commercial Workers (UFCW) locals, and an Office and Professional Employees Union (OPEIU) local—all had significant membership at Providence facilities, but had little experience in working together to win recognition and fair contracts at the Catholic health care provider. Working with SUN staff, leaders of the five unions put together a coordinated campaign plan. In February 2000, more than fifteen hundred Providence workers at three hospitals signed a solidarity newspaper ad. Workers in the different bargaining units distributed joint literature and coordinated bargaining and workplace actions. SUN staff assisted with community outreach and publicity.

For the CLC to coordinate effectively on an individual affiliate's campaign, there must be a high level of trust between the leadership and staff of the affiliate and the central body, and a common agreement on the strategic approach. With close coordination between the affiliate and the CLC, the campaign is better able to benefit from all the assets of the labor community. An example of this is SUN's role in the Teamsters' port-trucker organizing campaign. SUN staff and KCLC leadership were involved in strategic campaign discussions with Teamster staff and leadership, and also participated in key meetings with the union's organizing committee. SUN staff and Teamsters worked together in developing the campaign's "white paper," and also teamed up on visits to port and elected officials. The team effort produced solid campaign events, and also showed a broader, more united front to policy makers, the media, and employers that the union needed to influence.

Initiating Organizing

Occasionally, the central labor body plays a more active role in initiating organizing drives. WashTech, the CWA affiliate, provides an example of this. In September 1997, prior to the launching of SUN, three Microsoft workers met with the KCLC's Union Cities organizer. They had done some internal organizing at the technology giant, convening meetings of several dozen workers in the previous year over various workplace issues. But they were not certain that they wanted to form a union, and local union organizers were far from confident that technology industry workers could be organized. Working out of the labor council's office, the workers organized a modest-sized committee of technology-industry employees and contractors. Two months later, the industry persuaded the state of Washington to eliminate overtime-pay provisions for computer professionals. The move prompted an outpouring of anger from technology workers—including more than eight hundred letters to the state denouncing the action—and the workers' organizing committee took off. In early 1998, CWA began discussions with the workers and later in the year signed a formal affiliation agreement.

Factors for Success

What are the factors that support CLC-driven organizing? What lessons from Seattle are transferable to other communities? First and foremost, there must be buy-in from affiliates. Some 69 percent of organized labor's funds lie within local and regional unions, and another 30 percent are controlled by international unions (AFL-CIO 1999). Central labor bodies, which control a statistically insignificant amount of union dollars, can encourage and cajole local affiliates to take on organizing, but do not have the power or resources to compel action. Affiliates must be committed to planning, staffing, resourcing, and engaging in organizing campaigns as well as to supporting the Union Cities objective of educating and activating union members. At the local level, international unions play a key role in encouraging local affiliates to undertake organizing drives and to back capacity-building initiatives that support organizing, such as Union Cities. Thus, CLC-driven organizing will be most successful when it is done in coordination with both international unions and their local affiliates.

The second key factor is leadership and commitment to working together. Both the CLC leadership and the principal officers of key affiliates need to support the concept of coordinated organizing efforts. In Seattle, the SUN project developed and achieved focus out of extensive planning discussions around Union Cities and Right to Organize. A broad range of organizers participated in the planning sessions, including principal union officers, staff and rank-and-file organizers, and community activists. The process of achieving broad buy-in to the objectives of Union Cities, and later, SUN, has proved to be as important as the actual words in the final planning document.

Relationships and interunion cohesion also get built through working together. As the planning process was advancing, Seattle-area unions increasingly found themselves working together on mobilizations and campaigns. Joint participation in picket lines, demonstrations, sit-ins, and campaigns built camaraderie and grounded the planning process in real-life experiences.

Key to building leadership and cohesion is risk taking. While there is a new surge of militancy and activism within today's labor movement, promoters of organizing need to appreciate the internal inertia built up within unions over the years and what it will take to overcome these obstacles. This manifests itself at all levels—from elected leaders unwilling to shift resources, to workers who will not get involved because they view their union as an insurance company. In this terrain, effective leadership creates the space for trying new organizing approaches, and for being willing to accept occasional failure as a learning experience.

The third key factor is a readiness to be flexible and inclusive. Cooperative organizing campaigns must be informed by local circumstances, such as the strengths and weaknesses of the area economy and the resources and relationships within the local labor movement. The SUN project began with an exclusive model, with unions applying to join SUN and to commit to specific numerical mobilization and training goals. The intention of having specific goals was to achieve accountability in the project; instead it was a deterrent, as several organizing unions initially chose to stay out of the project. By revamping the SUN statement of commitment six months into the project, the AFL-CIO and the KCLC achieved broader participation and an enhanced ability to draw on the combined resources and talents of the entire labor community.

The fourth factor is the involvement of rank-and-file union members in the process of developing organizing campaigns and in advancing systems of interunion cooperation. More than hard dollars, union members are the decisive resources in a winning organizing campaign. No number of experienced, professional union organizers can make more credible, effective house visits to unorganized workers than can a cadre of trained union members who can speak from their experiences in the community and on the shop floor.

As a testing ground for new, cooperative organizing models, Seattle is an exceptional example, with more local and national organizing resources than most communities can claim. But the lessons of Seattle do not depend on massive infusions of labor dollars. The beginning ingredients—a commitment to organizing, local and CLC leadership, and involvement of rank-and-file members—can be found or developed in dozens of communities across the country.

Reversing labor's half-century slide is not an overnight proposition, however. Only time, experimentation, and risk taking will determine what combination of resources and initiatives will produce tangible gains in union density and living standards for working families. What is clear, however, is that labor's rebirth depends on figuring out how people like Harry Lucia and Barbara Judd can organize and win bargaining rights.

Both in the traditional manufacturing and trade sector and in the growing technology sector, organizing campaigns require new models and approaches and a new scale of efforts. The CLC-based model offers hope for such innovation and ambition.

Bibliography

Aero Mechanic. 1994. "Free Traders Go Home Hungry," April–May 1994.

AFL-CIO. 1997. "Union Cities, Strong Communities." Pamphlet.

AFL-CIO. 1998. "Seattle Organizing Center Statement of Commitment." May 1998.

AFL-CIO. Web A. 1999. http://www.aflcio.org/publ/press96/pr0124.htm.

AFL-CIO. Web B. 1999. http://www.aflcio.org/publ/speech96/sp0411.htm.

AFL-CIO. Organizing Department. 1999. *Change to Organize Slide Show.*

Anne E. Casey Foundation. 1997. "Strategic Investment Plan." December.

Bureau of Labor Statistics. 1980. *Handbook of Labor Statistics.* Bulletin 2070, December.

Bureau of Labor Statistics. 2000. http://stats.bls.gov/news.release/union2.nr0.htm.

Bureau of National Affairs. 1997. "Union Membership and Earnings Data Book." City of Publication.

International Brotherhood of Teamsters, Local 174. 1999. "Why We've Parked Our Trucks—and Are Working to Make this Strike a Success." Pamphlet, September.

King County Labor Council. 1997. "Union Cities Organizing Plan for the King County Labor Council, AFL-CIO." September 3. Press release.

King County Labor Council. 1998. "KCLC Organizing Survey Results." March 26. Press release.

King County Labor Council. 1999. "Right to Organize." March 17, press release.

King County Labor Council, AFL-CIO, and Teamsters Local 174. 1999. "Bustling Ports, Suffering Drivers." August, White paper releases.

Labor's Voice. 1997. "Organizing Conference Energizes Local Labor Movement." Spring, 4.

Labor's Voice. 1998. "Worthy Wages = Quality Care." Summer, 2.

Labor's Voice. 1998. "Personal Insight: Musician Libby Poole-Pressley Shares Her Experience." Summer 5.

Lynch, Jim. 1999. "Revitalized Organized Labor Ready to Test Clout in Olympia." *Seattle Times*, January 22.

Rosenblum, Jonathan. 1997. "A Tale of Two (Union) Cities." Presentation made at King County Labor Council Union Cities Meeting, July 22.

The Scanner. 1993. "Jobs With Justice: Labor and Community on the March for Workers' Rights." December. Newsletter.

Seattle Union Now. 1999. "SUN Statement of Commitment—Amended." January 12.

Seattle Press. 1999. "U.S. Immigration Raids Bell Town Construction Site," June 2–15, 3.

Video. 1999. Videotape of event, in possession of author.

9

The South Bay AFL-CIO Labor Council

Labor's New Laboratory for Democracy in Silicon Valley

Amy Dean

As the American economic and political landscape undergoes dramatic changes, the metropolitan region is rapidly growing more important as a center of power and innovation. Through its central labor councils, the American labor movement has a great opportunity not only to adapt to this new geography of decision making but also to provide a new role for working people in the development of regional economic strategy.

The highly flexible, fast-growing, and loosely networked world of Silicon Valley, one of the premier centers of the information technology economy, challenges organized labor's established ideas of how to represent workers' interests. Working together through the South Bay labor council, the region's labor movement—which is strong in traditional sectors such as construction trades, health care, retail, and service—despite low density in the computer and information sectors, has tackled the problems of Silicon Valley's grossly uneven development by building a new political force that promotes a strategy for more equitable metropolitan growth (Bureau of Labor Statistics 1999; Labor Research Association 1999).

Central labor councils, as they attempt to revive and recreate themselves, clearly must help the labor movement organize new workers, educate its existing members, and build more political power. Just as important, however, they must also project a vision, program, and strategy for intervening in decisions about how the economy grows. These local struggles for a more just community can become the building blocks of a national movement reflecting what working families need and want for their futures.

Profound changes taking place in the American economy are making metropolitan regions a crucial focus for union strategy. Increasingly, these regions, more than established political units like cities or states, have become the building blocks of the global economy. Regions are important in part because the new economy reflects not just new products and technologies but also a new organization of capital. In the era of industrial mass production, corporations often tried to function as vertically integrated producers. Ford's massive River Rouge automobile plant—which took in raw materials to make steel, glass, and other materials; manufactured most component parts; and then assembled the cars—typified this ideal in one industrial operation. Companies integrated research, design, production, marketing, finance, and service as much as possible.

Although there were always concentrations of industries, like auto manufacturing, apparel, or machine tools, in geographic districts of varying sizes, increasingly regional economies provide the integration that corporations once tried to achieve on their own. The computer and information technology industries of Silicon Valley, for example, consist of a regional network of firms that are often highly specialized and rely on subcontractors as well as temporary or contract employees for as much work as possible, reducing themselves to a set of core workers and functions (Capelli et al. 1997; Moss forthcoming 2001). Firms regularly spin off from one another, and workers move from employer to employer. While businesses are highly competitive, they also rely on their networks of contractors, and they count on the ready availability of a pool of trained workers and skilled providers of products and services in order to grow fast or shift strategies. New businesses are formed or branches of larger corporations locate operations in the region in order to tap into this network of people and firms (Pastor et al. 1999; Storper 1997).

At the same time, these businesses and the region operate in a global economy. Capital is fluid, and firms can relocate manufacturing operations to Malaysia or software engineering to India to take advantage of lower wages but also highly skilled regional economies. These regions compete with one another, however, not only on the cost of labor but also on the richness of the physical and social infrastructure. The more advanced the technology and skilled the work, the more the local infrastructure counts. That infrastructure can include not only advanced transportation and communication, but also land-use planning, lifetime education opportunities, adequate housing and public amenities, and social institutions from local government bodies to intermediaries in the labor market.

The basis for wealth in the new economy is knowledge. Both businesses and regions compete with other firms or communities to attract or create the knowledge workers they need. Some firms may provide opportunities to learn on the job, but as businesses trim their long-term workforce to a minimal core and more work becomes temporary, much of the training essential in industries that prize innovation inevitably comes from outside the company's walls (e.g., American Society for Training and Development; National Alliance for Fair Employment).

Increasingly, workers in the new economy identify with an occupation, a profession, or a set of skills more than with an industry or certainly a company. This has always been true for some workers, from doctors to carpenters, but it is true for an even wider range of occupations in the new economy—programmers, systems analysts, technical writers, or even janitors. As the nature of work and of employment relationships change, there is a new need for intermediary institutions that provide workers with connections to employers and to their evolving occupations (Carre and Joshi 1997; Harrison and Weiss 1998).

There is a new politics of regions as well as new regional economics, and the two are linked in many ways. Metropolitan economies typically sprawl far beyond existing political jurisdictions such as city or county governments. As urban geographers have shown, regional economies are more likely to thrive if there are political institutions that integrate the regions and reduce social and economic inequalities (Orfield 1997). Also the potential for innovation in government is greatest at the regional level. Over the past two decades, there has been a shift in responsibilities for many public needs from the federal government to localities, and with political stalemate in Washington, it has become more difficult for the federal government to take on the leading role it once had as innovator. Now, sometimes by default, local and state governments must adapt to challenges previously considered national problems. At the same time, there are movements—some led by reform-minded business interests, others by more progressive citizen groups—to create more effective governing institutions that reflect regional realities. These groups include Working Partnerships USA, Silicon Valley Manufacturers' Group, Joint Venture Silicon Valley, and the Greenbelt Alliance.

As always, one of government's most important roles is that of expanding the abilities of people to do things, often described in business terminology as investing in human capital. There is a critical need for regional governmental institutions that can adapt to the new economies of regions in two ways. First, workers need education and training to be able to respond to regional labor markets. Government should coordinate regional learning networks, reducing duplication and addressing the needs both of local labor markets and of individuals, from preschool through adult worker-training programs. Education and training should not simply serve the immediate needs of a region's business but also provide people with the skills and understanding to expand their career opportunities, their power at work, and their ability to use democratic processes to shape the future of their communities.

In Silicon Valley, the new economy has generated much wealth, but it has also increased the divisions between rich and poor and between those with stable, highly skilled jobs and those with unstable jobs, both skilled and unskilled. For example, the median wage in Silicon Valley actually declined slightly between 1990 and 1998, from $17.20 per hour to $17.01 per hour, even though these years included a recession followed by robust economic growth (Bureau of Labor Statistics 1999).

Not only are most workers in the middle- or lower-income brackets not sharing in the prosperity, their jobs are becoming less secure. During that same period, when the new information economy was growing explosively, the fastest-growing industry in the state was temporary help providers—growing more than half again faster than the computer and data processing industry (Benner 1998).

The jobs pay poorly on average and offer few benefits. In Silicon Valley, personnel supply services was one of the fastest-growing industries, with a 280 percent increase in the number of temporary workers over the past sixteen years. Over 15,000 temporary employees in 1997 earned less than $10.00, with a median hourly salary of $7.19, or $14,955 annually (Employment Development Department 1994, 1995, 1997). In addition, less than 20 percent of temporary workers received health insurance from their employers, compared with 50 percent of full-time employees (UCLA 1997). Overall, temporary employees were two to three times less likely to have any health insurance coverage whatsoever (UCLA 1997).

Even supposedly permanent jobs were lasting shorter periods of time, and there was immense churning of jobs: While the computer industry grew rapidly from 1993 to 1998, it also had the third-largest number of layoffs nationally (Benner et al. 1999). Despite a surprisingly tight labor market, workers who lost their jobs on average spent a longer period unemployed in the 1990s, compared to laid-off workers in the previous two decades. Also, while the new network economy involves growing numbers of small companies, conditions for workers at those small firms typically is worse than at big companies.

The old mechanisms for providing job or income security and for supporting a lifelong career have weakened for all workers, but that is especially true in the economic sectors that are innovative, are growing fast, and are heralded as the most promising future prospects for American workers. Those industries have relied disproportionately on short-term employment and have thus invested even less in workforce development than industries more influenced by union bargaining. Ultimately the federal government will have to fund new programs to give workers more security and to enact policies that will reduce inequality, but the labor movement in general, and state federations and central labor councils in particular, can take the lead in fashioning policies for their regional economies and providing models for national strategies.

Central labor councils are uniquely positioned, given the changes in politics and economic life in recent years. Also, while there is a disquieting decline in voting participation, local and neighborhood activism is on the rise, whether it is work to improve local schools or a fight against an unwanted electric power plant. People are more likely to be involved in politics when their activism leads to results they can see. They are often more cynical about their ability to make a difference in state or national politics. Yet citizen activism so far rarely focuses on the region, even though there has been some growth in regional political structures, such as the Valley Transportation Authority (VTA), and industry is increasingly organized regionally, as in Joint Venture Silicon Valley. Indeed, the emergence of the high-tech industry lobby accentuated the importance of the Santa Clara County labor movement giving voice to its priorities for the region.

In order to rebuild organized labor's presence and highlight its value to the regional economy, the central labor council decided to pursue two parallel tracks simultaneously. The primary mission, reflecting the basic agenda of the AFL-CIO Union Cities strategy, was to strengthen the core capacity of the labor movement. Local labor councils constitute a strategic crossroads of labor—typically geographic and industrial dimensions to build real social power for working people. In Silicon Valley, we realized that we had to help unions strengthen their traditional work of organizing, bargaining, and political mobilization both by coordinating the work of the region's unions and, to complement their work, by providing additional capacities such as research, strategic communication, and recruitment of political and community support.

This central, fundamental effort to develop the capacity of the central labor council and its affiliates had four dimensions: mobilizing union members, providing support—including a favorable public climate—for organizing, engaging in political action, and leveraging relationships in the community.

In order to build a strong and vibrant labor movement with a different kind of activism that engages more members, the labor council continuously trains union leaders and members in ways to inspire active involvement by more members, to develop strategic mobilization plans in each local union, to establish work-site committees, and to develop and maintain good lists of members to turn out for demonstrations and political action. The labor council also works to strengthen organizing work in the region by establishing an organizing committee (which meets monthly to assess the needs of local unions) and by providing support during organizing campaigns. For example, when the Service Employees were organizing at Stanford Hospital against stiff employer resistance, the union was able to focus on worker-to-worker organizing contacts at the hospital, and the labor council provided assistance with communicating to the press, research, mobilizing community and political support, and organizing external campaigns to pressure the hospital. In early 2000 the Interfaith Council (an alliance of regional religious, labor, and civil rights leaders), Jobs With Justice, and Working Partnerships (a nonprofit research and advocacy institute) organized the Workers' Rights Board of civic and elected leaders to investigate disputes. Eventually the council would like to institutionalize the board as a local community body that could speak out on labor-related issues and give legitimacy to concerns not covered by the cumbersome National Labor Relations Board.

The labor council has also tried to develop the political capacity of the labor movement by linking the needs of local unions to the process of endorsing political candidates, by democratizing endorsements through engagement of rank-and-file union members, and by connecting political endorsements to long-term strategic goals of the labor movement. Initially the labor council simply tried to introduce the particular interests of local unions into the endorsement process. Then we began to educate candidates, inviting anyone who had declared the intention to run for office to learn about labor's perspective on issues before an endorsement was even considered. Increasingly we insisted that candidates not only offer verbal support for the rights of workers but also commit themselves to march or picket on behalf of workers who were trying to organize. Finally, in the late 1990s the Labor Council and its allies began developing a Community Economic Blueprint that encompasses a broader vision of what we want on issues such as transportation funding, welfare reform, housing, and land development.

During this time the labor movement has developed its own capacity not only to work on campaigns but also to carry our political work into the legislative and policy debates after elections. In addition to organizing political committees at workplaces, making door-to-door precinct contacts in working-class neighborhoods, and reaching members by telephone and direct mail, the labor council has also recruited candidates and conducted courses on how to run political campaigns at its Political Training Center. Our political committee, made up of representatives of thirty-seven affiliates, defines the key issues and targeted races. It raises money to support political staff—usually six in the primary and a dozen in the general election, who help train and mobilize rank-and-file members and oversee the campaigns in neighborhoods and workplaces.

Developing labor's political capacity also included building a force bigger than the labor movement itself. Key allies included immigrant rights organizations, students, housing activists, the faith community, trade and human rights organizations, some community-based groups, and even a few progressive segments of business.

The South Bay AFL-CIO also recognized that labor had to be a bigger player in shaping the economic landscape of the region, rather than simply reacting to decisions by business and political leaders. If we were to succeed in reinventing labor, we realized that we would have to go beyond reviving labor activity and provide a more substantive vision of how the regional economy should develop. Thus the second parallel track of central-labor-council action involved working with allies to develop a strategy to influence the process of regional economic decision making. In doing that, we had to play a role that transcended the interests of the individual unions by engaging regional economic issues that might seem far removed from union contract disputes or organizing. Given the ways in which the new economy, facing few constraints from unions or business, has increased inequality, the South Bay AFL-CIO decided it had to make social equity an issue in every debate about public subsidies, infrastructure investment, and regional policy. In particular, the labor council had to help set the terms for economic expansion and to change the social and political climate of the region in ways that would strengthen and expand the labor movement. We had to carve out a larger domain as the moral voice for workers in the community.

The labor council played a leading role in establishing Working Partnerships, an independent research and advocacy institute that has been essential for promoting this broader vision. Working Partnerships conducts research on broad trends affecting the future of the region, helps to build new democratic structures of shared governance, and provides a vehicle for experimentation with new ways to give workers a voice at work and in the community.

Working Partnerships research helps lay the foundation for labor and community campaigns by reshaping discussions about the local economy and public policy. In 1995, for example, a report by Working Partnerships was the point of departure for a campaign to make businesses that receive public subsidies and tax rebates accountable for the number and quality of jobs they created (requiring all jobs to pay at least $10 an hour) (Benner and Rosner 1998). In 1996 another report on contingent workers as the "shock absorbers" of the new economy focused attention on the quality of jobs created in Silicon Valley and led to the county employees' negotiating benefits and new protections for casual labor (Benner 1996). Another report, "Growing Together or Drifting Apart?", looked at growing inequality and the ways in which prosperity of the region was not shared, especially by people of color. It went beyond the workplace to examine trends in housing, education, and transportation and their impact on working families (Benner 1998). In "Walking the Lifelong Tightrope," Working Partnerships researchers showed how workers in the new economy throughout the state of California were exposed to greater insecurity but with fewer social supports than in the past (Benner, Brownstein, and Dean 1999). Most recently, working with the Center on Wisconsin Strategy (COWS) in Milwaukee, the Silicon Valley team will look at the function of different kinds of intermediary

institutions in the labor market, including unions and job-training programs, and assess how successfully they can positively affect wages,
benefits, and work opportunities.

These reports are contributing to the development of a Community Economic Blueprint for Silicon Valley. In 1997 Working Partnerships initiated
a series of discussions with community leaders and activists on planning
for developing the area and its infrastcucture. The Blueprint reflects our
conviction that the community and its values must drive development and
empowered people can create a vision for public policy that affects social
and economic well-being more comprehensively than traditional business-
driven policies. The process is producing successful community based initiatives. The first Blueprint initiative, providing access to health insurance
for 100 percent of San Jose's children, mobilized hundreds of people to join
Working Partnerships and the labor council in winning political commitment and funding (Gaura 2000; Slambrouk 2000; Guido 2000). The second initiative secured public resources to expand mass transit to economically
underserved neighborhoods.

The Blueprint process continues to generate a wide range of local
and regional initiatives, including inclusionary zoning to create very
affordable housing, community standards for contingent workers, and
subsidized child care for low-income families with decent wages for
care givers. Support for these initiatives comes from the continued involvement of community members and labor affiliates in defining the
problems and directing the solutions. As economic development becomes
more regional and regions replace the work of firms, so can the organizations that represent the interests of working people address a wide
range of issues to improve economic well being.

Research is one step in developing new structures for more democratic
governance that include labor unions and their community allies. Working
Partnerships is one building block, but so are neighborhood groups and
organizations like the Interfaith Committee. The structures that the labor
council wants to promote are most evident in issue campaigns. In early
2000, the labor movement proposed measurable social equity returns from
public subsidies to a new $1 billion development by Cisco Systems in San
Jose. This illustrates work linking public subsidies to better wages and
working conditions. More broadly, to promote "smart growth with equity"
and to ensure that low-income workers share in smart growth, a labor-community coalition is designing guidelines for projects that benefit from public funds. Guidelines will measure the number of jobs generated, the quality
of jobs, and access of low-income residents to jobs.

Community participation in these new democratic structures has emerged mainly as a result of the Labor-Community Leadership Institute, sponsored by Working Partnerships and San Jose State University. In each nine-week session, prominent local figures—from the head of the NAACP to an elected county sheriff—take part in classes on the regional economy and conclude with a class project involving social action. By the end of 2000, more than one-hundred and eighty people had graduated, and Working Partnerships had launched two new institutes for neighborhood groups and for leaders in faith communities.

In keeping with its drive toward greater equity, organized labor wants to use public institutions to help raise pay standards for the region. In 1999, the South Bay central labor council and its allies won the nation's highest "living wage"—$10.10 an hour with benefits, $11.35 without benefits—for companies with contracts with city government. The legislation also required any contractor who won a competitive bid to retain the current employees. Through 2000, the ordinance as affected forty-three contracts over six-hundred people. Due to the retention policy, more than five-hundred workers have been assured job stability. Future applications may include coverage of the San Jose Redevelopment Agency and exempted large lease agreements, such as the airport.

The ordinance also provides a "labor peace" proviso to prevent disruption of valuable services. For example, in 2000, when the Hayes-Mansion Hotel and Conference Center sought the city council's approval to amend their lease agreement, HERE 19 and the labor council demanded city agreement hinge on the hotel operators signing a Memorandum of Understanding agreeing to Labor Peace. As a result, there is an organizing campaign under way at the hotel involving three-hundred workers. Using the labor peace to help leverage organizing has been the largest benefit to date of the living wage.

Given the political stalemate in Washington, it is unlikely that labor law will be reformed in the near future. Living wage ordinances are thus even more significant as strategies capable of improving labor conditions and strengthening workers' rights at the local and regional levels.

Beyond creating a climate more receptive to union organizing, the South Bay AFL-CIO also recognizes that conditions in the new economy may require experimenting with new models of worker representation. Working Partnerships is now the primary vehicle for a major campaign to address the needs of temporary workers, the fastest-growing part of the labor force. Although there are temps at all levels of the corporation, from technical workers and managers to home-based manufacturing subassemblers whose children help with piecework, clerical and administrative workers—roughly fifteen thousand in Silicon Valley—make up the largest group (Employment Development Department, Santa Clara County). Altogether 40 percent of the region's workers, disproportionately women, African Americans, who number fifteen thousandl, and Latinos, are in contingent employment relationships, with about triple the national level employed through temporary agencies (Benner 1996; Bureau of Labor Statistics 2000). Welfare reform swelled the ranks of temporary employees, but industry trends suggest that contingent employment will continue to increase in any case. Although they are frequently exploited and mistreated, temps have been difficult to organize into unions, in part because of traditional union structures and restrictive labor laws.

The labor council's Temporary Employment Project includes two new institutions—a job-placement agency and a temporary workers membership organization—and a campaign for a code of conduct for temporary agencies. Launched in 1999, Working Partnerships Staffing Services helps connect temporary workers and employers, like any of the other two hundred staffing agencies in Silicon Valley, but it provides workers much more. Whatever the employer pays the agency for a temp, the worker is guaranteed a minimum of $10 an hour.

Much like the established hiring halls of the building trades, the staffing service hopes not only to place temporary workers in the best possible jobs but also to shape conditions of the labor market. Eventually we hope to work with community colleges and employer groups, for example, to establish widely recognized certification of different skill levels in clerical work to create career ladders of advancement. In addition, temporary workers can join Working Partnerships Membership Association and gain access to a health plan and other benefits, training, and the opportunity to advocate improvements for temporary workers. For example, the Membership Association and the South Bay AFL-CIO are asking the Santa Clara County Board of Supervisors to establish a code of conduct for placement of welfare-to-work clients. Under the proposed code, the county would have to place former welfare recipients with agencies that pay a living wage; offer access to affordable benefits, including health care; provide training; and treat employees fairly, including no discrimination (either for race and gender or such actions as previously reporting unsafe conditions at work) and advance notice of when the job ends.

Central labor councils can help rebuild the labor movement by supporting organizing and providing technical assistance to individual unions. They can build alliances with community groups, environmentalists, religious organizations, and other citizen groups, and they can mobilize union members and working people in general more effectively for politics. All these efforts are enhanced when they are linked together—for example, when labor presses politicians to join a picket line to support workers who are organizing or demands that developers pay workers well and protect the environment. Rebuilding the labor movement, creating coalitions, and mobilizing forces in a more coordinated and effective fashion are all necessary for working people to gain greater power in their communities. But it is also necessary to use all of the public-policy levers over the economy—taxes, budgets, and incentives—to connect the prosperity of industry and the well-being of the community and to influence private decision making to enhance social values. At the same time, generating the vision in a collaborative fashion in itself gives more power and legitimacy to labor and its allies.

Members and leaders of labor unions, working in part through their central labor councils, have to go beyond thinking of themselves as niche players lobbying for labor interests narrowly conceived. They must become the force that coordinates the broadest movement in every region to make sure that prosperity is broadly shared and that the economy benefits the majority of workers and community residents. With the growing importance of regions in both economic and political life, the solutions that labor creates in these new laboratories of democracy may provide models for the national rebirth of progressive politics attuned to the desires of working Americans.

Bibliography

Benner, Chris. Shock Absorbers in the Flexible Economy: The Rise of Contingent Employment in Silicon Valley. Report. Working Partnerships, USA, San Jose, CA, May 1996.

———. "Growing Together or Drifting Apart? Working Families and Business in the New Economy. A Status Report on Social and Economic Well-Being in Silicon Valley." Working Partnerships USA, San Jose, CA, and Economic Policy Institute, Washington, DC, 1998.

Benner, Chris, Bob Brownstein, and Amy B. Dean. "Walking the Lifelong Tightrope: Negotiating Work in the New Economy. A Status Report on Social and Economic Well-Being in the State of California." Working Partnerships USA, San Jose, CA, and Economic Policy Institute, Washington, DC, 1999.

Benner, Chris, and Rachel Rosner. "Living Wage, an Opportunity for San Jose. A Report on the Benefits and Impact of a Living Wage Ordinance on the City of San Jose." Report. Working Partnerships USA, San Jose, CA, 1998.

Capelli, Peter, Laurie Bassi, Harry Katz, David Knoke, Paul Osterman, and Michael Useem. *Change at Work.* New York: Oxford University Press, 1997.

Carre, Francoise, and Pamela Joshi. Building Stability for Transient Workforces: Exploring the Possibilities of Intermediary Institutions, Helping Workers Cope with Labor Market Instability. Cambridge, MA: Radcliffe Public Policy Institute Working Paper Series, Working Paper No. 1, 1997.

Employment Development Department, Santa Clara County, CA, 1994, 1995, 1997, OES (Occupatinal Employment Statistics) data, WPUSA calculations.

Gaura, Maria Alicia, "San Jose Urged to Move on Child Health Care," *San Francisco Chronicle,* June 9, 2000, 1.

Guido, Michelle. "Health Care Insurance for Children Proposed." *San Jose Mercury News,* May 31, 2000, 1.

Harrison, Bennett, and Marcus Weiss. *Workforce Development Networks: Community-Based Organizations and Regional Alliances.* Thousand Oaks, CA: Sage, 1998.

Moss, P. "Earnings Inequality and the Quality of Jobs." In William Lazonick and Mary O'Sullivan, eds. *Corporate Governance and Sustainable Prosperity.* New York: Macmillan, forthcoming 2001.

Orfield, Myron. *Metropolitics: A Regional Agenda for Community and Stability.* Washington, DC: Brookings Institute, and Cambridge, MA: The Lincoln Institute of Land Policy, 1997.

Pastor, Manuel, Peter Dreier, Eugene Grigsby, and Marta López-Garza. *Growing Together: Linking Community and Regional Development.* Minneapolis: University of Minnesota Press, 1999.

Slambrouck, Paul Van, "Providing Healthcare for All Kids," *Christian Science Monitor,* June 18, 2000, p. 1.

Storper, Michael. *The Regional World: Territorial Development in a Global Economy.* New York: Guilford, 1997

UCLA Center for Health Policy Research, based on data from the Current Population Survey, March 1997. Unpublished paper.

Web Sites

American Society for Training and Development, *http://www.astd.org.*

Bureau of Labor Statistics, 2000, http://stats.bks.gov/news.release/union2.nro.htm.

Labor Research Association, "Economic Notes," February 1999, table at *http://www.laborresearch.org/content3g.html.*

National Alliance for Fair Employment, *http://www.fairjobs.org.*

10

The Atlanta Labor Council

Building Power Through Mirroring the Membership

Stewart Acuff

One of the most common mistakes we in the labor movement make is seeing political action and/or political power as ends in and of themselves. They are not. Effective political action for the successful central labor council (CLC) is the strategic use of power aimed at building more power and creating more movement. It is but part of a broader strategy to contest for power for working people in a community, city, or region—one of several ways unions and CLCs develop the power necessary to deliver, to win, to address the issues of working people.

The mistake is thinking political action ends when the polls close. That mistake leads us to shy away from challenging the very officials we helped elect for fear of losing access. That mistake prevents us from developing a comprehensive strategy of building and exercising power that effectively weaves together ongoing coalition work, direct action and mobilization, and political action in a broad, long-term, comprehensive strategy to continually build and exercise power.

Therefore, effective political action is much more than the mechanical, rote implementation of phone banks, precinct walks, rallies and news conference, and poll work—as important as all that is. And the most effective political action includes an intentional integration of the CLC into the life of the community and intentional leadership development and leadership opportunities that allow the community to see itself reflected in its labor movement. In Atlanta we have worked to develop diversity in the leadership of our labor movement. We have worked to integrate the components of power building and struggle: ongoing direct action and mobilization, reciprocal coalition work, and political action. And we have been intentional about the integration of the labor movement into the life of our community.

For much too long, working Americans have been shy about the concept of power. The word has often reminded us of corruption or excess or selfishness. It has sounded unseemly. But power is critical to the ability to get things done, to accomplish goals, to win. A local labor movement that refuses to contest for power relegates itself to irrelevancy. Conversely, a local labor movement that is comfortable with the concept and exercise of power with leaders who understand how to build power, use it, and leverage it can learn to win.

In the labor movement we aim to accomplish several goals: to raise the standard of living and quality of life for working families, to push wealth downward, to generate movement for social change, to advocate more effectively for social and economic justice, to open up space or room for organizing more workers, to build more power. We build power for workers and their unions by organizing. The strength of the labor movement is directly related to its number of members. But we exercise power through mobilization, militancy, and political action. And we further leverage that power through coalitions and alliances—with either like-minded organizations or friendly political leaders.

Power is not a static, easily quantifiable commodity. Its appearance or perception can become real. The long-term strategic purpose of political action by a local CLC is to exercise power to improve the lives of working families, to promote change and justice, and to assist organizing.

In a local community, worker power works like this: A labor council, its affiliates, and its activists work in targeted school-board campaigns. They are successful in providing significant assistance to a newly elected board majority. That board majority enacts prevailing wage standards for school construction. Those standards make it possible for union contractors to do the work of opening up opportunities for building trades recruitment and organizing. That organizing locks up a larger percentage of the labor market for construction unions, providing incentive for more contractors to work union, recruiting more members, building more power. Then the new school board adopts a policy of neutrality in the organization of school staff. Janitors, bus drivers, cafeteria workers, and others organize, building more labor power.

Atlanta Olympics

It really did work that way in the 1996 Centennial Olympics in Atlanta. The CEO of the local Atlanta Olympic Committee was a silk-stockinged lawyer named Billy Payne. He selected as his chief operating officer a banker named A.D. Frazier. They planned for the first Olympics to be paid for solely by corporate sponsorships with no public funds. They had no intention of accomplishing the $1.7 billion "public" works project with union labor. They had every intention of having all the work done at the very lowest labor cost. They believed they were accountable only to the International Olympic Committee and their corporate sponsors. The Atlanta labor council met with Payne and Frazier. They were adamant. The labor council turned to Mayor Maynard Jackson and the Atlanta City Council. Mayor Jackson supported the labor council. He said publicly, repeatedly, that the work on the Olympics should be done union. The city council passed a resolution urging the Atlanta Committee for the Olympic Games (ACOG) to do the work with contractors that paid prevailing wages, offered health insurance and pensions, and provided training and a safe workplace.

But neither the mayor nor the city council could order the ACOG. Payne and Frazier ignored them. The labor council built community support. Payne and Frazier ignored the community. Finally, after a year and a half of patiently building support, the labor council took militant action. After a series of mass demonstrations including a ten thousand–person march, a takeover of ACOG's offices, a tent city with community activists, and a credible threat to stop groundbreaking on the Olympic Stadium, an agreement was signed for the construction of the stadium. That was the biggest piece of the work but only half of the construction and less than one-fifth of all the work. Right after the signing of the stadium agreement and the groundbreaking, the campaign for the 1993 Atlanta mayoral election began. Maynard Jackson was not running for reelection. He had had open-heart surgery and decided to return to the private sector.

After getting an agreement to support the labor council in the Olympic fight, in other organizing, and with public employees, the labor council endorsed Bill Campbell early—two months before qualifying. A single-member-district city councilman, with 41 percent more name recognition among Atlantans, Campbell wasn't given much of a chance against the business and establishment candidate, Michael Lomax, chair of the Fulton County Commission. But with labor council affiliates and activists providing much of the ground and field support, Campbell won. He came to the first meeting of the labor council after his inauguration—press in tow—and announced his appointment of the labor council's president to the executive board of the ACOG.

With the president of the labor council on its executive board, with the backing of the city's political leadership, and with the proven threat of militant mass action, the policy of ACOG began to change. Where possible, the work on the Olympics was done union. The building trades grew and stabilized, reclaiming commercial work after the games. The stage hands union, the International Alliance of Theatrical Stage Employees (IATSE), had its final wall-to-wall project. Transportation and communications were done union. And because it had taken such a huge, public, and long fight, the stature and importance—and perceived power—of the local labor movement was increased.

Organized Labor's Niche

Most important local political campaigns are divided into several areas of responsibility: fundraising, free media, paid media, direct mail, phone banking, volunteers recruitment and maintenance, and field and get out the vote (GOTV) efforts. Unions and union volunteers can play an important role in most of these areas.

Clearly unions raise money and participate in fund raising. In some cases unions play a very significant role in raising money. But unions cannot hope to compete with the business community in fund raising. In the 1996 federal elections, unions were outspent seventeen to one by business. By mailing endorsement notices, issues comparisons, and other political education, unions can augment a campaign's direct-mail effort to a strategic bloc of voters. And unions can be a good source of volunteers for phone banks and other headquarters work.

But it is in the broad arena of field GOTV that unions and union volunteers can add the most to any campaign. That is where the strength and capacity of the labor movement is best matched with the needs of most campaigns.

Volunteers

The labor movement and unions are a rich source of volunteers for progressive candidates' campaigns and the Democratic Party. Active union members learn valuable organizational skills, organizational discipline, and they develop the will to engage in a long-term effort to achieve important goals. Unions, at both the local and the national level, engage in consistent member political education. In union literature, worksite leaflets, newsletters, and union newspapers, and at meetings, unions constantly educate, motivate, and mobilize their members on legislative issues and candidates.

Central labor councils are constantly called on to assist in grass-roots lobbying and other issue campaigns. Political leaders often drop by delegate meetings to ask for support, to check in, or just to touch base. Central labor councils often lobby at the city, county, state, and federal level. CLCs even get involved in nonunion community legislation and campaigns at the request of allies and coalition partners. It has often been said that the two best places to catch up on politics in Atlanta are the weekly Concerned Black Clergy forum and the monthly Atlanta Labor Council meeting. There is almost always a community partner or political leader at labor-council meetings.

All this political and legislative activity makes labor-council activists a well-prepared, engaged, and motivated pool of potential political activists. Besides their efforts in labor-council voter registration and get-out-the-vote efforts and union member education and mobilization, union activists make great general campaign volunteers.

It is not at all unusual in Atlanta and other cities for CWA (Communication Workers of America) members to staff or run phone banks using the skills they have developed on their jobs. It is not unheard of for union activists to develop ongoing capacity to make them more effective volunteers. One union family I know specializes in putting up campaign signs. The father cuts dozens or hundreds of stakes in his garage workshop; the son puts up the signs. The range of personal efforts union volunteers can and do make is almost limitless. Union volunteers drive the candidates, put up signs, pass out leaflets, man phone banks, register voters, canvass precincts, fill up rallies, even provide security.

During the final days of the 1992 presidential campaign, Bill Clinton went on a three-day nationwide blitz of rallies. On October 31, he stopped in Atlanta for the largest rally of the entire campaign. Twenty-five thousand people filled the Decatur, Georgia, high school football stadium.

For four days union volunteers had passed out leaflets at public transit stations before work and on their lunch breaks, or had canvassed Democratic neighborhoods after work. Other volunteers had managed or staffed phone banks. But on the day of the rally, union volunteers provided the political security, doing all those things that the police and Secret Service cannot do: removing the opposition's banners, neutralizing mischief makers—even holding up the barricades as the candidate reached out to shake hands in the crowd and the crowd surged to him.

Phone Banks

Union volunteers are most often identified with phone banks. That's partly because before John Sweeney was elected president of the AFL-CIO, the only political activity labor councils were encouraged to do was work at phone banks to reach undecided union members in marginal districts from union halls. While making these calls is important, it is obviously a very limited activity. The calls do little to mobilize on a mass scale. And because they were made from union halls, candidates, campaign officials, and party leaders rarely saw the callers, making it almost impossible to use them as tender for power.

Don't get me wrong. Phone bank calls to union members are still very important. But they must be tied to a broader campaign effort—particularly in places like Atlanta where union density is low and the labor movement must have an impact bigger than its membership if the labor council is to exercise real power. But because of this experience, union volunteers do great work calling voters in targeted precincts in get-out-the-vote efforts around issues. Union volunteers do great running campaign phone banks making persuasive calls on behalf of their candidate. Phone banks are most effective as part of a broader strategy that also includes face-to-face contact, mail, and media.

Signs

Two or three or four union volunteers in a pickup truck with a couple of power staplers, a couple of three- or four-pound, short-handled sledge hammers, and a thermos of coffee can put up a mighty lot of candidate signs every evening after work or on a Saturday or Monday night before the election.

Jimmy Dedeaux, an Atlanta Labor Council activist, professional bus operator, and member of the Amalgamated Transit Union, and Jim Chamberlin, a member of the Painters' Union, both pickup truck owners, are well known to progressive political candidates in Metro Atlanta for their willingness to pound signs for prounion candidates. Starting about six weeks before election day, they fill their weekends with sign duty. The night before election day, they and scores of others blanket targeted, strategic areas with appropriate GOTV, issue, and candidate persuasion signs.

Although it seems simple—sometimes like overkill—the hundreds of signs that Dedeaux, Chamberlin, and others erect reinforce a candidate's message, provide a constant reminder, and help define a community's interest in the election. Signs, particularly in voters' yards, are a form of individual endorsement that says collectively how the community sees the election.

For traditionally oppressed constituencies, a community response or collective opinion is extremely important in an election. Working-class voters and minority voters are usually very sensitive or attuned to the consensus opinion in their community about an issue or a candidate. Signs help to demonstrate a community's consensus. When David Duke ran against Edwin Edwards for Governor of Louisiana, the A. Philip Randolph Institute, an organization for black union members, ran a very effective get-out-the-vote campaign. One of the tactics was to blanket black communities with a sign that said: "Vote! They're counting on you to stay home!" Every utility pole in every black community in New Orleans wore one of those signs on election day.

Leaflets

Leaflets can be used effectively in a whole variety of ways and for a whole variety of purposes. Since the 1996 election cycle, unions—through labor councils, state federations of labor, and the national AFL-CIO—have capitalized on the newly rediscovered value of face-to-face leaflet distribution at unionized worksites. Steve Rosenthal, an AFL-CIO political director, says his research indicates that face-to-face leaflet distribution from one union member to another is the most effective means of political communication for union members.

The AFL-CIO has gone to great lengths to base the message of these leaflets on issues and to design them for union members to increase turnout for worker-friendly candidates. While the AFL-CIO produces the leaflets, union activists distribute them—in leaflet lines at shift change and in break rooms at lunch. These leaflets in a workplace serve the same purpose as mass sign distribution in a neighborhood—they define a constituency's interests. That is one reason it is so important that they be issue based. In precincts with high union-member density, issue and candidate leaflets are very effective when delivered by union activists to the homes of union members using precinct walk lists identifying the houses inhabited by union members. Since this method involves unions and their members communicating with other union members, there are no election law restrictions and it is very effective.

But, in cities like Atlanta, even in working-class precincts with low union memberships, issue-based leaflets are very effective at mobilizing communities to vote. Issues must be carefully and strategically selected so that the leaflets resonate with other messages the voters are receiving to make them most effective.

Church Leafleting

I have to say a word about church leafleting. In parts of the South, Atlanta for instance, historically church leafleting has become very important at election time. Black and white evangelical churches and their parking lots have become battlegrounds on Sunday mornings in October. It is an indication of just how racially polarized our nation has become that the leaflets, issues, and candidates represented at black Baptist churches are almost always directly opposite those at white Baptist churches—or Methodist, or Holiness, or whatever. But in many places in the South, leaflet distribution in church parking lots on Sunday is essential. And a few union volunteers can cover a dozen churches if they know where they are going and what they are doing. That is why labor council activists are so important. They know where they are going. They know the pastors, deacons, and usher boards who may patrol the parking lots, and they help define a community's consensus.

Close to election days, leaflets are also very useful on Saturdays at neighborhood shopping centers and grocery stores. Those businesses are neighborhood based—thus contributing to the community consensus–and masses of people pass through on Saturday. A couple of union activists can quite effectively communicate with literally hundreds of working-class voters at a neighborhood supermarket on a Saturday. Multiply that by twenty teams and you have a citywide blitz.

Precinct Work

Some labor councils call it labor-neighbor. Some call it canvassing. Some call it precinct walks. In Atlanta we call it Street Heat. Whatever you call it, it is the mobilization of union activists in targeted precincts with leaflets, a common message, and good shoes to get your voters to the polls.

A smile and a simple, compelling speech or message delivered by a labor-council activist or a couple of labor-council activists is an extremely effective voter-mobilization tool. Even for voters who are not home, a leaflet focused on issues important to them left at their door can be a very effective message. In Atlanta, our labor council has a formula for precinct targeting. We start two months before election day on Saturdays in reliable, very stable precincts with leaflets that attempt to define the issues and choices. As we get closer to the election we move to precincts with traditionally lower turnout, and we end a week before the election in very low income communities. The closer we get to the election, the more days of the week we walk as well.

One of the highlights of almost every election is walking precincts with candidates. The candidate is pumped by the volunteers, and the volunteers are pumped by the candidate. At every house, the voters feel the energy and it just swells. One Saturday in October 1998 twenty Atlanta Labor Council volunteers walked Ralph David Abernathy Boulevard with Congressman John Lewis. We went door-to-door to residences and small businesses asking for votes, passing out a card endorsing the Democratic ticket, and putting up signs—all the while stopping traffic and blocking traffic on one of Atlanta's busiest streets. That day of collective work with one of America's movement legends kept those twenty volunteers going stronger than anything else we could have done—or given them.

Direct Mail

Labor councils, national unions, and the AFL-CIO can all do very effective and important targeted, direct mail to their members. As long as it is union-member education, it is unrestricted. Mailing to union members is particularly effective in getting union members to focus on economic issues instead of social issues or guns or any number of other extraneous issues. Direct mail to union members is very effective at exposing the candidates' records on labor issues. It is very important that direct mail to union members focus on those labor issues where the candidates' records and members' interests overlap. That sounds self-evident. But it is silly to do direct mail that simply parrots a candidate's message to the broader public. Direct mail to union members is the chance to make the case in a compelling, straightforward manner.

Money

Not much needs to be said here. Unions and union members should contribute all they can to their candidates. But we will never compete with corporate America on the basis of money. Therefore, campaign contributions, while important, are a poor way to exercise or express power. People—activists and voters—are our vehicle to power to win.

Direct Action on Opponents

Very infrequently an opportunity arises in a political campaign that warrants a public demonstration of outrage. And who is better equipped with experience, activists, leadership, picket signs, and bullhorns to deliver that demonstration than your local central labor council. This tactic must be used judiciously and with extreme caution because it can easily backfire. The last thing you want to do in an election is make your opponent appear sympathetic. But there are times when a candidate's behavior is so egregious that community outrage is not only understandable but necessary. Such was the case in October 1998 when the Republican candidate for governor, Guy Milner, who had made his fortune running a temporary service agency and helping employers destroy full-time, permanent jobs tried to buy support in Atlanta's African-American community. First, he recruited black homeless people from shelters and halfway houses to hold signs for him so he could appear to have black support. Then he did not pay them when promised. Next he scheduled a rally/press event in the heart of Atlanta's African-American community to unveil his agenda on civil rights, using these same homeless folks as part of his visual—all while his party attacked affirmative action and his running mate for lieutenant governor ran an openly racial television campaign. It was just too much.

So labor-council activists showed up, shouted him down, focused on the real issues of the community, demanded prompt payment for his human props, stole his show, and captured his media. Sometimes the behavior is just so egregious.

Field and GOTV Coordination

Given all we have just said, who are more natural candidates to coordinate all this activity than those who produce the activity? Labor activists, organizers, and leaders have the skills, the experience, and certainly the contacts to make them naturals for campaign field and GOTV coordinators. There's nothing in the list of field and GOTV activities that union organizers do not have to do or at least make happen when organizing workers at the workplace. Why not transfer all that experience to the electoral arena?

Experienced union activists and organizers are usually—or always—much easier to work with than the endless stream of twenty-five-year-old graduates of elite universities on their way to ego gratification and Congress, who are most often given field and GOTV responsibilities. Of course, their next campaign will be fund raising, then campaign management, then candidate status.

The truth of the matter is that most campaign professionals—managers, consultants, and so on—and candidates do not take this work nearly as seriously as they should. It is often ignored until two weeks or just days before election day when someone panics and buckets of money are given to a very diverse cast of characters promising to "deliver the/a vote." If a CLC takes this work seriously, recruits the activists, developments the skills, trains and motivates the activists, and hones its capacity from campaign to campaign, it can deliver another source of political power for workers. And that power is magnified when the coordination comes from the council instead of from someone else who will claim credit for the work done by organized labor.

Election Day

It all comes together on election day when every piece of fieldwork and GOTV has to be in place and when tight organization is essential. Election day is a culmination of weeks of GOTV work.

Election day begins the night before. On election eve after the last door has been knocked on and the candidate has shaken the last hand at the public transit stop, one group of volunteers hangs specially made "GO VOTE" reminders on mail boxes and door handles. Another group begins a night-long effort of putting up yard signs on utility poles and in rights-of-way. Yet another group sets up the war room to coordinate election day GOTV activities. Large wall charts are made of key precincts with anticipated vote totals updated at two-hour intervals during the day. The space is enclosed to ensure confidentiality and phone lines are extended into it.

Also during the night, walkie-talkies are assigned to volunteer GOTV leaders. Election day begins at 5:00 A.M. for the coordinator and key volunteer leaders. Assignments are finalized. Doughnuts, coffee, and fruit are prepared. Volunteers arrive at 6:00 A.M., are assigned to teams and given their targeted precincts, and hit the street between 7:00 and 7:30 A.M. One group holds signs at important commuter intersections. Another group works public transit stops. At 9:00 A.M. all GOTV volunteers—except those working phones—move into targeted precincts, knock on doors, leave door-hangers when knocks are unanswered, and provide rides for elderly or poor voters. After 10:00 A.M., vehicles with sound systems work back and forth between the crews with music and messages reminding people to vote and designed to create energy, excitement, and urgency. Workers vote after work. The most heavily populated, solid, and dependable working-class precincts are worked the hardest after 4:00 P.M.

Meanwhile, throughout the day, poll workers go to targeted polls and record aggregate vote totals. In precincts where those totals do not match expected turnout, extra precinct teams with sound are deployed as crash or blitz teams to get out the vote. All this is coordinated out of the war room

At the election night party—hopefully a victory party—those given the most respect should be the volunteers in sweaty union T-shirts or sweatshirts who spent the day turning out the city's progressive constituency and building power for workers.

Politics, Diversity, and Community

The problem is how to translate and leverage political work to increase the power of working people. It is essential to have in place an organization that is capable of capitalizing on the electoral work. No matter how good your political program or how effective your strategy, it is almost impossible to be a politically successful CLC if the face of your CLC and its leadership does not look like the face of the community you live and work in.

America's cities are much too diverse for a CLC to look just like the oppressors. No matter how good the promises or how moving the rhetoric, a monochrome local labor movement is a contradiction of expressed goals of progress, justice, and liberation and just cannot build the trust necessary to move forward together with a racially and culturally diverse community.

This means that a politically successful CLC should be a part of its community and the community should see itself in the CLC. To even try to do otherwise is foolish. Traditionally and historically, African-American political leaders, voters, and communities have been organized labor's most important and reliable allies. You can make a similar case for other ethnic and racial minorities as well, particularly Mexican Americans in the Southwest, and Latinos in New York.

These connections between the CLC and the community and its leaders can be made in a number of ways, most importantly through leadership diversity and coalitions.

Diversity

The day is past when a labor movement led only by older white men can be successful. At every level, most of America's labor movement has finally learned that its face should look like America's workers who increasingly are nonwhite.

That is particularly true in America's cities where the largest CLCs operate. The leaflets just will not ring true if everyone passing them out is white. You defeat your own purpose if everyone passing out leaflets at African American churches is white. It is very hard to develop the trust necessary to get through tough political fights if the candidate is of color and all the labor leadership is white.

The successful CLC political program cannot be directed or designed by leadership that has long since left the city and severed all ties except the location of the office. Therefore, the most important first political step of a successful CLC is the development of leadership diversity. This requires three things: (1) an internal political commitment to change, (2) opportunity for leadership growth, and (3) active recruitment of women, youth, and people of color as leaders. (1) A commitment to diversity requires leadership. Labor leaders must step forward and articulate the need and define the self-interest of the labor movement in diversity. Although there are plenty of moral and justice-based reasons to embrace diversity, the best argument is one based on fundamental self-interest.

No labor council can talk about the interests of a community that is foreign to it. No labor council can expect to be taken seriously by a community that is foreign to it. No labor council can expect to provide political leadership to a community that is foreign to it. Any labor council is much stronger when its interests coincide with the interests of the broader community. Those interests are best articulated by labor leadership that is part of the broader community.

Otherwise, labor council activists and volunteers are working at cross purposes with the community, perhaps in opposition to it. The labor movement is not strong enough on its own anywhere in America to fight employers, ideological conservatives, opportunistic politicians, and their natural allies.

Within the local labor council it is particularly important for white leaders to define this interest and to make these points. In fact, forcing people of color or women to make this case internally can be disastrous and lead to frustration, anger, marginalization, division, and a precipitous decline in power. This makes it so much more important for white leadership to step forward and define the labor movement's interest in diversity. (2) A white labor-council leadership must make room for women and minority leaders to develop, practice leadership, and build trust among labor-council delegates, activists, and other leaders. The labor-council president is in the best position to do this by exercising his or her prerogative on committee appointments and committee chairs. Appointed committee leadership is a great place for activist, able, and energetic minority and female trade unionists to grow and develop. It also gets activists and delegates accustomed to accepting leadership from women and people of color.

It is a short step from committee leadership to a place on the majority slate at election time. Once in the leadership, the task of executive officers is to put together the votes. At the Atlanta Labor Council, both the secretary-treasurer and the recording secretary are African Americans. White men are no longer in the majority on the executive board. (3) The labor movement is full, chock full, of talented, skilled, and committed women and minority leaders. More and more local unions are led by women and people of color. But, very often, they must be searched out and recruited for broader leadership in a labor council.

Coalitions

The other most effective way labor councils can be part of the community is through coalitions with grass-roots, community-based, justice-oriented organizations.

There is often some confusion about what kind of organizations labor councils should link up with. If the labor council wants to be part of its community and to allow the community to see itself in the labor council, its appropriate organizational partners will be grounded in the community, led by people from the community, and focused on social or community justice. It makes no sense for a labor council to look for such partners at the local United Way.

Many American cities have a Jobs With Justice coalition already established. Jobs With Justice coalitions exist to link labor with the community, to engage in militant direct action when necessary, and to defend workers' rights, especially the right to organize. Jobs With Justice coalitions are linked to one another by a small national office and staff in Washington, D.C., that was first established primarily by several of the most progressive national unions including the Communications Workers, the Service Employees, and the American Federation of State, County, and Municipal Employees.

Coalition work requires attention, patience, work at relationships, trust, and reciprocity. Though very valuable, it is not easy. That is only one reason that Jobs With Justice serves such a useful purpose in doing the hard work of bringing labor and community together.

Whether it is Jobs With Justice or some other formulation, the longest-lasting, most stable community coalitions either begin with or quickly incorporate personal relationships between organizations. Those personal relationships are often necessary to allow a coalition to weather the multiple stresses inherent in multilateral movement work. Those relationships require trust and patience to develop. Not only do the personal relationships strengthen the coalition, they also enrich it, making it more organic and natural, less engineered or manufactured.

It is inevitable in the life of any coalition that lasts for more than one campaign that one or more partners will give more and get less than others. It is essential that those who have received the most reciprocate and actively look for ways to pay back the others. Failure to reciprocate is the surest way to break up a coalition and leave its members bitter and antagonistic.

Electoral coalitions can be especially valuable in defining a candidate and his or her values and commitments, helping to broaden appeal, linking more constituencies, attracting more voters. And when the coalition partners are activist organizations, you increase the number of volunteers available for the essential grass-roots political activity.

A labor council that gets out early in a campaign for a well-established friend or that is trying to develop a broader electoral base for a union member running for office must have a broad and deep community relationship and a history of reciprocity and trustworthiness in the community. In other words, a labor council's chances of electoral success require a history of good coalition work.

Direct Action

Effective political action does not end when the polls close on election day. Effective political action is not confined to effective campaign work—or just to electoral work. Truly effective political action has neither a beginning nor an end but rather a series of tactics tied to issues and time frames inside a larger strategy.

Friends in office, like enemies, must be held accountable. Accountability cannot be adequately achieved exclusively in the context of an electoral campaign. It requires coalition work, media work, intense lobbying, presence, and direct action.

We must never lose the threat of direct action in politics. We use it in contract campaigns and issues campaigns—and sometimes in organizing. But we also must use direct action in the context of politics.

When Georgia Democratic governor Zell Miller broke a campaign promise in 1995 to SEIU Local 1985 and the entire labor movement by deciding to privatize state government, SEIU Local 1985 did not just wring its hands over his betrayal or ask for mercy, it fought back with a powerful campaign of direct action. The union brought two hundred people to the governor's office and took it over. Union members did a pray-in with members of Concerned Black Clergy. And they marched on the governor's mansion with one thousand people, holding a candlelight vigil and rally and blocking Atlanta's most exclusive street.

The direct action coupled with effective and intense lobbying helped prevent establishment of Governor Miller's blue-ribbon privatization panel made up of Georgia's leading business people. The campaign had the most important effect of turning the people of the city against privatization. Following the event, 57 percent of Atlanta's voters were opposed to privatization.

Direct action is probably even more important when used against enemies. The Atlanta labor movement tried to defeat Newt Gingrich at the polls for years, almost succeeding in 1990 at the tail-end of the Eastern Airlines strike. But he changed districts in 1992 moving to a very safe Republican suburban district, won office again, and began plotting his 1994 Republican revolution. He and his cohort captured the Congress in 1994 and began their assault on working America with efforts to cut Medicare, Medicaid, education, OSHA, and the National Labor Relations Board and to end the forty-hour work week and environmental regulation. We in Atlanta thought we had a particular responsibility to fight back.

So at the height of Gingrich's power in January 1995 we began to plan a major action against him to express rage, to shatter the appearance of consensus or acquiescence, and to try to galvanize action and activists. We circulated a memo to the leadership of the labor council arguing for an office takeover. We conducted two dozen personal conversations weighing the hoped-for result against the anticipated backlash, and we intensified planning. Then we debated the proposed action at the February 1995 Atlanta Labor Council meeting. With unanimous approval, we began to build turnout.

On March 15, 1995, about three hundred union leaders and activists jammed themselves into three chartered buses and rode from the IBEW (International Brotherhood of Electrical Workers) Building near downtown Atlanta to Gingrich's suburban district office. Spilling out of the buses and blocking traffic, we rushed his office and took over. We held the office for only thirty minutes. Two demonstrators were arrested, including a civil rights legend, the Reverend James Orange. Charges were later dropped. But that action galvanized activists all over America. Almost immediately, Gingrich's congressional confederates became targets of action, and he himself was faced with pickets and demonstrators across the country on his book tour.

The draconian nature of the Gingrich policies and the expression of rage eventually turned the tide. When Gingrich made it clear he would hold the government of the United States hostage to his policies, he and his "revolution" were finished.

Politics and Organizing

It is only since the Sweeney, Trumka, Chavez-Thompson AFL-CIO administration that the labor movement has recognized that politics can play an important role in organizing. Always before, union organizers left politics and politicians alone.

But with the newly rediscovered emphasis on organizing and the stark realization of the necessity to grow again, organizers, unions, and the AFL-CIO have begun to use political action as an important strategic component of organizing.

Political friends of labor can pressure employers who violate workers' rights to organize. They can embarrass abusive employers. And as Jobs With Justice has shown with its worker's rights boards all over the country, politicians can help to shame immoral and illegal employers. Jobs With Justice workers rights boards, community hearings or accountability sessions, rallies, public letters, media, or off-the-radar conversation with friendly politicians can all help pressure employers to do the right thing and recognize workers' rights.

Friendly political leaders and the bonds built between union activists and elected officials at the ground level while doing political campaigning can be essential to organizing victories. The Atlanta Labor Council would never have been so successful with the 1996 Olympic Games without the election of Bill Campbell and his appointment of the labor-council president to the executive board of the Olympics Committee, and nowhere near so many workers would have been organized.

And politics was a critical part of the victory of flight attendants in getting a first contract and successfully organizing Air Trans Airlines. Four years after winning their union election, the flight attendants still were not union members, still did not have a first contract, and still had not resolved the issues that led to their efforts to organize. Headquartered in Atlanta, Air Trans had begun as Valujet, a low-cost, no-frills alternative to Delta and the other major carriers. Management considered the union a frill. They wanted no part of it. For four years the Association of Flight Attendants fought management. Finally, the association was released under the Railway Labor Act by the National Mediation Board to strike on Labor Day weekend, 1998. As part of strike-assistance efforts, the Atlanta Labor Council planned a community hearing on Air Trans for Labor Day. A panel of community and political leaders was recruited to hear the evidence publicly of Air Trans' violation of workers' rights to a union contract. State Representative Nan Orrock, City of Atlanta Community Affairs director Michael Langford, and National Organization for Women leader Claudia Shauffler all agreed to serve on a panel anchored by Congressman John Lewis.

Media coverage was intense. Airline labor disputes always attract reader attention. The company knew well in advance through news stories, airport leafletting and rallies, and bargaining that John Lewis and other leaders would publicly examine their violation of workers rights. At 1:00 P.M. on Saturday, forty-five hours before the scheduled start of the hearing, a settlement was reached. After a four-year struggle, the Air Trans flight attendants finally got their union.

Conclusion

Power for workers at the local level is built by organizing. It is exercised by mobilization and effective grass-roots political action. Power for workers at the local level is leveraged through coalitions and community allies.

For maximum success, a CLC must move all these elements together in a broad, long-term strategy focused on building power to raise our standard of living and quality of life, to fight for justice, to push wealth downward, and to generate movement. Effective political action does not end with election day, does not stand alone, and is not separate from the broader community.

About the Editors
and Contributors

Stewart Acuff is deputy director of the AFL-CIO Midwest Region. He was president of the Atlanta Labor Council AFL-CIO between 1991 and 2000, where he was instrumental in rebuilding the city's labor movement. From 1985 through 1991 Acuff was the executive director of the Georgia State Employees Union, SEIU Local 1985, building the power of the union of twenty-five hundred state workers despite no collective bargaining, no dues check-off, and no recognition. As interim organizing director of SEIU Local 250 in northern California, Acuff led successful organizing efforts of nursing homes and hospitals.

Amy Dean leads the labor movement in Silicon Valley, where she is the chief executive officer of the South Bay Labor Council. As the regional federation of labor in Silicon Valley, the South Bay AFL-CIO, the fifteenth largest in the nation, represents a hundred and ten local unions with a membership of over a hundred thousand working families. When elected to her position in 1995, Dean was the youngest person and first woman to lead one of the top labor federations in the country. Dean serves on the general executive board of the national AFL-CIO. She is public policy fellow of the Japan Society and fellow of the Koret Israel Prize and the Wexner Heritage Foundation. Amy Dean has appeared repeatedly on CNN, *The News Hour*, National Public Radio, and *Good Morning America*. Her work has been featured in the *New York Times*, *Wall Street Journal*, *Washington Post*, *San Francisco Chronicle*, *West Magazine*, *Los Angeles Times*, *El Pais*, *Le Monde*, *Yomiuri News*, *Business Week*, *Working Women's Magazine*, *Mother Jones*, *Fast Company*, *Forbes*, and *Business 2.0*. Dean has published numerous articles and has contributed chapters to several published books.

Stuart Eimer recently earned his Ph.D. in sociology from the University of Wisconsin-Madison. He is Assistant Professor in the Sociology Department of Widener University, Chester, Pennsylvania. His research focuses on the AFL-CIO, labor councils, living-wage campaigns, and the labor movement in politics. He has written: *Industry, Space and Organization: The Rise and Fall of the Greater New York Industrial Union Council, 1940–1948* and has published articles in the *Labor Studies Journal* and *WorkingUSA*.

Fernando E. Gapasin earned his Ph.D. in sociology. He has been active in the U.S. union/labor movement for over thirty years and has served in every capacity. He is presently a president of a social service union in Los Angeles, a faculty member at the Center for Labor Research and Education, and in Chicano Studies at UCLA. He was formerly a faculty member at Pennsylvania State and a researcher for the AFL-CIO's Union Cities program.

Stephanie Luce is an assistant professor at the Labor Center and a research associate at the Political Economy Research Institute, both at the University of Massachusetts at Amherst. She received her Ph.D. in sociology in 1999 from the University of Wisconsin at Madison. Luce has done extensive research on the political and economic impact of the living-wage movement and has coauthored *The LivingWage: Building a Fair Economy* with Robert Pollin.

Immanuel Ness is Assistant Professor of Political Science at Brooklyn College, City University of New York. His research focuses on labor, politics, and immigrants and organizing. His books include *Trade Unions and the Betrayal of the Unemployed*. He is a contributing author to the authoritative *Organizing to Win*. He has edited the *Encyclopedia of Third Parties in America*. Ness is also the author of numerous articles on labor and politics in *Labor Studies Journal*, *Working USA*, *Social Policy*, *The Nation*, and *New Political Science*. He is currently working on a book on immigrant organizing and union jurisdiction in New York City. Ness is also conducting research on privatization's impact on people of color. He received his Ph.D. in political science from City University of New York.

Wade Rathke is Chief Organizer of the Service Employees International Union (SEIU) Local 100 and ACORN (Association of Community Organizations for Reform Now), both headquartered in New Orleans. He also serves on the Executive Council of the SEIU. Local 100 has a multistate jurisdiction (Louisiana, Texas, Arkansas, Mississippi) and primarily organizes low-wage service-sector workers. For the past quarter century, ACORN has organized low- and moderate-income communities throughout the United States.

Joel Rogers is the John D. MacArthur Professor of Law, Political Science, and Sociology at the University of Wisconsin–Madison. He is also founder and director of the Center on Wisconsin Strategy (COWS), a research and policy institute, and is incubator and manager of "real-world" experiments in policy reform, dedicated to promoting "high-road" economic development. Rogers has written widely on American politics and public policy, political theory, and U.S. and comparative industrial relations. His most recent books are *America's Forgotten Majority: Why the White Working Class Still Matters* (2000) and *Working Capital: Using the Power of Labor's Pensions* (2001). A contributing editor of *The Nation* and *Boston Review*, a MacArthur Foundation fellow, and a longtime social and political activist as well as an academic, Rogers was identified by *Newsweek* as one of the one hundred Americans most likely to affect U.S. politics and culture in the twenty-first century.

Jonathan Rosenblum is director and lead organizer of Seattle Union Now, AFL-CIO. He has served as a Union Cities organizer for the King County Labor Council, AFL-CIO. He has also been an organizer for Washington State Jobs With Justice and the Service Employees International Union. Prior to full-time organizing, he worked in the newspaper industry and was a member of the International Typographical Union, Chapel 379.

Roland Zullo is an assistant research scientist at the Institute of Labor and Industrial Relations, University of Michigan. A former member of the United Steelworkers of America and the American Federation of Teachers, Zullo has taught numerous labor-education seminars and has instructed graduate-level coursework in the areas of collective bargaining, labor management relations, and industrial relations theory. He received his Ph.D. in industrial relations from the University of Wisconsin in 1998.

Index